Agorafabulous!

Agorafabulous!

*DISPATCHES FROM MY BEDROOM

Sara Benincasa

wm
WILLIAM MORROW
An Imprint of HarperCollins*Publishers*

HarperCollins books may be purchased for educational, business, or sales promotional use. For information please write: Special Markets Department, HarperCollins Publishers, 10 East 53rd Street, New York, NY 10022.

FIRST EDITION

Designed by Diahann Sturge

Library of Congress Cataloging-in-Publication Data

Benincasa, Sara.
Agorafabulous! : dispatches from my bedroom / Sara Benincasa. — 1st ed.
p. cm.
ISBN 978-0-06-202441-1
1. Benincasa, Sara—Health. 2. Agoraphobia—Patients—United States—Biography. I. Title. II. Title: Dispatches from my bedroom.
RC552.A44B46 2012
616.85'225—dc23

2011033172

12 13 14 15 16 OV/RRD 10 9 8 7 6 5 4 3 2 1

For my parents, Lillian and Jonathan, and my grandmother Jean
And for Sam

So keep fightin' for freedom and justice, beloveds, but don't you forget to have fun doin' it. . . . And when you get through kickin' ass and celebratin' the sheer joy of a good fight, be sure to tell those who come after how much fun it was.

— Molly Ivins, *Mother Jones*

Contents

The Thing Before the Rest of the Thing

I didn't know what to call this part of the book. I guess you could call it a preface, but that sounds too fancy to me. I've already got an introduction (that comes later) and this obviously isn't a table of contents. You might call it a foreword, but don't *other* people usually write forewords? You know, like the author's famous friends. I've got some of those, but they're usually pretty busy signing autographs and swimming in great vats of their own money, Scrooge McDuck–style.

Anyway, I want to tell you some important stuff up front, before we get to the rest of this tragicomic journey into the depths of my lady-soul. This story is mostly true. I tried my best to keep it real, as the children say, but I'm not a fucking journalist. I didn't have a damn tape recorder on me during every conversation.

Please also keep in mind that when a lot of the stuff chronicled in this book actually happened, I was crazy as a loon. On meth. In a crack house. I had to fill in some of the fuzzier memories with my best guesses as to what actually happened.

A few of the characters represent amalgamated mishmashes of people I once knew. I changed some names, places, and identifying details for a couple of reasons. I still talk to some of the people in this book, and I'd like to keep it that way. I don't talk to some of the others, and I'd *really* like to keep it that way.

Rest assured that the grossest, meanest, ugliest, most foolish things that *I* do in this story all actually happened in real life. I subscribe to the notion that if you can laugh at the shittiest moments in your life, you can transcend them. And if other people can laugh at your awful shit as well, then I guess you can officially call yourself a comedian.

That is all. Thank you. I hope you like the rest of my book. If not, feel free to use it for kindling to warm yourself in the cold night when the Revolution comes. And oh, it's coming.

Agorafabulous!

Introduction

When I was seventeen years old, I met the hottest guy in seriously the entire *world* at a free academic summer program run by the state of New Jersey. The camp, held at a public university down the Jersey Shore, was called the New Jersey Governor's School on Public Issues and the Future of the State. It doesn't sound like the place to find Adonis, but there he was: a dreamboat straight-A football captain named Kevin, whose extracurricular activities also included coaching little kids' sports teams and volunteering at a convalescent home for nuns. When he turned seventeen that summer (he was young for his grade), his mom brought a cake with a car on it, because he and his twin sister were finally going to get their driver's licenses. He told me once that his sister was the only person he really trusted. She and I had the same first name, except hers had an "h" at the end and mine didn't.

He was very nice, too nice to be true, and the other students at Governor's School—Type-A student-council brats, mostly—wondered what his deal was. You couldn't be *that* smart and *that* hot and *that* nice and not secretly be crazy, or a werewolf, or something. I found it deeply disappointing that he failed to offer to relieve me of my virginity. And at a certain point, his plastic perfection started to weird me out. Oh, I totally still would've let him put his fingers down my pants, but a strange kind of resentment arose within me, as well. As a funny (read: insufficiently hot) girl, I wasn't privy to the mating behaviors of popular alpha males. But I was savvy enough to intuit that I was never going to be Kevin's girlfriend.

Eventually, I did find a boyfriend. He wasn't as hot as Kevin, and we never had sex, but he played tennis and was good at finger-banging. Plus, we liked a lot of the same books, Philip Roth's *Goodbye, Columbus* chief among them.

Governor's School ended, and we all went off to our respective high schools to start our senior years. Kevin entered a new high school in a new town and was immediately nominated for Best Looking, Most Likely to Succeed, and Best Personality—a stunning trifecta of high school laurels. I heard about it and thought, with slight annoyance, *Of course.*

Then, one night in the spring, he walked into his garage, filled a bottle with gasoline, brought it upstairs into the bathroom, locked the door, poured some of the gasoline down his throat, soaked himself in the rest, and lit a match.

When they broke the door down, he was still alive. He still responded to his name. The end took a little more time in coming—less than a handful of hours, but if you measure time in pain, I imagine it felt like years to him—because indeed he was still there, after the fire, still conscious, still feeling everything. I think he wanted it that way. Not for him the quiet chemical sleep of too many pills; not for him the instant, violent relief of the shot to the head. If his death taught me anything, it's that when life doesn't hand us the punishment we think we deserve, we are wholly adept at delivering it unto ourselves.

In the weeks that followed, I heard rumors about things he had supposedly done and things that had supposedly been done to him, but they were rumors only, confused teenagers' attempts at explaining the inexplicable. I have always regretted not going to his funeral. We were never very close, but maybe it would have made more sense, being there, seeing his family and all his friends. Maybe *he* would have made more sense.

I've thought of him often in the intervening years, through friendships and love affairs, college and graduate school, times of joy and times of breakdown. I don't know if I believe in God. I don't know if I believe in Heaven. I don't know if I believe that Kevin is watching me, or that he hears me when I speak his name. He didn't watch me often on earth, so I don't know why he would feel the need to do so from any other plane of existence. Maybe I should've worn tighter shorts the summer I knew him.

What I do know is that Kevin was very much on my mind during the times when I walked myself to the edge of the abyss and stared down, feeling my toes curl over the lip, seriously considering giving myself over to the yawning absence of anything. And so Kevin has been with me, in one form or another, perhaps just as a thought, on numerous occasions.

He was with me when I stacked empty cans and jars against the wall of my tiny apartment because I was afraid to take the recycling outside—or do anything outside the confines of my home. He was there when I began urinating in cereal bowls and shoving them under my bed because I was frightened of using the toilet or even the sink. He was there when I admitted, finally, that sometimes I thought about doing secret and terrible things to myself—and I didn't put those things into words, because I didn't want to, and I didn't need to. He sat with me while the knives whined their siren song from the drawer and I rocked back and forth, gently, sort of ignoring them but mostly just waiting.

Kevin was there somewhere, perched in the back of my mind, reminding me that clear-cut choices are few and far between, and I had better not fuck this one up.

CHAPTER ONE

In Simplest Terms and Most Convenient Definitions

Lee Redmond of Salt Lake City, Utah, had the world's longest fingernails. She stopped cutting them in 1979, and, according to the Guinness World Records website, they measured a total of 28 feet 4.5 inches by 2008. At 2 feet 11 inches, her right thumbnail was the longest of them all.

When Redmond initially secured the world record, she announced plans to cut her nails. In the August 10, 2006, edition of the *Deseret Morning News* (Salt Lake City's more conservative paper), she described her daily activities, including grocery shopping, cooking, and taking care of her husband, an Alzheimer's patient. She said of her nails to reporter Tammy Walquist, "It's strange how they become you. It's almost your identity. It'll probably be a trauma after twenty-seven years to cut them off." She then changed her mind, unwilling to part with them. She turned down tens of thousands of dollars to slice them down to socially acceptable length on live television.

On Tuesday, February 10, 2009, the sports utility vehicle in which Redmond rode was involved in a collision. According to the SLC police, Redmond was ejected from the vehicle and sustained serious but not life-threatening injuries. She survived, but her nails did not. Each one broke off near the finger.

When I heard about Lee Redmond's accident, my first thought was *not* "Jesus, how the fuck do you insert a tampon with two-foot-long fingernails?" (That was my second thought.) My first thought was, "Why on Earth would anyone *choose* to be a freak?" To my mind, freaks generally come in two categories: those whose freakishness was visited upon them and those who devote considerable time and effort to creating and maintaining their freak status. I am one of the former, and I have never been able to understand the latter.

When I was a child, I began to experience panic attacks that increased in frequency and intensity over several years. This condition eventually led me to develop a fear of leaving my small studio apartment, and finally of leaving my bed—even to go to the bathroom. The ensuing complications were, well, pungent.

By the time I was twenty-one, I was a full-on obsessive, cowering, trembling agoraphobe. How serious was it? Well, because I was too frightened to go to the hair salon, I let my roots grow out—which, gentle reader, is truly a sign of desperation in a born-and-bred daughter of New Jersey.

The word *agoraphobia* comes from the Greek *phobia,* or fear, and *agora,* or marketplace. In simplest terms and most convenient definitions, my psychiatric diagnosis is that I'm afraid of the mall. Which, I can assure you, is untrue. New Jersey claims to be a state, but it is actually a gigantic slab of cement upon which malls sprout like blisters and corns on the stubby, scrubby feet of overworked, chain-smoking strippers. These malls are interconnected by a complex, ill-conceived system of congested roads. You are not allowed to take a left turn anywhere in the entire state. If you try, the rest of us will run you over on our way to the Macy's white sale.

If you opened up my chest and examined my heart, I'm fairly certain you would find stamped therein a precise map explaining how to get from the Bridgewater Commons Mall to the low-rent Quakerbridge Mall, to the high-endiest of high-end malls, the Alpha and the Omega, the Mall at Short Hills (valet parking! Neiman Marcus! Sit-down restaurants!). I feel at home in these temples to materialism. They have many bathrooms, and if you get anxious you can always find pain-numbing food or a soothing, well-chlorinated fountain.

In fact, my own life is so entwined with mall lore and magic that everything-must-go closing sales at mall shops fill me with an unbearable sense of despair. There is nothing I despise more than a once-great mall gone to ruin, the victim of a poor economy or a competing mall in the neighboring town. These are ghost malls, and they haunt my dreams. Their stores—empty husks of commerce—are tragic reminders of our own mortality. I can't handle the recent spate of recession-era store closings. I'm still not over Structure, and that old warhorse died over a decade ago.

I believe that there should exist an end-of-year memorial montage for all the mall stores we've lost. You know, like they have at the Academy Awards ceremony each year. And I believe this montage should be set to Sarah McLachlan's "In the Arms of the Angels." A solemn voice—mine, perhaps—should intone the names of the deceased as images of their gone-but-not-forgotten merchandise flash across the screen. "Circuit City," I'll whisper. "Tower Records. Virgin Megastore." Viewers will weep. It'll be fucking beautiful.

To sum up: my diagnosis notwithstanding, I'm not really afraid of the marketplace. Quite the opposite, in fact. But I have been afraid of many other things. Here are some of them, in a handy chart form that will get you up to speed:

Things of Which I Have Been Afraid (Abridged)

Feared Thing	Degree of Fear	Am I Over It?	Solution
Leaving my home	Severe	Mostly	Prozac; Xanax; Klonopin; cognitive behavioral therapy; bringing a stuffed giraffe named Mary with me wherever I go.
Having a wet head	Moderate	Yes	Avoiding the shower; using a high-power hair dryer with a diffuser for less frizz and extra curls.
Driving	Severe	Mostly	Deep breathing.
Being a passenger in a car	Severe	Mostly	Insisting on driving.
New York City	Severe	Yes	Realizing that most people here are even crazier than I am. It's rather comforting, really. I'm among my own.

Lincoln Tunnel	Moderate	Mostly	Moving to Manhattan so I wouldn't need to use the tunnel to visit, as I am already here.
Holland Tunnel	Moderate	Mostly	See *Lincoln Tunnel*.
Flying	Severe	Mostly	See *Leaving my home*.
Taking the bus	Severe	No	Not taking the bus, except when it is absolutely unavoidable.
Taking the subway	Moderate	Yes	Taking cabs unless I'm in the mood for interaction in close quarters, in which case I take the subway and enjoy it. But I'm rarely in the mood for interaction in close quarters that does not involve consensual sex with another adult person.

Vomiting	Moderate	Yes	Realizing that it can excuse you from leaving your house. Also, the feeling of relief that ensues afterward is the closest thing to a natural Xanax I've ever experienced.
Sex	Severe	Yes	Fucking people and enjoying it.
Being pregnant	Severe	No	Fucking men and enjoying it while using prophylactics. Alternatively, fucking women.
Having an abortion	Severe	No	See *Being pregnant*.
God	Severe	No	Consorting with atheists and other hell-bound types, like comedians.

Source: Personal storage bank of memories, 1982–present. (I don't really remember anything before that. I'm sure I was afraid of many things, including but not limited to light, shadow, and babysitters.)

When I say that I've been afraid of these things, I don't mean that I had a vague idea that it would be painful or distasteful to endure them. Nor do I mean that I simply disliked these activities or concepts. Rather, I developed, to one degree or another, a terror of these events/acts/experiences. In the case of leaving my home, flying, taking the train, taking the bus, taking the subway, driving, and being a passenger in a vehicle, I developed an actual phobia. There are funny Greek names for each of these individual phobias, but it's more convenient to group them together under the label of agoraphobia.

I didn't just wake up one day and realize that I was an agoraphobe. For me, agoraphobia crept up after a decade of experiencing panic attacks in a diverse and exciting array of situations.

Panic attacks happen when your body shifts into an ancient and somewhat entertaining state known as the "fight or flight" response. It's actually a good reaction to have if, for example, a bear is chasing you and it is the year 1000 B.C.E. and you live in the woods and have only a wooden spear to protect yourself. Your heart starts beating very fast and blood flow is diverted from your extremities to your heart and upper respiratory system, so you can breathe more quickly, and your legs get tense, and you start to get nauseous, because your digestive system goes out of whack (your body isn't going to waste time digesting your food—there's a fucking *bear* after you! Run!), and your pupils actually dilate a little bit to let in more light in case you have to run through light and dark. In the woods. Where you live.

It's all very evolutionary and interesting, and, like bicycles and electroconvulsive therapy, it can still be useful in some cases. For example, if you're walking down the street late one night and are approached by someone who expresses a sincere and heartfelt desire to rape you, you should probably go into fight or flight, and run the fuck away as fast as you can. Unless you're into that sort of thing, in which case you probably write a blog that only appeals to a very small segment of humanity.

A panic attack is the fight-or-flight response in a situation that does not require fisticuffs or the hurling of primitive weaponry. Sometimes a situation triggers a painful memory. For example, a soldier who is home from a combat zone might find that he becomes frightened and has a panic attack when he hears a news chopper flying over his city. Post-traumatic stress disorder, or PTSD, sometimes includes this sort of response.

Quite often, however, the panic attacks are related to a more general feeling of not being in control of a situation. Many sufferers find they have panic attacks in crowds. I once had a doozy of a panic attack while driving through the desert in Texas. Having grown up among hills and trees, I found it terrifying and more than disconcerting to actually *see* the horizon. I later spoke to a tall Texan/Native American lesbian semi-pro softball player, who had freaked out on a car ride back East when she *couldn't* see the horizon for the trees. And if you know any Texan/Native American lesbian semi-pro softball players, you know they don't scare easy.

Somebody who has had enough panic attacks (and "enough" can mean one or one hundred) might start to avoid the places where he or she has had those panic attacks. After all, if every time you walked into a particular store you were punched in the stomach, you'd probably find another store to visit, right? (Again, unless you're into that sort of thing.) And thankfully, our homogenized chain-store culture enables one to find pretty much the exact same shit in half a dozen big-box outlets.

If you live in the average American town, you've got a Walgreens, a Rite-Aid, a CVS, an Eckerd, the drugstore at Walmart, and some local family-run pharmacy that's on the verge of closing due to the presence of the previous five. Unfortunately for you, the mysterious impulse that causes the panic attacks is within you, not the stores. You'll keep having those panic attacks no matter where you pick up your birth control. Eventually, there won't be any stores left to try. (Then you'll probably obtain it using the agoraphobe's greatest friend: the Internet. But you might miss actual human interaction after a while.)

For me, it was approximately a decade-long trip from "I'm afraid of X" to "I'm afraid of other places that look like X" to "I'm afraid of every place that is not my bed, and have resolved to stay there for the rest of my life, thank you very much." I prayed that this mysterious mental malady would be lifted from me spontaneously, or that I would somehow suddenly become normal. It didn't happen.

When I was twenty-one I finally concluded that I was a freak of the most terrible type, designed not to be displayed and celebrated but to be hidden in the darkness, an ugly, stinking waste of flesh. If college was supposed to be the best time of my life, I couldn't imagine how awful it must get afterward. It sure didn't seem like the sort of thing worth sticking around for. I wondered how it had taken me so long to realize that I was broken beyond repair, and that I didn't belong on this planet with all of the real humans. I imagined my future as one of dependence, fear, and disability. I would always be a burden on the saner individuals charged with my care. I would always be different, in a bad way. I might kill myself, if only I could summon the courage to choose death. Instead, I chose to do nothing but wallow in the rising swamp of my own shame. I hid in my bedroom, with garbage piling around me, rocking back and forth in bed, singing an old, half-remembered hymn as I prayed for sleep to come and blot it all out.

Of course there had been warning signs—plenty of them,

over the years. Maybe I was too young or naive to recognize them, too afraid to speak up and admit that I needed more help. My brain sent up one big, giant, flaming-red signal flare when I was eighteen, the week after the beautiful boy from summer camp killed himself. But everybody around me found ways to explain it away. It was heat exhaustion; it was fatigue; it was homesickness. After all, no one goes crazy on vacation.

CHAPTER TWO

Sicily on Five Freakouts a Day

The story of American immigration goes like this: impoverished, oppressed peasants flee their respective filthy countries and struggle until they achieve the American dream of working sixteen hours a day, seven days a week. And as they toil in the fields and factories of this great nation, they say to themselves, "The Old Country was a terrible place. Here in America, I live in luxury!" They smile and shed a tear, partly from emotion and partly from the industrial airborne carcinogens that will eventually kill them.

A few upwardly mobile, American-born generations later, one of their descendants gets a bright idea.

"Hey!" someone says. "We ought to visit the Old Country. We can smile at the adorable native people and eat the adorable native food and consume the adorable native alcoholic beverage of choice. Then we can vomit on the nearest historical landmark. If we're lucky, we can buy a T-shirt at the site of the mass grave where Great-great-grandma was killed by opposition troops! Perhaps the charming locals will show us a bit of their famous hospitality rather than stab us on sight."

Thus did I end up in Sicily, the Alabama of Italy. It is a fact that my grandmother, whose people were from southern Italy but not Sicily, used to refer to my grandfather's Sicilian-American mistress as "that black bitch." There is also a charming saying that ancient racists of mainland Italian descent enjoy repeating: "Sicily ain't southern Italy. It's northern Africa!" This is generally followed either by a knowing cackle or a disgusted wave of the hand. It is a unique pleasure to come to understand as a child that your elderly relative is not using the Italian word for eggplant in a complimentary fashion when describing citizens of Sicily or, more often, Harlem.

Since many humans have never actually heard of Sicily, it is perhaps instructive to do a quick tour through this large island's colorful history. It doesn't sound like the sort of place where one would willingly send one's buxom virgin[1] eighteen-year-old daughter on an "educational trip" (at least not a trip from which one hoped she would return), but the real Sicily actually has more to it than pasta and automatic weapons.

In terms of conquest, Sicily is the geographic equivalent of the drum-circle bong—everyone's hit it at least once. The Phoenicians and Carthaginians had it, as did the Greeks and Romans (who brought Jewish slaves). Then came the Vandals and Goths (not to be confused with the influential punk band and sad-eyed Hot Topic kids), followed by the Byzantines. After that, the Arab Muslims showed up. A few more Jews arrived and behaved nicely without bothering anybody, which has generally been an

---

1 Unless you count oral sex. Which, being Catholic, I did not.

unsuccessful course of action for them throughout their history. Then the Normans staked their claim. Through marriage, Sicily passed to the Swabians, who are noted for having the goofiest-sounding name in history. Then the French took over—which didn't turn out so well.

On Easter Monday in 1282, the Sicilians (whatever the hell that meant by then) decided to kill all the new French residents. The island was independent for, oh, six seconds, at which point the Kingdom of Aragon (not Aragorn, the foxiest dude in *The Lord of the Rings*) kindly stepped in. Aragon and Spain joined forces, and Sicily became Spanish property. In the fourteenth century, the Black Death made its legendary European debut in Sicily. The plague killed a bunch of people, which made the Spaniards feel competitive. Bloodthirsty, mass-murdering Queen Isabella and her kill-happy hubby Ferdinand implemented their own extermination method, loosely titled "Get Out of Here, You Fucking Jew (Or I'll Stab You)."

After a couple centuries of earthquakes and pirates, Sicily went to the Austrians (or, presumably, the Austrians went to it). Then the Spanish showed up again, but there were no Jews left to banish or kill, so their heart wasn't in it. Sicily was independent for another brief moment, after which the mainland Italians popped in and took over. The economy collapsed, the Mafia rose to prominence, a fuck-ton of immigrants bounced and went to the United States, and you probably know the rest from your favorite Francis Ford Coppola educational filmstrips.

In short, Sicily is no stranger to illness, drama, or evil female overlords. My own trip would incorporate all three.

Surprisingly, my journey to Sicily was not a punishment but a reward. I'd actually asked for the trip as a pre-graduation present. My school was cosponsoring a journey to the *Regione Autonoma Siciliana* with an outside tour company, a business devoted to turning culturally illiterate young American rubes into sophisticated international travelers. Via bus, train, and ferry, we would take in the faded glory of the most violent segment of a majestically corrupt nation.

It was my first trip abroad, unless you counted the time we'd visited the Canadian branch of my family when I was eight. And while I'd long grown accustomed to the swirl of fear and nausea that always arose on car rides to Manhattan and bus rides to Philly and plane rides to Florida, it did not occur to me that a European vacation might magnify my usual troubles with travel. In fact, I rather thought it might diminish them. After all, those other trips had involved my tall redheaded Irish-American dad and short dark-haired Sicilian-American mother, who commenced vacations only after marinating in a highly acidic vat of tension for a solid seventy-two hours. This trip would put more than four thousand miles between my parents and me. It would be like a marinara-flavored preview of college, where all my homebred quirks would disappear. The thought gave me comfort.

A week before the trip came the news that Kevin, the heartbreakingly beautiful boy I'd met the previous summer, had doused himself in gasoline and died via self-immolation. I cried until my stomach ached and my eyes burned. As a good Catholic, I had been taught that suicide was the only unforgivable sin a human could commit.

"Do you have your passport case and your money belt?" my father asked. "Jesus, I can't believe you haven't packed yet."

"You really need to check what time your bus leaves for the airport," my mother said.

"I don't think I want to go," I said.

"Oh," they said. "You're going."

Whether or not Kevin was bound for Hell, I was certainly bound for Sicily.

The plane ride wasn't bad. I slept most of the time, relying on an extra-heavy dose of Dramamine, my drug of choice. I'd never smoked pot or been drunk, but I'd ingested impressive amounts of anti-nausea medication since I was very small. This was acceptable, because over-the-counter medications have been rubber-stamped by a completely scrupulous and unbiased government authority, while marijuana is typically stolen from the desiccated corpses of South American toddlers/drug mules, all of whom have been strangled to death and then ritually fucked by men with large vans and candy.

Dramamine wasn't the only drug swirling through my system on that trip. I'd been taking a prescription anti-depressant/anti-anxiety medication for two years. The pediatrician had written me a scrip when I was sixteen to treat my occasional bouts of intense depression and my more-than-occasional panic attacks. The irrational fear and crippling sadness kept coming, and the pediatrician kept increasing the dose. I didn't know that other drugs might help me. I was convinced that I was taking the only drug in the world designed to treat my weird problems, and that if the drug couldn't fix me, nothing could. But most of my friends didn't know I was taking it, and I certainly hadn't informed the other students on the plane. I kept the bottle hidden in my backpack, next to my carefully concealed stuffed giraffe, Mary.

When we finally landed, I rose unsteadily to my feet and trudged in a daze behind the other passengers. It wasn't until I'd passed through immigration and assembled with my schoolmates that I happened to catch a glimpse of the horizon through an airport window. As I watched intently, it wobbled. I caught a split-second glimpse of something menacing hovering just beneath the sun.

"I don't think I'm okay," I said to Mr. D'Angelo, the guidance counselor who'd volunteered to chaperone our trip.

"What, you got *agita*?"[2] he asked. "You want some Imodium AD?"

I thanked him politely and accepted his offer. I hadn't eaten in several hours and didn't have anything sitting in my stomach or bowels, but I was raised to put complete faith in the power of name-brand OTC medications.

As we waited for the bus and I chewed slowly on the antidiarrheal tablets, I took stock of my fellow travelers. It was not a particularly promising crew. The crowd was made up mostly of students from the junior class, one year behind me. Some seemed lovely and some seemed dull, but I didn't know most of them particularly well. There was some loud kid so scarred by acne his face looked like a pizzelle iron. There was a cute boy from the lacrosse team. And then there was one small, tightly wound knot of females with whom I was all too familiar.

Every school has it, that group of Madisons and Michelles and Jennifers and Jessicas and Adrianas and Ariannas and Taylors and Tiffanys. I supposed the reincarnated souls of Spanish inquisitors, Nazi commandants, and medieval Chinese proto-waterboarders

---

2 Italian-Americans argue over the origin of the term *agita* (AH-jih-da). The most common explanation is that it comes from the verb *agitare*, "to agitate." Some folks say it is a Southern Italian mispronunciation of the noun *acido* (AH-chee-do), or acid. It means that you're really nervous, your stomach hurts, or you've got the shits. Mr. D'Angelo assumed my malady was of the more scatological variety.

had to end up somewhere. Our particular trip was enlivened by the presence of a foursome of bitchtastic bottle blondes from the girls' tennis team. This cuntsquare of future real estate agents and PR associates was led by junior class homecoming princess Amber Luciano. That she shared some DNA with the man who split New York into five crime families and ordered countless murders of his rivals—well, that was no surprise, once you got to know her.

I was generally liked in my own grade (I cracked jokes in class and wrote funny editorials about the cafeteria for the school newspaper) but had few friends on the trip to Italy. And I was certainly not loved by Amber, who seemed particularly irritated by people who liked clowning around for laughs. She disliked them even more than she disliked people who made art on their own time, people who wore vintage clothing, people who listened to non–Top 40 music, and people who read books. And Amber really hated people who read books. I once heard her say in an English elective, "I have a *boyfriend.* I don't have time to waste on a fuckin' *book.*"

If I'd been accompanied by my own tight-knit coterie of friends, I would have taken delight in mocking Amber in whispers from across the bus. But I was alone, and my power as an outgoing senior was limited. Amber and her lieutenants knew a lame duck when they saw one.

We boarded the bus, and Amber immediately staked her claim in a set of seats far enough back to be cool, but far enough up to be away from any bathroom stink. I eyed her warily as I chose my own seat. When I struggled to put my bag in the overhead compartment, I heard a sudden burst of laughter from the bitch contingent. Foolishly, I turned my head to look. They were covering their mouths and giggling to each other while staring straight at me.

"Oh my God, shut up, she saw," one of them whispered loudly.

Great. Fucking great. I'd finally gotten a hearty laugh out of Amber Luciano. At least my bottle of crazy meds hadn't popped out.

I sank into the seat and thought of Kevin, who would undoubtedly have been in these girls' social circle if he'd gone to my high school. He might even have dated one of them—Amber, obviously. It was true that aside from their superficial assets, they had little in common—he was genuinely kind, and she had the soul of a troll. But the most attractive people in any school always had to pair off. It was like an unwritten law.

Mr. D'Angelo boarded the bus last. He was a guidance counselor at the school, a position generally awarded to football coaches and other paragons of emotional intelligence in order to justify their higher-than-average salaries. He had probably taken one requisite psychology course in college back in the 70s, in order to complete the requirements for his General Studies major with a Human Health minor. I assume some sort of nominal further training was required, like a half-hour workshop at the local Board of Education offices one random Sunday afternoon. If he had any legitimate expertise in dealing with the unpredictable twists and turns of adolescent development, he did an excellent job of hiding it.

"A-right, a-right everybody," he boomed in his thick South Jersey accent. "Listen up. We got eight days together. That means we got 192 hours to accomplish the following goals: (A) learn something; (B) demonstrate respect for this ancient local culture; (C) have . . . A GOOD TIME, AMIRIGHT?" He smiled broadly at the last part, like it was a rabbit he'd pulled out of a hat. A smattering of applause emerged from the passel of ungrateful teenagers seated before him.

"And when do we go to the beach?" Amber demanded.

Mr. D'Angelo smiled and chuckled. He was the type of man who found the questions and "problems" of teenage girls to be infinitely amusing. This is certainly a wonderful quality for a high school guidance counselor to possess, since he is unlikely to encounter any troubled adolescent females in his chosen line of work.

"Well, Amber," he said. "We go to the beach on Wednesday."

It was Sunday morning. Amber and her coven let out a burst of disappointed groans.

"Not 'til Wednesday?"

"I didn't go to the tanning booth, 'cause I thought I'd get a full week at the beach here! Oh my God, I'm gonna be pasty by Wednesday."

"This is bullshit."

No one has ever really figured out why white people from New Jersey are so obsessed with staying tan. When MTV's investigative journalism documentary series *Jersey Shore* became a hit, I fielded countless inquiries from friends, acquaintances, and even press, who wanted to hear an Italian-American female comic explain the mystery of tanning culture.

"Fucked if I know," I told one reporter, who woke me up from my cherished pre-gig nap. "Most of the guidos I grew up with were racist idiots. They didn't even talk to brown people, so I don't know why they'd wanna look like them." He chose not to run that quote in his newspaper.

"Hey hey, watch your mouth!" Mr. D'Angelo said sharply to one of the girls. "On this bus we say *bullcrap,* not that thing you just said. Or else we say *garbage*."

"Fine," the girl said. "Bullcrap. It's friggin' bullcrap that we can't go to the beach 'til Wednesday. This whole place is an island, right?"

I've always over-identified with authority figures. Maybe it's because I desperately seek their approval. It is a fact that when I was getting laid off from a radio station, I spent half the meeting assuring my boss that he'd done a really wonderful job and that I totally understood why my show was being canceled. I added that he was handling the layoff quite nicely and that I was sure the New York State Department of Labor would provide helpful answers about unemployment insurance. And even though he'd decided to shit-can me, I genuinely liked the guy.

I didn't particularly like Mr. D'Angelo, but he was in charge and I'd long ago developed a disdain for students who flouted rules of hierarchy and procedure. I played by the rules because rules were the only thing that kept everything from descending into anarchy and chaos and violence. Why couldn't everybody else understand this? Amber's open defiance was so frustrating.

That's probably why, when one of Amber's friends opened her mouth to complain again, I found myself saying aloud, "Jesus, if you wanted a tan you could've gone to friggin' Florida. We're in Europe, for Chrissakes. Just enjoy it for what it is." I heard a sharp intake of breath around the bus. Even Mr. D'Angelo looked surprised.

I rarely use the terms *friggin'* or *for Chrissakes* in my adult life (unless I'm drunk or hanging out for an extended length of time with my family in our native homeland). However, at the moment, I was immersed in the curious pidgin jibber-jabber of New Jersey, and was not averse to occasionally groaning, *"Madonna mia!"* in public when irked. I didn't get that far, though, because I was stopped by the icy-cold stare of hatred that shot from Amber's eyes to my face like frigid poison. I had committed the highly unusual transgression of crossing a popular girl in public. This would have been normal for a person who genuinely didn't give a flying fuck what people thought of her. I, on the other hand, gave a desperate, needy flying fuck.

"Well, maybe if you could fit in a bikini you'd want to go to the beach, too," Amber shot back. Her friends giggled uproariously. In retrospect, I think Amber's primal instinct was simply to call any adversary fat, regardless of actual size. At the time, though, it was like a flaming-hot arrow had struck deep in my chest. I worked very hard to hide my pudgy little belly under my clothes, and was extremely self-conscious about the fact that I weighed nearly (gasp!) 120 pounds. Many years and several pounds later, I'd like to smack my younger self in the face, immediately after kicking Amber in the teeth.

"Everybody calm down!" Mr. D'Angelo boomed. "We don't want no attitude from any of youse on this trip." Mr. D'Angelo didn't usually speak like that, but the reality of his choice to spend a vacation with forty whining teenagers seemed to have hit him. It was enough to loosen anyone's grip on standard American English.

"She's the one being a fuckin' bitch," Amber said, just loud enough for me to hear. Mr. D'Angelo had already turned his back on the lot of us and ambled to the front of the bus to chat with our Sicilian bus driver in loud smatterings of messy Italian. I don't know if he had missed her words or if he simply didn't want to deal with the situation any longer. I leaned against the window and felt my stomach lurch within me. This wasn't good. This wasn't good at all.

The trip to the hotel took about two hours and saw us stuck in a tiny village that was probably far too accustomed to large tour buses full of Americans. Our driver had a bit of trouble with a particularly gnarly turn and nearly ran into someone's charming five-hundred-year-old cottage, which appeared to be part of the most recent wave of development. The entire town turned out to help, coaching the driver by shouting directions and offering the kind of wild gesticulations for which Italians and Sicilians are known the world over. When we finally inched past the cottage and straightened out on the road, the kindly townsfolk waved good-bye. I imagine that, as we sped away from the miraculously unscathed fifteenth-century home, the butcher leaned over to the cheese monger and said, "At least it wasn't one of the nice *old* places."

This was my first trip to Europe, where everything is old. Everything is particularly old in Italy, and even older in Sicily. I guess that's one of the bonuses of being rather close to the continent where human life began. After unpacking at the sixteenth-century hotel, where I shared a room with Leann, a shy girl who kindly assured me that it was okay to be nervous and that it was nice to hear somebody stand up to Amber for once, we were off to see our first batch of ruins. We were joined by a jumpy, painfully sweet English tour guide, Mr. Brixton, who actually wore a tweed jacket in eighty-degree Sicilian heat.

Mr. Brixton said, "Over here you'll see the remnants of an Arab settlement. The Moors had a distinctive architectural—Amber, your cell phone likely won't receive reception here, I'm afraid. Would you like to use mine instead? Oh, it's no trouble at all, Mr. D'Angelo, I assure you. Now, where were we? Ah yes, Moorish architecture . . ." Amber spent the next thirty minutes screaming at her boyfriend back home about a variety of perceived slights, including but not limited to not reserving a *white* stretch limousine ("With a fuckin' sunroof so we can take cute photos, dammit!") for the impending junior prom.

The trip continued on like this for a few days, and while I couldn't sleep a wink at any hour, I found solace in writing. I dutifully took photos of all the historical sites we visited and then recorded my impressions of them at night in my little journal. There were the casual little slights from Amber: the loudly annoyed exhalation of breath whenever I made a comment, the rolling of eyes whenever I asked a question, the little whispers when I walked past.

In retrospect, maybe Amber was my first passive-aggressive heckler. Every comedian has to deal with the occasional rowdy audience member, but the passive-aggressive hecklers are the worst of all. They sit and sneer at you in disgust and whisper loudly to their friends while you're onstage. You either barrel through your set and ignore them, or you call them out on their bullshit. I didn't know I wanted to be a comedian until I was in graduate school, but it turns out I received my earliest exposure to shitty audience members way back in high school.

But Amber's little demonstrations of disgust were all endurable compared to the ever-increasing dread that sat with me on the bus and walked with me through battlefields, gravesites, and churches.

Anxiety is a strange traveling companion. If you stop and consider the grisly stories you've heard since you were small, there are many terrible possibilities on any trip. The tired, overworked pilot could fall asleep and crash the plane (this was before 9/11, so I didn't really pay terrorists much heed). The bus could plunge off a cliff. The hotel could collapse in an earthquake. All these things have really happened to real humans at various points in time, so why wouldn't they happen to you? One can argue statistics and probability, but an unquiet mind predisposed to irrational terror is unlikely to be swayed by facts and figures.

Talking about one's fears can alleviate the tension to a small extent, but who wants to air these concerns in the presence of thirty-nine of one's adolescent peers? Teenagers are fully consumed with playing the roles they've so carefully crafted. They are unlikely to break character to speak gently to the crazy girl. Many teens need someone else to demonstrate cowardice so that they can know for sure that they are not the weakest member of the group. Display that kind of vulnerability and the Ambers of the world might pounce. Better to keep it locked inside, to pretend to have a headache instead of admitting you are afraid of the museum because there's nowhere to lie down in case you actually do get a headache. Fear built on fear begets all kinds of little falsehoods.

Wednesday arrived, and with it a particularly harsh sun. This one was going to be extra hot, and we had a flat, dusty field of pottery shards to explore. On the upside for the popular girls, it was Beach Day. Amber would finally get to reveal the bikini she'd bought especially for the trip and smile coquettishly at the Sicilian men who would undoubtedly approach her. She would say cruel things in English that most of them wouldn't understand, and her best friends would howl with laughter, doubled over in their own, slightly-less-adorable bikinis. I had been advised that bathrooms would be few and far between, and thus had resolved to take off my cover-up only to covertly pee in the ocean.

The field was as dull as expected, despite Mr. Brixton's attempt to enliven the morning with discussions of drinking containers throughout the ages. I felt really hot, tired, and thirsty. I hate feeling any of those things, and feeling them in combination is about as desirable as a bout of constipation. The only part I didn't mind was the sweat, because it cooled me down a little on the rare but lovely occasion that someone walked past me swiftly and created a tiny breeze. It became hard to focus on what Mr. Brixton was saying. Something was tugging at the edge of my consciousness, gnawing at me with increasingly pointy teeth.

I felt strangely light as we trudged back to the bus, as if my body were trying to detach from the earth but was held down by my sneakers. I was like a balloon attached to one of those little Baggies filled with sand. It sounds vaguely pleasurable, but there was no joy in the wholly unfamiliar sensation. It wasn't until I sank into my dark blue–upholstered seat that I realized a voice inside my head was growling at me.

I couldn't make out the words, exactly, but I didn't need to. When a fierce dog with gnashing fangs and a foaming jaw growls at you, do you pause and ask it to enunciate? Something very dangerous and unfriendly had a message for me, and it wasn't verbal so much as it was tactile. I could *feel* it. The feeling was the frightening evolution of the grinding travel anxiety with which I'd long been familiar. This was not my first panic attack (I'd had them since I was ten, though I'd only gotten the official diagnosis and the attendant pills at sixteen), but it very swiftly announced itself as the worst one I'd ever experienced. All of a sudden, I felt true, real, unabridged, non-condensed, fully realized terror. And as one might imagine, I found the sensation *slightly* disconcerting.

I was lucky. I'd grown up in a very safe environment with all the benefits and advantages any person could want: nice family, nice food, nice home, nice education, nice prospects. I'd never been mugged or assaulted. I'd never starved or fallen desperately ill. I'd never faced war or poverty. When I copped an attitude and my father yelled at me for being spoiled, I even agreed with him. Of course, I usually followed it up with a shout of *"You made me this way!"* but that just better served to illustrate his point. I had a job at a bookstore that allowed me 15 percent off whatever I wanted to read (and I wanted to read *everything*). I was headed for college in the fall, and I'd just gotten a secret, totally cool Celtic tattoo on my lower back, a very original place that no other girl I knew had yet decorated. Besides the wrath of Amber, the lack of a boyfriend, and the dead camp friend thing, I didn't have a single problem.

And yet there I was, choking on my own fright. I felt as if my lungs were constricted, as if I'd never be able to breathe properly again. I wondered what that would be like. What if I could never take a deep breath? What if this was always how it was going to be, this dry, squeezed gasp for scraps of oxygen? My fingers began to tingle and my palms began to sweat. And then the bus began to move.

Dying on a bus had never seemed like a good option to me. I'd considered it several times, simply because every panic attack felt like the prelude to a little death (and not the sexy French version of the phrase). I'd had a kajillion panic attacks on buses. It was why I sometimes "missed" the bus on purpose in the morning throughout middle school and high school, forcing one grumpy parent or another (usually my dad) to deviate from his or her own schedule and risk being late to work. I knew it inconvenienced them, but after a while it became such a habit of mine that I didn't even stop to think about what I was doing. It was an automatic impulse. Once I got older, friends had cars and were more than willing to shepherd me to and from school in exchange for a sympathetic ear during a pregnancy scare or a weekly free dinner at the Flemington Family Diner (a wondrous Jersey-Greek institution that we all nicknamed "Flem Fam"). I didn't have a car, myself; my parents opined that a car was something you earned on your own, through hard work and careful savings. I'd done none of the latter, preferring to spend my earnings from the bookstore on—well, more books.

While avoiding the school bus had gotten easier as I'd gotten older, avoiding the bus in Sicily was an impossibility. I had signed up for a "journey into history via air-conditioned luxury motor coach," which, as it turned out, was tourism-speak for *regular old bus tour.* And as our bus lurched into action, I knew once and for all that this journey would be my last.

We had all worn our bathing suits underneath our clothes

that day, and I had donned a turquoise bikini top with matching boy-shorts that I hoped would de-emphasize my stubbornly protruding belly. The J. Crew bathing suit, like my Delia's T-shirt and Express denim shorts, was soaked with sweat from the trudge through the field. As I gripped my seat, willing myself not to writhe in terror, my body went cold. The sweat, formerly such a comfort, now felt like a thin layer of ice coating every inch of my body. I began to shiver. I realized with a start that my bowels were about to evacuate. This made sense, as I'd heard people sometimes crapped themselves upon dying, but I was tormented by the thought that I might not actually expire for a few minutes post pants-pooping. Propelled by the desire to *not* spend my last few moments writhing in my own shit while thirty-eight human teenagers and an adolescent monster named Amber looked on, I called out, "Mr. D'Angelo?"

"Yeah?" he hollered back over the noise of the bus. We were bumping over a mountain road that offered gorgeous views of the sea, which smashed against the rocks three hundred feet below.

"Could you come here for a second?" It was hard to push the words out. I had to close my eyes after the "Could you . . ." in order to finish. Thankfully, the other students seemed immersed in their own headphones and/or portable game players.

Mr. D'Angelo lumbered down the aisle and peered at me. He looked surprised, then concerned.

"Don't take this the wrong way, but you don't look so good, kiddo," he said. "You gonna throw up?"

I tried to speak, but I felt as if I were breathing lukewarm water. I was choking on my own words.

"What was that?" he asked, putting a hand behind his ear.

"Agita," I got out finally, in a scratchy whisper.

A remarkable shift took place on his face. What had been

confused concern was now replaced by a sort of confident, calm determination. I imagine it's the look a veteran firefighter gets on his face when he and his truck pull up to a blazing house in the woods. "First thing we do is we keep it from spreading," he says to his younger teammates. "We can lose the house, but it ain't gonna take the forest down with it. I want the three of you to spray down the trees to the rear. You two head to the left side and you two head to the right. I'll turn the hose on the house. With a little luck, we can avoid a real mess here."

"Change of plans!" he announced in a kindly roar. "Mr. Brixton?"

"Yes?" the tour guide asked, looked vaguely frightened.

"Tell the driver we gotta stop at a gas station. A filling—petrol—you know what I mean, yeah?"

"Certainly," Mr. Brixton said, looking relieved. This was a request he could handle. I wonder if he'd been scared that Mr. D'Angelo would announce a game of Shirts vs. Skins tackle football, with Mr. Brixton captaining Skins. I could sense that Mr. Brixton hadn't been the most accomplished student in gym class (we can smell our own).

"Who wants to use the bathroom?" Mr. D'Angelo asked brightly. Some of the kids were drowning in sonic oblivion, so he kicked his already considerable voice up a notch.

"HEY! WHO! WANTS! TO! GO! TO! THE! BATH-ROOM?!" he roared.

"I thought we were going to the beach!" Amber shot back.

"We are. We're just making a quick pit stop, because some-body doesn't feel good." I suppose this was his counseling training kicking in—confidentiality, and all that. Of course, it wasn't hard to figure out to whom he was referring, since he was standing beside my seat and I had long since taken on a pale-green hue.

He turned and walked to the front of the bus, leaving me alone to face the rest of the kids.

Amber groaned. "What the hell is *wrong* with her?" she demanded, throwing her head back and rolling her eyes. I sank lower in my seat and focused on holding my bowels tight. The nausea had cleared a little bit, replaced by stabbing pains in my gut. My heart still pounded fiercely, but the shenanigans in my lower alimentary canal distracted me from the growly inner voice that had so frightened me earlier. *If I can just get to a toilet,* I thought, *I'll be okay.*

"Seriously!" Amber nearly shouted. "What is wrong with you? This isn't just your trip. Everything doesn't stop because you ate too much!" Through the thick fog that clogged my ears, I heard a few other kids grumble. Amber's hot stare bored into me, and a couple of shameful tears spilled down my face. I could control my bowels or my eyes, but not both. One way or another, I was about to explode.

In my experience, angels arrive in the most curious form at the oddest of moments. They keep their wings folded neatly at their back, and save your ass using brains, brawn, or quiet calculation.

Leann, the nice girl with whom I'd shared a room the past few nights, said, "I could go. I want to wash my hands." She held them up. They were covered in a fine dust from the field trip.

Amber looked at her. Leann was one of those girls who were so humble and quiet that even the mean kids like Amber didn't pick on them. She posed no threat to the popular kids' dominance, and she could be depended upon to do all the work for any group project. She would also spot you money if you needed some for lunch, and she wouldn't ever expect you to pay her back.

"Just look at my nails," Leann added. Amber's eyes widened

in dismay. In the handful of classes I'd been condemned to share with Amber, I had never seen her devote much energy to anything other than her fingernails, which she maintained through an elaborate ritual of filing, painting, and gluing. Teachers frequently sent her into the hall for disobeying their command to keep her bottle of nail polish sealed during class. If her parents had allowed her, I'm pretty sure she would have taken the cosmetology classes offered in our school's vo-tech department. But they wanted her to go to college, so she slogged through French III while sketching nail designs in pen on the top of her desk. She was quite adept at intimidation and manipulation, but Amber's one true passion was the female fingernail.

Amber moved toward Leann, grabbed her hand, and held it up to the light. "Ew, you're right," she said with a genuine look of concern. "They do look bad. You can't go to the beach like that." She examined her own nails. "Shit, I lost a rhinestone back there."

"I have extras in my kit," her friend chimed in. "With glue."

"You think they sell those trucker pills at the gas station, NO-DOZ?" a third member of her contingent asked. "I fucking love those."

"I have cramps," said the fourth bottle blonde. "You think they got Midol?"

And because the four most popular girls in the junior class were now also falling apart, it was okay to delay the beach in order to go to the bathroom.

The driver brought us to a filling station and parked in the sun-baked lot. Mr. D'Angelo helped me disembark, and Leann put her arm around me and walked me to the bathroom. The other girls rushed ahead of us and were done with their handwashing by the time we reached the door. They commenced nail triage in the shade of a nearby tree.

"You go first," I told Leann. We were bonding, a little, but we were nowhere near the zone that allows one person to comfortably withstand the sound and smell of another's assplosion within the confines of a tiny restroom. Come to think of it, I don't know if I've ever reached that zone with any human other than my mother, and I was a baby then so I don't retain the heinous memory.

"No, you," Leann said. She smiled conspiratorially at me. "I don't really need to wash my hands," she whispered, and patted me on the shoulder. Gratefully, I lunged into the bathroom, locked the door, and let it all out.

There was an enormous initial feeling of relief. I felt weak and light-headed, but my intestinal system was mercifully at peace. Anxiety is wonderfully chameleonic. It can disguise itself as any number of maladies: insomnia, indigestion, fatigue, physical pain, or even addictions of every imaginable sort. And once you treat the insomnia or the addiction or whatever physical manifestation the anxiety has thrown up as a smokescreen, you are left with the beastie who started it all. Most of us do not want to face down the ugly, pathetic little demon that we've unwittingly allowed to run our lives. Most of us would rather talk to our doctors about irritable bowel syndrome, or complain to our chiropractors about knots in our back, or stay home from work because we're just "too tired" to go in that day. These symptoms are very real, but they all spring from one nasty little source that must be addressed. Otherwise, getting rid of one bothersome ailment just leaves room for something equally or more awful to pop up in its stead.

On that day in Sicily, with the specter of a beautiful, burning boy floating in the back of my mind and a high school archnemesis repairing her nails a few yards away, I hadn't the slightest idea of how to confront the real culprit behind my embarrassing tummy trouble. I didn't know how to talk back to the voice that had babbled terrible, inscrutable words within my head before the pain in my lower half drowned it out. And so, after I did all the things you're supposed to do in the restroom and rose from the toilet, the voice came back. It was louder and more distinct.

"You piece of shit," it hissed. "You fucking loser."

I turned on the sink and washed my hands, hoping the sound of the water would drown it out. The trouble with screeching internal voices is that they've bypassed the whole auditory system and actually emanate from within your brain. Throwing up aural roadblocks doesn't help. The harsh noise is already inside you.

I raised my hand to open the latch to the bathroom door.

"You can't go out there," the voice snapped. "Everything will hurt again. You can't go out there. It'll be worse than before. You have to stay here. You have to stay right here. You'll never make it anywhere. Why did you think you could come here? You're broken, and everybody knows it. You'll never see home again. You're going to die in here."

People with mental illness are privy to very special knowledge that the rest of the population—poor, average souls that they are—never gets to enjoy. We have the most stunning revelations in the most mundane circumstances. We're sort of magical, really. Thus was it revealed to me that I could not leave this particular restroom in this particular filling station on this particular giant island in this particular ocean on this particular day in this particular year.

So I sat down on the toilet.

I sat and I sat, and then I sat some more. I sat so long that the nail brigade tired of its labors and boarded the bus. I sat so long that I grew accustomed to the fetid smell of the hot bathroom. I sat so long that Leann gently knocked on the door and called my name not once, not twice, but three times.

"Just a minute," I said. "Just a sec."

In reality, I sat no more than twenty minutes. But stuck in that bathroom with only my hateful inner monologue for company, as my heart pounded in my ears and I perspired rivers, as my clothes took on the lingering scent of the shit and piss around me, I felt certain in the knowledge that to leave was to die. So I had to stay.

Then I heard the bus horn honk loudly and violently, four times in a row. Even in my stupor, I was a little surprised. Our driver was a mild-mannered guy. I couldn't picture him laying on the horn like that.

I heard footsteps approaching the door.

"Hey, Sara?" came a nervous voice that I recognized as Mr. D'Angelo's. "Um, I know you're not feeling well, but uh, I was wondering if you were maybe gonna wrap it up in there?"

Then came another voice, equally nervous.

"Sara," Mr. Brixton said. "I'm terribly sorry to rush you, but your classmates are rather eager to get to the beach and, well, I wouldn't say one of them has *overpowered* the driver, but she certainly seems unafraid to express her displeasure with the horn, and these small villages really do not appreciate the buses to begin with, and I'm afraid that the noise will rather antagonize . . ."

"If it's a woman's thing," Mr. D'Angelo offered, talking over Mr. Brixton, "it turns out the station does sell Midol or whatever, so I can go buy you some with a soda, and you can just take a nap on the bus if you don't wanna come out to the beach with us. It's just, the gang is getting restless and . . ." His words were interrupted by another blast of the horn.

God bless adolescent rage and peer pressure. If there was one thing in my life that frightened me more than anything my untamed brain could conjure, it was the very real disapproval of my peer group. Amber and her friends had never been on my side, but now it sounded as if the whole group was turning. And I couldn't abide that, no matter what my inner voice howled in protest.

I rose from my perch on the toilet seat, shakily opened the latch, and stepped out into the blazing sunshine. Then the earth tilted in front of me, and I hit the ground.

It was probably the most dramatic exit I've ever made from a lavatory. The response was appropriate: Mr. Brixton let out a very small, very controlled English shriek and Mr. D'Angelo gasped, "Oh, shit!"

"Can she hear us?" Mr. Brixton asked.

"SARA!" Mr. D'Angelo yelled. "CAN YOU HEAR US?"

To my disappointment, I found that I had not lost consciousness and could, in fact, hear him loud and clear. I had landed with one cheek on the ground, and I could feel a couple of knee scrapes begin to gently ooze blood. It was my knees that had given out in the first place, so I figured they deserved whatever they got. It seemed a rather inauspicious time for them to take a lunch break, and I dimly thought I might have a talk with them once we reached Heaven or The Great Calzone in the Sky or wherever people go when they die in Sicily.

Mr. Brixton knelt down and rummaged through his briefcase. For a moment, I caught a glimpse of thirty-nine befuddled, fascinated teenage faces pressed against the glass windows of a luxury air-conditioned motor coach. Then he stood up again, blocking my view with a large map.

"There's a hospital about seven kilometers away," he said. "I took a traveler there two summers ago when he had a heart attack."

"Shit," said Mr. D'Angelo, scratching his head. He held my wrist for a few moments. "Well, she's not having a heart attack."

"Probably not," Mr. Brixton said. "But it'll be free to visit, and they're very good."

"Free? You mean, like, they bill you later?"

"No, it's totally free. The man ended up needing surgery and he didn't pay a penny."

"No shit! Is it like that in England, too? Here, sweetheart, see if you can stand." While Mr. Brixton educated Mr. D'Angelo on the finer points of socialized medicine, the two men helped me to my feet.

"How you feelin'?" Mr. D'Angelo asked as the three of us, now a unit, slowly moved as one across the parking lot.

"Better," I said woozily. "How come the ground keeps moving?"

"Oh dear," said Mr. Brixton.

"She's talking and breathing and her pulse is okay," Mr. D'Angelo said. "She probably just ate the wrong thing, or not enough. You know how these girls are." We were nearly to the bus.

"I certainly do," Mr. Brixton said with a sigh. "My own niece thinks that Kate Moss is just the most beautiful thing in the world. Hardly eats a thing, and smokes like a chimney."

"Kate Moss looks like a bag of bones," Mr. D'Angelo said, shaking his head. "I don't get these magazines. Why would I wanna be with a girl who looks like she's dead?"

"I couldn't agree with you more," Mr. Brixton said. Before they could continue their discussion of unhealthy body image in women's fashion, the driver came down to help them get me on the bus.

My recollection of what follows is a bit hazy. I do remember being deposited in a seat near the front. I have a vivid memory of the driver picking a lemon off a nearby tree, halving it, and placing each half on my wrists. I think it was supposed to help with nausea.

I also remember Mr. D'Angelo announcing, "All right, kids. Another change of plans. We gotta skip the beach."

An enormous hue and cry arose on the bus.

"What the fuck?" Amber shouted. "Why can't we just drop her off at the hotel and then go?"

"We're not going to the hotel," Mr. D'Angelo replied. "We're going to the hospital." He paused. "Now sit down and shut up." There was a steely note in his voice that did not invite argument, even from entitled, angry, aggressively pretty New Jersey homecoming princesses used to getting their way.

We sped off to the hospital, whizzing around hairpin turns at a pace that would have terrified me if I hadn't been off floating in some la-la land beyond fear. It was very quiet now inside my head. My mind had detached from my body, and any sensation I felt—the tingling, sweating, shaking—seemed to be happening to someone else. My thoughts moved through mud.

If I'd been able to string two coherent ideas together, I might have wondered just what sort of hospital I was about to visit. Sicily is not generally known as the epicenter of First World medical care. I sincerely doubt that any Italian, upon learning of his or her diagnosis of cancer, has ever said, "Well, to Sicily we go! They can fix anything down there." I'm also fairly sure no one else of any other nationality has ever uttered these words.

Had I been capable of such imaginative thought, I might have envisioned an open-roofed shack with walls woven of leaves and vines. A toothless, wrinkled old brown *strega* would sit out front with a shotgun, a bread knife, and a jar of fermented blood oranges. The patients who showed promise would have the sickness cut out with the knife, with some booze to dull the pain (and another swig to keep the witch's spirits up). The direst cases would simply get a swift prayer and a shotgun blast to the temple.

What I got instead was a modern facility with a roof, doors, and electricity—the whole works. Uniformed nurses brought a wheelchair to the door as soon as the bus rumbled to a stop. Mr. Brixton, Mr. D'Angelo, and the driver helped a nurse load me into the chair. The driver returned to the bus, and Mr. D'Angelo shouted over his shoulder, "Everybody stays on the bus until we get back! Anybody gets outta line, I'm sending youse home tonight!"

"Can he put the A/C on, at least?" one of the boys asked. The air was deadly still and oppressively hot.

Mr. Brixton exchanged a few quick words in Italian with the driver and then called back, "I'm afraid not, children. He cannot run the air-conditioning while the bus is parked and off. Perhaps now would be an ideal time for a nap." He added quickly, "And he has advised me that the windows do not open."

An exasperated collective whine arose, and the bus door clanked shut behind us.

I remember swiftly gliding into the hospital, which was smaller than the giant places I knew from back home. We had an ever-growing county medical center, as well as the renowned Robert Wood Johnson Hospital, where I went to get some sort of mild, non-scary cancer hacked out of my skin once. It was no big deal, just a local anesthetic and a few snips. I may as well have been at my regular doctor's office, except for the super high-tech cameras and wide-eyed medical students taking notes. Also, my doctor's name was Babar, which was kind of awesome.

Other than that, I'd only gone to hospitals to visit new cousins in the baby wing and dying old relatives in the cancer wing. Something about being in that wheelchair just seemed wrong, like I was taking up a real sick person's space. Even in my hazy daze, I felt like a fraud. I was going to die, sure, but they shouldn't waste the wheels on me. They could just lay me out someplace. Maybe they could hook me up with a blanket and a stuffed animal and just let me expire quietly.

They did lay me out soon enough on an examining table in a room with spotless steel cabinets and bright overhead lights. A circle of faces peered down at me—Mr. D'Angelo, Mr. Brixton, and no fewer than three suspiciously attractive nurses, each of whom wore bigger hair and more makeup than I'd ever seen on a nurse back home in New Jersey (no small feat, incidentally). Someone took my pulse. Someone else shined a small flashlight in my eyes. A third someone looked at my tongue. I should have told one of them that I was on prescription medication, but my remaining shred of vanity stilled my voice. Besides, I was about to die. That secret could die with me.

"I suppose we ought to give her some space," Mr. Brixton whispered to Mr. D'Angelo.

"You're gonna be fine, kiddo," Mr. D'Angelo said. He patted my hand. "Don't worry." The sudden fatherly gesture of caring made a lump swiftly rise in my throat. I felt tears prick the back of my eyes, and had the vague realization that the body to which I was loosely attached was going to begin crying.

I stared up at the lights, blinking. The faces moved away, and the nurses spoke to one another in lovely-sounding syllables that I could not decipher. Soon, I could barely hear them anymore. My ears were shutting down. I was relieved to realize that my body was giving up.

Maybe I could just fall asleep here and not wake up ever.

Then came a sudden whoosh of cold air and a great crashing sound as the examining room door burst open. The energy around me changed suddenly, became electrified. I saw, without seeing, that Mr. Brixton and Mr. D'Angelo stood up straighter. Slowly, I turned my head to the side and gazed for the first time upon Dr. Sophia Loren.

That wasn't her actual name, of course. I don't think I ever got her real name. What I got was the same eyeful Mr. Brixton and Mr. D'Angelo were getting: a stunning, deeply tanned olive-skinned woman with huge, luscious clouds of shining brown hair, giant, heavily made-up eyes, pouty lips, and va-va-va-voom cleavage that owed its perkiness to nature, a well-constructed push-up bra, or a talented surgeon. She wore a tight purple V-neck shirt and a black miniskirt beneath an open white lab coat. I dimly noted her large gold hoop earrings and three-inch-high black stilettos.

Then she whipped out a pair of black-rimmed glasses that looked more like a prop than a necessity, and it dawned on me that I had unwittingly wandered onto the set of a porno movie. There was nothing about the scenario that didn't scream *adult film,* down to the bevy of hot chicks in nurse costumes. Out of deep-seated Catholic guilt and terror, I had long resisted my occasional feelings of sexual attraction toward women. But in my weakened state, I found myself vaguely turned on.

Then Mr. D'Angelo opened his mouth and promptly took the wind out of my Sapphic sails.

"HELLO. ARE YOU THE DOCTOR?" he asked in the loud, slow voice that Americans reserve for non–English speakers (as if screaming in a foreigner's face is going to increase his or her comprehension of our mongrel tongue).

Dr. Sophia cast the most dismissive glance at him that I have ever seen a woman give a man, and I'm including women who roll their eyes at cat-callers on the street. She didn't roll her eyes, but she did look straight through him, like a lioness who had heard the sound of a small, non-delicious animal but couldn't quite place its origin.

A hush again fell over the room. Mr. D'Angelo shut his mouth. Mr. Brixton uttered not a peep. Even the three lovely nurses were completely quiet. Had this been a BDSM porno, it would have been clear who was the dom and who were the subs.

Dr. Sophia's eyes came to rest on me, and she raised an eyebrow slightly. Regally, she held out her hand. A nurse quickly skittered up and gave her a clipboard and a chart. Dr. Sophia looked down at it, frowned slightly, and approached the table slowly, with her head cocked slightly to one side. She was wearing a significant amount of perfume, and her scent reached me before she did. She smelled like the most annoying part of a department store, but on her it was somehow sexy. With a body and a face like that, she probably could've carried off Eau de Raw Sewage.

Then she was right beside me, staring at me with an emotionless, analytical curiosity. I felt like a crossword puzzle. She bent down low, then even lower, until her face was mere inches from my own and the scent of her perfume threatened to overwhelm my nostrils. We locked eyes for a long moment.

I blinked first.

"Homesick!" she exclaimed in lightly accented English, straightening bolt-upright. Behind me, I sensed Mr. D'Angelo and Mr. Brixton jump in tandem.

"Sedative!" she ordered, scribbling something on the clipboard and handing it back to a nurse. Within a minute, a nurse handed me a cup of a yellow liquid and a cup of water.

I drank the yellow stuff, which tasted bitter and astringent, and then the water. Dr. Sophia smiled broadly and touched me for the first time. It was probably too early for the yellow stuff to have begun to work, but I felt a narcotic sense of calm wash over me.

"Better now," she said, smoothing some hair back from my forehead. "You go rest, take deep breaths, walk by the ocean. No stress!"

"No stress," I repeated, awed.

She turned to Mr. D'Angelo and Mr. Brixton.

"No stress!" she said firmly, glaring at them.

"No stress!" Mr. Brixton replied promptly. Mr. D'Angelo nodded mutely.

And then the queen swept out of the room, followed swiftly by her three ladies-in-waiting. It was as if none of them had even been there at all.

The room was silent for a few moments. Then Mr. D'Angelo said, "And this is all free?"

"Completely," said Mr. Brixton. "Of course, they pay very high taxes to fund it."

"See, that I wouldn't like," Mr. D'Angelo said.

I sat upright and grinned at both of them.

"Are you feeling better then, Sara?" Mr. Brixton asked.

"Yesssss," I said. I stretched out the *s* because I realized I'd never taken note before of how fun it was to make that sound.

"Yesssss I ammmmmmm," I added, delighting in the *m* sound.

"Excellent!" Mr. Brixton said, clapping his hands together.

"You look much better," Mr. D'Angelo said. "More color in your face. Let's go back to the hotel and call your mom and dad. And you just take it easy for the rest of the day, okay? No stress."

"No stressssss!" I chirped, smiling at the cabinets.

We left the hospital, with me leading the way. Anxiety felt like a distant memory. I couldn't believe I'd felt so yucky earlier in the day. What had I been so worried about? Everything was fine. The hospital was fine, the sky was fine, the sun was fine.

I was fine, Dr. Sophia was fine, everybody was fine. My pills were fine, and I could tell they were really starting to work for me. I was finally okay! It was so nice to be awake! Look at those clouds! Look at those trees! I was in Sicily! How exciting! I felt so blessed. Back home, Kevin was dead, and that was sad, but I was here and alive and that was just wonderful. I should really go to a church and say thank you to God for this blessing of being alive and in Sicily. Oh my God, was that a bird, *singing*? That bird in the tree was *singing.*

We got to the bus, and I insisted that Mr. D'Angelo and Mr. Brixton board first. Then, smiling, I hopped up the steps, said hello to the driver, and turned to face the students.

All told, we'd been gone for about thirty minutes. Ordinarily, that's not a long time to wait. But inside a tin box on wheels baking in eighty-degree heat, with the engine and air-conditioning off and windows that were not designed to open, surrounded by dozens of sweaty, irritable teenagers, I think the time passed rather more slowly than it did inside the cool, airy hospital. Thirty-nine pairs of eyes stared at me with expressions that ranged from irritated boredom to white-hot hatred (you can guess where the latter gaze came from). In the midst of my sublime new happiness, I recognized that my peers—who were all going to be my dear friends after this trip—needed some inspiration. And I was the only one truly capable of giving it to them. With that in mind, I decided to make a speech.

"You guyssss," I began, beaming as I stood in the aisle. "I know it was ssssso hot on this bussss, and I'm ssso sssssorry you're all hot and sssssweaty and ssstuff. Thank you for waiting for mmme. The great news isss that I feel ssssso mmmmuch better! I really think the resssst of thissss trip isss gonna be soooo awesssommmmme." And with that, I dropped into a seat and stared happily at the ceiling.

"Oh my God," Amber said. "And she got fuckin' *drugs*? Why the fuck does she get everything and I get bullshit?"

The driver turned on the engine and the A/C. Most of the students clapped with a mixture of sarcasm and relief. Leann leaned across the aisle and said, "I'm so glad you're feeling better! I finished all my postcards while we were waiting. I have some extra blank ones if you want any."

"Thanksssssssss," I replied happily.

"Can we get to the goddamned beach now?" Amber demanded.

"Actually, Amber," Mr. D'Angelo said, glancing at his watch, "we gotta head back about forty minutes in the other direction and get Sara settled in at the hotel, so we're not gonna have time for the beach today. But we're still taking the tour of the Museum of Agricultural Implements at four—not you, Sara, I want you to stay and chill out, just nap or go shopping or whatever you want, that goes for the rest of the week too. Leann, you can stay with her if you want, or you can come with us. No stress!"

"No ssssstressss!" I said.

"No stress," Leann said. She sidled up and put a comforting arm around me.

A few rows behind me, I heard Amber start to cry in angry, gulping little gasps.

"This sucks," she sobbed, stamping her foot. "This fucking sucks."

Her friends were silent. I smiled gently to myself, and soon the gentle bouncing of the bus, the warm pressure of Leann's arm, and the rhythm of Amber's sniffles lulled me into a deep sleep.

CHAPTER THREE

Bowls of Pee

If the whole point of college is to learn unforgettable life lessons, here's the main one I took home: when you piss in a cereal bowl and let it cool down to room temperature, it behaves a lot like chicken noodle soup under the same conditions. The solids settle to the bottom, and a layer of fatty scum forms on the surface, like the algae that blooms in untended suburban swimming pools in August.

Fresh urine can smell sweet, but it ages in a decidedly bitter fashion. If you leave it in the bowl for a few days, the acrid stench will peel the skin off the insides of your nostrils. If you get in the habit of shoving the bowls into the closet or under your bed, it won't be long before the whole room is choked with stink. The best advice I can give you is to open all the windows, get a fan going, and hold your breath till you've dumped the stuff down the drain and filled the bowl with scented dish soap. Then you can give a ragged exhalation and cautiously inhale again, and all you'll detect in the air is a foul trace, a barely-there remembrance. It won't be that bad. Memories of terrible things are almost always easier than the things themselves.

When I was twenty-one, I got into the habit of voiding my bladder into chamber pots of my own invention. I was afraid to use the bathroom, because I'd had one too many panic attacks there. I wasn't a religious person, but I was into the kind of hippie spirituality sold in the New Age section at mainstream bookstores. Therefore, I diagnosed my bathroom with a case of seriously bad vibes, and devised a far more soul-nurturing habit of pissing in my bedroom, in dinnerware. They were actually a very nice set of plain white bowls from the Le Creuset outlet back home in Flemington, New Jersey, where I grew up. My mother had bought them for me as a housewarming gift when I moved into that apartment, a twelve-by-ten-foot room with a sink, a hot plate, a mini-fridge, a slim closet, a twin-size mattress on a rolling cot, and a small window with a view of a smoke-choked alley. The bathroom, a feat of space maximization, was the size of an airplane lavatory with a very slender shower stall tacked on. The medicine cabinet had room for a toothbrush, some toothpaste, and a bottle of the pills I still took every morning without fail. When I sat down to pee—back when I still used the toilet—my knees bumped the door. It was impossible to have sex in that shower, a fact I confirmed more than once through trial and error.

Bathrooms, regardless of size, had always been my place of refuge from the fits of terror that stalked me throughout late childhood and adolescence. I developed rituals to stave off the attacks. I sang the same old church hymn, "Be Not Afraid," under my breath, over and over again. I rocked back and forth, holding myself. I hit myself in the face to shake my brain loose. (Not *hard*—I used a totally normal level of force, like you do.)

When things got really bad, I'd lean my head on the wall, or even on the roll of toilet paper itself, and cry. No one bothers you in the bathroom, because only pervs try to engage with other people in bathrooms.

My friend James Urbaniak, who voices Dr. Venture on the cult Adult Swim hit *Venture Bros.,* once played a toilet freak on an episode of *Law & Order: SVU.* (That's the rapey one, not the courtroomy one or that other one.) His character installed a secret camera in a bathroom so that he could watch ladies go to the toilet. After the inevitable lurid sexual assault that occurs on every episode of *SVU,* the cops find the camera and trace it to James's character. They burst into his apartment, where his sister, played by the wonderful Amy Sedaris, is trying to hide him. Anyway, turns out the toilet freak isn't the one who committed the violent sex crime. But we don't find this out before Christopher Meloni hauls him downtown and slams his no-good pervy ass up against the bars. (James told me that Meloni pushed him so hard that the bars, which are made of plywood, actually bent and had to be replaced.)

I remember watching this episode back in 2004, a few years after I'd had my own fit of freaky toilet behavior, and feeling a strange sort of kinship with the voyeur character. I didn't get a sexual thrill from watching other people use the bathroom, but I did share his view of the restroom as a special place, set apart from less exciting rooms like the living room or the dining room. These rooms were prosaic and uninspired places where one was expected to make small talk with any number of irritating companions. But in the bathroom, even if another person sat not six inches from you in a neighboring stall, you were blessedly alone.

So you can imagine my irritation when I discovered I *wasn't* alone in my tiny bathroom in that cramped studio apartment in Boston. I'd moved into the place in May, and as the months passed I gradually became aware that something was following me wherever I went, sitting on my shoulder or atop my head. I didn't know what the something was, but it was definitely a bad something, the sort of something you don't want perching on your body. It would say things, unintelligible things that I could feel but not understand. And sometimes it would get rather loud.

My solution was to keep my life noisy, filled with chatter and bustle. I had just finished my sophomore year at Emerson College, a school for writers and actors and assorted other deviants. It was a colorful, loud, silly place. In the hall between classes, one tiny gay boy or another was always imitating a character from *Rent* or *Hedwig and the Angry Inch.* And when that wee flamboyant lad warbled a few bars of the show tune that had gotten him through locker-room beatings in high school, he would inevitably be joined in his crooning by a chubby girl from across the hall. Thus did countless blessed fag/hag unions form in the precious space and time between Page to Stage 206 and Mid-Century Chicana Queer Poetry 307.

I knew I couldn't sing, and I was pretty sure I couldn't act (not that I'd ever tried), but I could write reasonably well, so I did that. I had long, curly brown hair and big boobs and a belly I was still convinced was terribly pudgy, three years after Amber Luciano had made a crack about my weight on that ill-fated trip to Sicily. I made out with boys, and got As and Bs, and found a bunch of friends who were infinitely better-looking and more glamorous than me. They did cocaine and wore really tight Diesel jeans and dabbled in the kind of stand-up comedy where you made a joke about a children's TV show people remembered from the eighties and then the audience laughed and then you looked at the audience like you hated them and then you made fun of a band you secretly liked and then you rolled your eyes and got offstage and drank whiskey. This was called alternative comedy, and it was very cool. There were a lot of alternative comics out in Los Angeles, and that was where everyone was going to move once they finished school.

I couldn't imagine moving to Los Angeles. I couldn't imagine standing on a stage by myself and telling jokes to strangers. I couldn't imagine wearing my jeans that tight, not with *my* belly. Instead, I went to the other students' shows and then went home and wrote poetry about feelings and cups of tea. I had a lot of both of those in college. I didn't write about the fits of fear, the panic attacks, because in writing class everyone got to read everyone else's poems and I didn't want any of these skinny, pretty people with frayed-on-purpose clothing and sharp tongues to know that I was the wrong kind of different.

And even in the summer after my sophomore year in college, even in the months when that different part of me grew teeth and claws and an ever-louder voice, I still loved Boston. I loved the orderly, easily navigable flora in the Public Garden; the familiar smells from the Italian restaurants and the twenty-four-hour bakery in the North End; and the floor-to-ceiling stacks of verse at the Plimouth Poetry Shop across the water in Cambridge. I got a job as a receptionist in a hair salon called Très Bien, which is French for "angry queen," and in between the stylists' temper tantrums I managed to enjoy myself. The weekly staff meetings were particularly entertaining. During one inspired lecture, the co-owner, Bruce, stared intently at each of us in turn while growling, "There's a lot of bad hair out there. And some of it comes from *the other salons on this street*!" Then he threw a bottle of Bed Head shampoo across the room and yelled, "But not from *this salon*!" I understood why one of the stylists, Alejandro, drank so heavily in his off hours (and, sometimes, during lunch breaks).

The money from the hair salon job funded some of my purchases at my favorite shops on Newbury Street: challah French toast at Trident Café and Books; trinkets at a little shop called Hope, where a man with long dark hair sold books and crystals and cards with fairies painted on them; and weird goth skull-and-bones candlestick holders in a dusty cave that specialized in refurbished antique coffins and ceramic gargoyles. My favorite item in that shop was a very expensive Victorian hair wreath, which included the intertwined locks of some long-dead mother and child.

For a short while that summer I had a therapist named Mabia or Mons or something similarly vulvic. Her name was fun to repeat in conversations with friends, but the woman herself, while perfectly polite, was not particularly entertaining. I didn't go to see her often, partly because she let too many quiet moments creep into our sessions and partly because going to see her didn't really seem to *do* anything. Besides, I had figured out a few secrets to staving off panic attacks on my own: urinating three times before leaving the house; murmuring a prayer I'd found in some book by Ram Dass; and carrying a small pebble I'd found on the shore of one of the tiny islands in Boston Harbor, where I'd choked on a French fry and been administered the Heimlich maneuver by a stranger.

I don't know when things began to curdle and spoil inside me that year. Certainly the ingredients had been present since childhood, but it's hard to say what finally flipped my crazy switch. It's tempting to blame it on September 11, 2001, but that's too pat and also quite stupid. I lost no friend or family member on that day. It was sad and it was frightening, but it also provided an excuse for me to stand in line for three hours with the boy I secretly loved, chatting glumly while we waited to donate blood at Massachusetts General Hospital. Once the initial shock of the news wore off, I found myself wondering if it was true that tragedy brought people together and, more specifically, if I could get him to tearfully make out with me. Anyway, it turned out he couldn't donate blood because he'd used coke too recently, but we still got to spend the afternoon together.

So it wasn't September 11 that did it, and it wasn't the invasion of Afghanistan, and it wasn't the release of Destiny's Child's blockbuster sophomore outing, *Survivor,* which was completely awesome and probably delayed my descent into madness. I still don't know *what* it was, just *that* it was. And so, in the latter half of 2001, I enjoyed an extended spell of what the Victorians might have politely called "hysteria."

One Tuesday in August, I woke up and stared at the stained ceiling, just as I always did. I had timed my alarm to give me fifteen ritualized minutes to prepare for and get to work, one block away. I liked to sleep as long as possible before facing each day. And then, every morning, I got up, rushed around, and dragged myself out the door to the salon, or to class, or to an appointment with Minses or Magina or whatever the fuck her name was. I was usually late getting to wherever I was going, but I always got there.

This day was different.

This day I woke up, stared at the ceiling, and was gripped by the certain knowledge that, if I left the apartment, something terrible would happen. I did not know what the terrible event *was*, only that it would occur, and with a fury. One might reasonably ask how I could have "known" such a thing, without any clear evidence. Well, one of the benefits of having debilitating anxiety is that you know certain facts that no one else in the entire world knows. You gain a hyperawareness, a sort of sixth sense, and a new world is revealed to you, festering and smoldering just beneath the surface of what the rest of the poor, benighted populace sees. That raving street-corner loon who screams that the end is nigh? He's just smarter than you are, and more perceptive to boot. That wackadoo who claims she's the reincarnation of Mother Teresa? She *is,* and she pities you for not having the special gift to see the truth. The anxious person who knows that, should he board an airplane, he'll die in a fiery, violent crash? He's absolutely right, and woe unto those who blithely take flights without contemplating imminent death.

So I didn't need evidence or logic to know that something singularly terrible lay outside my door. I just needed my inner knowing, my sixth sense, the still small voice that shrieked, "YOU'RE GONNA FUCKING DIE!" upon my awakening. With brilliant insight like that, who needs "evidence"?

I called in sick to work. It seemed an astute move, considering the threat of destruction and all. Bruce at Très Bien took the absence in stride, offering a slightly harried and vaguely sincere "Feel better" before hanging up the phone. I rolled over and went back to sleep. I dreamed of raising my arms like wings and taking flight, looking down at all the McMansions and planned subdivisions in my hometown. It was a nice dream, a recurring one, and one of my favorites.

When I awoke, it was dark and the clock read 12:00 A.M. I'd slept fourteen hours, a new personal record. My stomach grumbled, and since I didn't keep much in my mini-fridge, I decided to put on some pajama pants and leave to grab food at a local diner. Something about the darkness of the night sky through my windowpane told me that it was safe to leave the house now. It wouldn't be safe forever, mind you, but it was safe for the moment. I figured I'd best take advantage of this grace period, and I brought my journal to the diner and had a lovely time downing French toast, scrambled eggs, and tea. I wrote and smiled and enjoyed being the type of person who eats eggs and toast and tea at a diner after midnight, with a journal in tow. I felt like a real writer.

I awoke the next morning at one P.M., which in addition to not actually being "morning" was three hours past the start of my shift. I felt a jolt of terror zap through me, and I called in.

One of the hair-sweeping, chain-smoking, rap-loving eighteen-year-old assistants answered the phone. It is a feat to speak exclusively in a ghetto Boston blackcent when you are the eldest daughter of an enormous Greek immigrant family, but Athena pulled it off with flair.

"Yo, Très Bien."

"Hi Athena, it's Sara." I did my best to sound weak and pitiful.

"You sound mad sick, yo. Was you supposed to come in today? Bruce is freaking the fuck out, for reals. I think Alejandro did Jell-O shots at lunch."

I thought fast.

"I'm at Mass General," I coughed. "I passed out last night. My neighbor called the ambulance. I was dehydrated."

"Oh shit. My baby's father went to Mass General last time he got shot. They was good. You wanna talk to Bruce?"

I most definitely did *not* want to talk to Bruce. "No thanks, I just wanted to apologize for not calling in earlier. I've been sleeping and—hydrating. On a drip. A—a water drip." It sounded plausible, to me.

"Feel better, girl."

I got off the phone and applauded my own quick thinking. I considered sneaking outside in a baseball cap and sweats and sunglasses, and enjoying an incognito day at the mall. But when I got to the door and grabbed the knob, I instantly recoiled, as if it were burning-hot.

The thing—hell, the *Thing*—on my shoulder, which was also the voice in my head, which was also the smartest and most intuitive part of me—you know, that gut feeling/inner wisdom source self-help books are always talking about—well, that Thing said, "Go back to bed. Sleep. If you go outside, someone will catch you. It's safer inside. You work hard. Take a second mental health day. It's good for you. If you don't, you might have a panic attack, you know. You'd better take it easy."

On Thursday, I returned to work, and was promptly fired by Bruce's deputy, his partner in codependence, Arlene. Arlene and Bruce shared a condo, a boat, a dozen friends, and a business. They also shared a pronounced disdain for their employees, especially ones who didn't show up for work and provided fake excuses involving dehydration.

"Here's a day's pay," Arlene said, furiously flipping cash out of the drawer. She pushed it at me and snapped, "Now get out." The other stylists watched with a range of emotions: sympathy, confusion, and, on one face, glee. (That was Alejandro, who liked me but loved drama far more.)

I wandered home in a daze, filled with a mixture of shame and relief. I'd been fired before, once, from a home décor store called Cute Stuff, which specialized in "distressed furniture." In practical terms, this translated to shoddily assembled handmade dressers wrought of wormhole-riddled wood, painted in whimsical, bright colors and with rusty-on-purpose knobs and handles. This was part of the lamentable Shabby Chic trend, which inspired millions of idiots to drop tons of cash on the equivalent of pre-ripped, pre-faded jeans with the goal of feigning an interesting personal history.

I wasn't fired from Cute Stuff because I disagreed with the store's aesthetic direction. I was fired from Cute Stuff because one time I had my boyfriend call in sick for me. Oh, and a pattern of lateness prior to that. But mostly because I had my boyfriend call in sick for me. He was nice. He played the violin and did lots of drugs.

After I got home from the salon, I called my parents to tell them I'd quit my job—for what reason, I can't remember, although I'm sure I invented something interesting to elicit sympathy and mild outrage at whatever alleged evil I insisted my boss had committed. I probably claimed my boss had thrown a shampoo bottle directly at me, which likely *would* have happened if I'd stayed on the job much longer, so it wasn't really a lie.

With the salon job gone, I had to cut back on the activities I enjoyed that cost pocket money—eating at the all-night diner, shopping at the bookstore, buying hippie groceries at Bread and Circus (soon to be purchased by some hippie company called Whole Foods). I enjoyed these adventures for the same reason I enjoyed the urban life: I could move among crowds, listening to other people without engaging them. It was a way to be an island outside the confines of my room.

I kept going to parties for a while, because you didn't have to pay for those. I never put any of the stuff on offer up my nose or down my throat, and the only people who seemed to be having a good time were the ones who did that. I did, however, spend a memorable evening that summer riding around in a budding celebrity chef's stretch limo with twenty of his nearest and dearest friends, but that was because he invited me really nicely and I don't say no to someone who makes a lucrative living by turning rabbits into haute cuisine.

He was really sweet, actually, and later that summer he toted some pals and me along to a party at his friend Dagger's house. Dagger was a working magician who flew all over the world, doing industry conventions and private events for the extremely wealthy. Dagger threw epic parties in his restored Victorian farmhouse in the country, a place that looked humble from the outside but which was a fully functional sex den inside. He had a giant cage installed in his living room and a fuck swing in his kitchen. I'm not sure why the fuck swing was specifically placed in the kitchen, but it did contrast nicely with the butcher-block center island.

Dagger, who was courtly and hospitable, set out crystal bowls filled with neat mounds of pills and powders and herbs of the illegal sort. When I excused myself to go to the bathroom, I noticed a closed-circuit television over the toilet. It was showing a live feed of some of my guy friends pouring wax on a stripper, accompanied by a gentleman who had previously been introduced to me as Sir Sinister. Sir Sinister had four-foot-long dreadlocks and he seemed to be on very familiar terms with several of the surgically enhanced working girls at the party. I sat down to pee, and watched Sir Sinister wave my friends out of the way so that he could mount the girl. By the time I pulled up my underwear, he was inside her. I called a cab and left.

On my twenty-first birthday I had sex with a boy I thought I loved or maybe could love, sort of, even though we didn't know each other that well. He was notable for both his sense of humor and for the polite way he ignored the piles of soda cans and cardboard piling up against my wall. (I kept telling myself I would recycle these things, that I would do the right thing and give them a second life as crap that would then be re-junked. The trouble was that my aversion to going outside was growing stronger by the week.) The sex was extremely fun, but it also misled me into believing that it is always an easy thing to climax during vaginal intercourse. Sadly, this is not true for most human women, and not for me, either, as I would eventually discover. The boy went back to his home city. The last time I saw him, he drunkenly confessed that he was in love with me. Then he threw up Carlo Rossi red wine all over my bathroom. A couple of weeks later, he told me over the phone that he hadn't meant it, and that he'd just been drunk. He never called me or wrote to me after that.

School started on September 11, except it didn't. I was late for my first class because I was gripped by the now-familiar fear of leaving my apartment, but I would've been only fifteen minutes late if there had been any class to attend. The cab driver who pulled over and picked me up was shaking furiously.

"And how do you like this day?" he spat. It sounded almost like an accusation.

"It's fine," I said cautiously. "It's really pretty out." It was, too.

He was appalled. "This is a terrible day!" he shouted, banging his hand on the steering wheel. "Everything is terrible today!"

"Oh," I said soothingly. "Boston traffic is pretty bad."

"It's not traffic!" he shrieked, and turned on NPR, loud. "They flew planes into buildings and they are blowing everything up!"

"They? Who's they?"

"Terrorists! Crazy sons of bitches!"

We sat in traffic and listened to the radio. By the time we reached my destination, he and I had gotten to know each other a little bit, in the way that you do with strangers in airports when blizzards or small TSA incidents ruin everyone's plans. I didn't know how to say good-bye, so I tipped him and got out of the cab and said, "Thanks for picking me up, Mohammed."

"No way is school open today, Sara," he said. "Go find a TV and watch the news."

He was right, and I did.

School was open the next day. I went, but I didn't go very often after that. My fear of going outside really had very little to do with the hijackings. In fact, seeing the entire nation gripped by fear made me feel more normal, somehow. For the first time, the world outside my head seemed as irrational and terrified as the world inside my head. And there *was* a world inside my head—there was the Thing, of course, and then there were the people I invented to help me when I was really feeling awful. One of them looked and sounded like my grandmother, but with an Irish accent, and she was always baking bread. Another one was some sort of Italian-American uncle with a Jersey accent, but he didn't last long. He was very encouraging, though. And then, of course, there was my own chattering, worried inner monologue, which never ceased, except when I slept.

I started sleeping a lot.

Sleep was my respite and my vacation. I loved sleeping. I loved the moment of dropping off into unconsciousness, even when it brought nightmares. I would wake up, frightened, but then the Irish grandmother's voice would sing me a lullaby and tell me that everything was going to be all right, and I'd relax back into slumber. I got really good at sleeping for long stretches of time. Years later, I would have a counselor who participated in super-marathons, running for one hundred miles over several days. I was like that, but with sleep. Marathoners learn certain tricks to keep themselves going, and super-marathoners become even more expert in the art of endurance. I learned that a good night's sleep—twelve to eighteen hours—could, in fact, be achieved without the use of sleeping pills. (I disdained sleeping pills as harmful chemicals. Because I enjoyed such a healthy, natural lifestyle.) The number-one key to eliminating obstacles to sleep was to eliminate excess energy in the body—the sort of mindless juice that led to time-wasters like showering and answering phone calls. And the number-one cause of energy in my body was food. So I stopped eating it. An ingenious fix, really, and one that worked brilliantly.

There is a unique and insidious delight to denying oneself readily available nutrition. I imagine this is quite different from being starved by some horrid outside force—a bad harvest, an occupying army, a modeling agent. I have led a life of comfort and privilege, with a roof over my head and a loaf of bread within easy distance. To deny myself my favorite foods—to deny myself any food—was to wield control over a part of my body that challenged me each day to sate its needs. I could not control my brain, or my soul, or whatever it was that demanded I wrap myself in blankets and rock back and forth a prescribed number of times before daring to fetch a glass of water. But I could control what I put in my body.

I don't know if I had an eating disorder in the traditional sense, but I think I can understand a little of the anorexic mindset. People with eating disorders appreciate the absolute pleasure of watching their flesh shrink against the bone. Yes, weight-loss champions on reality television shows testify about the joy of going from a size fourteen to a size six, how they learned to eat healthful meals and how they've grown to love exercise, but that's not the sort of reduction I mean. The pain of self-denial turns exquisite when you feel the points of your hip bones pressing against thin skin. As my grades tumbled and my waking hours shrank, as my crowd of friends diminished and my garbage pile rose higher, I lay beneath layers of quilts and felt myself getting smaller and smaller. Shrinking was wonderful. And I was watching myself disappear.

I did eat, a little bit, sometimes. I had dwindling food supplies, but occasionally hunger would drive me to open up a year-old can of beans or scrape the mold off a piece of bread. I didn't get too down on myself for eating, because it wasn't adding more substance to my body and it certainly wasn't giving me any of the dreaded energy. When I ate, I nibbled in bed and thought about dying.

Lying in bed was vastly preferable to moving about my apartment, which had, unfortunately, turned into a hotbed of conflict. This was mainly due to the hostility of certain objects in my home. For example, the television stared at me plaintively, begging to be turned on when I most definitely did not want to turn it on. Television fried your brain and made you do stupid things, as I explained to it at three A.M. one morning. The answer was apparently not to its satisfaction, because the TV copped an attitude that made me feel weird whenever I looked at it. I covered it with a tie-dyed cloth so that I wouldn't have to look at it anymore. I had a similar altercation with my computer, which also earned itself a drop cloth.

It wasn't that these appliances actually *spoke* to me out *loud* or anything *crazy* like that. It was more of a vibe. You know when you know someone at work doesn't like you, even though they've never *said* anything explicitly rude to you? It was like that. My household objects were giving off bad vibes. And pretty soon I realized that the Thing that sat on my shoulder had somehow managed to take over my bathroom, which was when I had to break things off with the toilet and start pissing in cereal bowls. Thankfully, the lack of solid food in my system made defecation a rarity.

By the time I started squatting over bowls and peeing, I was too enmeshed in my own half-imagined new world to stop and wonder whether it was a healthy activity. It was just something I did, like turning on the same CD as soon as I woke each day (or night, depending) and playing the same song over and over until I fell asleep again a few hours later. Because I was a white girl from suburban New Jersey, my omnipresent musical companion was the Dave Matthews Band. In the waning days of the fall semester, I listened to their hit single "Satellite" countless times. The repetition was soporific, and guided me through the terrible few hours when sleep simply would not come.

One December evening, there came a loud banging at my door. It was rather like the indelicate door-knocking of stern detectives on television cop shows. None of my friends had called or shown up in some time, since it had become abundantly clear I wasn't going to answer voice-mail messages or emerge from my increasingly noxious lair. I spoke to my parents on occasion, always briefly. I'd claim I was in a hurry to get to class or a party, and then I'd hang up the phone and crawl back into bed. So the combination of shock at the knocking and concern regarding its cause actually propelled me out of bed and to my door. I opened it up, and came face-to-face with Alexandra.

I had two best friends at Emerson College, and Alexandra was one of them. She was a talented comedic actress and a trained dancer, and she had excellent strawberry-blond curls and a strikingly beautiful face. She came from a colorful Jewish family of singers and writers and musicians, and she had been to faraway places like Bali and Arizona. Everyone wanted to know her or make out with her, but she was sparing about allowing either privilege. I was not so selective with my favors, and I always admired her restraint. She was often as bound up with tension as I, but she dealt with it through dance, comedy, acting, and sushi.

She also had another strong passion, and it was this aspect of her personality that must have roared most loudly within her when that door swung open: Alexandra loved cleaning. She did it every day. It stopped just shy of a compulsion, and instead manifested as both a hobby and a great talent. Her room was always meticulously well-ordered. She swept, she dusted, she polished, she vacuumed. And in so doing, she created a welcoming personal space that was as lovely as it was unpretentious. Her place was resplendent with little Buddhas, her friends' black-and-white photography, reproductions of Victorian fairy paintings, books and rings and smooth stones and beads and tiny beautiful abstract sculptures. Her home was never cluttered, dirty, or unfriendly.

It is also a fact that Alexandra detested peppers with an intense hatred. Freshman year, our friend Christopher thought it would be a great April Fool's Day prank to squeeze pepper juice in Alexandra's immaculate clothing drawers and impeccable bed. Another girl in the dormitory, a loudly anti-abortion, conservative, evangelical Christian, thought this was the height of hilarity. When Alexandra entered her room that evening, she froze and sniffed the air, instantly detecting something terribly wrong. When Christopher and the other girl entered and found her trying to hold back a gag as she emptied her underwear drawer, they busted out laughing. Alexandra made friends sparingly and was deeply loyal to those who entered her inner circle. Christopher was one of these; the other girl was not. Alexandra turned her fierce green eyes on the girl and said, "This is exactly as funny as me putting a dead fetus in your bed." The girl ran off, terrified. Alexandra turned her gaze on Christopher. "I'll deal with you later," she said in a low, steady voice. Christopher backed away slowly and hid in his room. Alexandra went out and talked herself down, over brown-rice tea and sashimi.

Alexandra's aversion to general disorder was barely evident when I opened my door, which was a testament to both her love for me and her talent at acting. She told me later that she didn't know there were bowls of urine festering under my bed, but I can't imagine the smell escaped her notice. I know she saw the pile of garbage and the empty soda cans that rolled at my feet, the stained clothes all over the floor and, most of all, my skinny, stinking frame. I hadn't showered in weeks, and I had been wearing the same urine-stained sweatpants and T-shirt for too many days to count.

She met my gaze and didn't blink. "We're going out to dinner," she said. It wasn't a suggestion.

"We are?" I asked, confused.

"You should put a coat on, and a scarf. It's cold."

The only thing that surprised me more than Alexandra's presence was the fact that I did what she told me to do. I put on a coat, a scarf, and Mary Janes (not generally known to work with sweatpants, but I didn't really have fashion on the brain) and followed her down the stairs and across the street to a Malaysian restaurant we'd often admired from afar, back when I was normal.

We sat down and stared at one another for a moment.

"So what's been going on with you?" she said. "I haven't seen you in forever, and I don't even know what you're up to. How's school going?"

"Pretty well," I mumbled, and a waiter appeared with menus.

Alexandra ordered a mango lassi. I ordered water.

"Don't you want tea?" Alexandra asked. "You love peppermint tea. They've got peppermint tea."

"No, water's cool."

"Are you sure you don't want peppermint tea? I've seriously never been out with you and seen you not get peppermint tea if it's on the menu." Alexandra's voice was rising to a higher pitch than normal, and a look of confused concern crossed our waiter's face.

"Water's fine."

"Are you gonna get dinner?"

"I'm not hungry."

"Not hungry?" On the last syllable, Alexandra's voice squeaked to new heights. "They've got all your favorite things. Look, they've got chicken with mango and coconut. And they've got noodles. Did you want noodles?"

"I'm fine," I said mechanically and, for a moment, I wondered how exactly I'd gotten out of my apartment. Had I walked, or floated, or what? It was hard to remember.

"I can come back . . ." the waiter said faintly, backing away.

"No!" Alexandra snapped. "We will get a plate of noodles and a plate of coconut-mango chicken, and we will share. And some peppermint tea. And no peppers."

"No . . . no peppers? Is someone allergic?"

Alexandra turned the full force of her gaze on him. *"No . . . peppers."*

His eyes widened in fear. "Yes, madam." He skittered away.

She turned and looked at me. "Are you feeling okay? You look really thin."

And for a moment, something dead inside me briefly flared back to life.

Out of all the parts of the story—the imaginary people in my head, the pissing in cereal bowls, the lack of showering—it is this part that embarrasses me the most. I've told this story on stages in cities from Los Angeles to Oslo, including many places in between, but I've never told this part. It's just too lame to cop to in person.

"I did this," I said, and showed Alexandra the place on my wrist where I'd cut myself earlier that day. I'd done it on purpose, but I hadn't even broken skin enough to draw blood. I wasn't a cutter—I always made fun of the goth girls who carved their creepy boyfriends' names into their arms—but I was bored and I was awake, and it seemed like an interesting experiment. What would that feel like? Would it hurt? I found that it did hurt, but only a tiny bit, and I filed the information away for later use.

Now that's awkward enough, but here's the truly humiliating part, the piece I've never admitted to anyone else—not to my parents, my friends, my therapist, or my very patient audiences: it was a butter knife. *A fucking butter knife.* What the hell kind of half-assed training-wheels shit is that? I've given myself deeper cuts while shaving my legs. It was nothing more than an advanced scratch. It wasn't even a fully realized effort to hurt myself, much less end my own life. It was pretty much the most pussy attempt at self-destruction ever.

But I showed it to Alexandra anyway.

Her expression was briefly horrified, and then switched to a look I'd never seen on her face before. It wasn't totally sad and it wasn't totally angry and it wasn't totally worried, but it might have had a little bit of all of these things put together, with something else.

"You need help," she said evenly, lowering her voice. "I don't know what is happening, but it's something really bad. You need to tell your parents what's going on, and go home."

At this, a feeling I hadn't encountered in a while—defiance—shot up within me like a geyser.

"You can't make me," I said, except maybe it wasn't me saying it, exactly.

The waiter appeared. "Mango lassi and water?"

"In a minute," Alexandra said, without breaking eye contact with me.

"No, I've got them right here," he said.

She turned and glared at him.

"I'll come back later," he said, and disappeared.

She turned back to me.

"Go home and call your parents," she said. "Tell them to pick you up. Because if you don't, I'll call them. And I don't care if they get mad at me or you get mad at me."

"I'm twenty-*one*," I said, and it came out like a hysterical whine.

"Not right now, you're not," she said.

I rose slowly, and noticed with detached interest that someone had shredded my napkin to bits and rained the pieces on the floor all around my chair. Then I trudged to the door, across the street, up the front stairs, and into my building. Once inside, I slowly ascended two flights of stairs before dropping to my knees to crawl up the third. I was too tired to remain upright. In my room, I accidentally kicked over a bowl of urine. Automatically, I fetched a paper towel and dropped it on the puddle. I watched the dark stain spread across the paper. Then I went to sleep.

I awoke three hours later to a ringing phone. My phone hadn't rung in a long time. For the second time that day, my surprise propelled me forward into an unusual action: I answered the call.

"Hello?" I said hoarsely.

"Hi, Ra-Ra!" chirped one voice.

"Hey, Ra!" boomed another.

It was my parents.

I had forgotten about my non-dinner conversation with Alexandra, so I couldn't imagine why they were calling me. Had I been of sounder mind, I might have noticed that the clock read 11:00 P.M., which to suburban middle-aged white people is like 4:00 A.M.: they're only up at that hour if something very big is going on. In addition, they were both on different extensions in the same house, something parents only do when they call to tell you something awful, like that your older brother knocked up that terrible girl who works with him at the carwash, or that your grandmother drowned the cat in the bathtub.

All these details escaped my attention.

"Hey, guys," I said, and it sort of came out smooshed, like *Hayguysss*.

"How's everything going, Ra?" my dad asked with a feigned cheer that, again, escaped my notice at the time.

"Great," I mumbled. "Awesome. Really, really good. Like the best."

"Whadja have for dinner?" my mother asked, her voice the same high-pitched mode of perky she used with her elementary school students.

I had to lie, because otherwise—otherwise—I couldn't think past "otherwise," so I mumbled, "Food. Really good food. Pasta and . . . hamburgers and . . . salad and . . . water and . . . other pasta." The Thing sat heavy on my shoulder and dug in its claws. "And watermelon ice cream," I added, inventing a dish that sort of sounded like the kind of interesting thing you'd eat in a city.

"You sure, Ra?" my dad asked, and his voice wavered a little.

Oh shit, I thought, alarm bells going off in my head. *He's on to me. This dude is psychic! How does he know I'm lying? I said "watermelon ice cream"! That's too good to be a lie!*

I thought fast, and came up with the perfect answer to shut him down.

"Yeah, I'm sure," I said, and cleared my throat elaborately.

There was a moment of silence on the other end of the line, and my mother piped in. "How's school going, Ra? You getting good grades?"

"Yeah. Yup. Oh, yes," I said. "Like As . . . Bs . . . one B-minus, because this teacher didn't understand what I was trying to say, but she's letting me do it over so . . . I feel pretty awesome about that." I punctuated every few words with a cough. I realized I hadn't spoken to them at such length in a very long time. It was surprisingly tiring.

"Good grades?" my dad said. "You sure about that, Ra?"

Goddammit, I thought. *This motherfucker's good. Maybe he really does have like the eighth sense or whatever. This is getting eerie.*

"Yeah," I said.

"Ra, is everything okay?" my mom asked, and I relaxed a little. Mom was an easy sell.

"Totally," I said. "I'm pretty busy right now, actually." I reached out and turned on "Satellite."

"You sure about that, Ra?" she asked.

Not her, too! What are these people, wizards? Are they fucking soothsayers or some shit?

I jerked my head to the side and caught sight of the paper towel I'd put over the urine spill earlier. It had dried and yellowed. The bowl of piss had been sitting there for two days . . . or maybe it was three, I couldn't remember. I'd kept telling myself I would wash it out in the sink, but the sink and I were having issues because it was giving off a hostile vibe and I just wasn't interested in the drama.

"You can tell us if something's wrong, Ra," my mom said.

And then I knew it was over and that they knew everything, even though, really, they didn't know the half of it. I thought they must be omniscient or something, that they could see all the bowls of pee and the dirty clothes everywhere and the garbage and all the rest.

"I don't think I'm feeling too well, Mommy," I said. This greatly confused the Thing on my shoulder, which commanded me to commence rocking back and forth. I obeyed.

"We didn't think so, honey," my mom said. "Would you like us to come pick you up?"

My shoulders dropped about a foot, which startled the Thing so much that it disappeared for a moment.

"Yes, please," I said, and I felt something I hadn't felt in a while—tears, real ones, bubbling up in my eyes.

"Your mother will drive up tomorrow, after she's done with work," my dad said.

I looked at the urine-soaked paper towel and then the empty

bowl and then at the full bowl sitting under my bedside table, and then I thought about all the sharper knives I had in the drawer, the ones I hadn't tried yet. And I thought about how much I wanted to die.

"I think I need you to come now," I said. "I don't know if I can last that long."

"You feel pretty bad, huh?" my mom said. It was as if we were discussing a nasty case of the flu, which is to say, she spoke to me just as if I had any normal illness and wasn't totally fucking bat-shit crazy.

"I think I might be really sick," I said, and began crying in earnest.

"Oh, honey," my dad said. "It's all gonna be okay. We're gonna get you some good help. You don't need to cry like that."

But I did. Because as soon as I told them how fucked up I was and that I needed them, I realized that I couldn't go home to New Jersey, because I couldn't leave my house. I could never leave that room ever again. I was going to die there, which would be really inconvenient, because they'd have to break into my house to retrieve my corpse, and that would probably involve a lot of paperwork and the police, and my dad really couldn't stand bureaucracy and my mom really didn't like stairs, and they'd have to climb the stairs to get me. It just really sucked how everything was going to turn out, and it was my fault.

"I'm sorry, I'm sorry," I kept saying. "I'm so sorry, I'm really, really sorry."

"It's okay," they kept saying. "It's okay. It's really, really okay."

"I want to—I want to hurt myself," I said through a sob. I was so embarrassed. "Please don't be mad at me."

"I'll be there in five hours," my mother said. "Read a good book." She made it in four.

It would be a few years before I'd sort out exactly how my

parents had gotten the red alert on the state of my brain. Apparently, Alexandra had gone home and called my other best friend, Katherine, who had grown up in New Orleans a pure and virginal Southern belle despite the fact that her childhood babysitter had been a drag queen and her mom and stepfather were prone to dressing up like identical French prostitutes for Mardi Gras. But while Katherine's mom was outgoing and sociable, Katherine was shy and bookish. Her idea of a fabulous weekday evening was curling her dark hair while sipping a glass of wine and reading a book by e. e. cummings. Her apartment in Boston was full of old framed Art Deco advertisements that featured elegant ladies powdering their noses. She seemed always to be surrounded by diaphanous pink fabric and stained-glass mosaics. She had an undeniable bosom and a regal bearing, and she usually smelled like night-blooming jasmine or some other delicate flower. Though they weren't especially close, Alexandra was fascinated by Katherine and often said in an awed tone, "She is just a real woman."

Between the girls, it was decided that I had indeed gone off the rails and that the best thing to do was for Katherine, who knew my parents better, to call my mom and dad. It pleases my vanity that this was a tag-team effort. Any average crazy person can worry *one* friend into action. But *two*? That's advanced achievement in the art of being nuts.

My parents fielded Katherine's call, spent a few moments quietly freaking out, and walked over to a psychiatrist neighbor, who advised them not to tell me that my friends had clued them in. I would need a support system, or so he said, and I needed to feel that I could trust my friends. The best thing for my parents to do would be to call me and see if they could draw the truth out of me on their own, without mixing anyone else up in it.

"Okay," they said. Then, I imagine, everyone threw a hand in, counted, "1, 2, 3, TEAM!" and broke the huddle.

My mom arrived in my dad's gas-guzzling SUV, but she did not come alone. She brought with her a large white teddy bear in a T-shirt that read GET WELL SOON. I don't know where one purchases a large white get-well bear on the Massachusetts Turnpike at two A.M. Quite frankly, I don't want to know what she had to do to get that bear.

She knocked at my door, and I opened it in pretty much the same state in which I had opened the door to Alexandra several hours earlier. I saw a look of dismay very briefly flash across my mother's face before she rearranged her features back into Fake Happy-Time Mom Face. You know the one—it's the expression every mom wears when family members who really suck drop by for a surprise visit, or when you ask her if she wishes she'd dated more before settling down. Fake Happy-Time Mom Face is a brilliant mask. I think they hand them out in maternity wards, along with pamphlets about not shaking your baby. My mother's Fake Happy-Time Mom Face comes complete with wide, cheery eyes and a pinched smile. Should I reproduce one day, I'll model my Fake Happy-Time Mom Face after hers. It's a good one.

I suppose it's clear by now that I wasn't exactly firing on all mental, physical, or emotional cylinders at this point. I'd actually forgotten about Fake Happy-Time Mom Face and thought she was just in a genuinely upbeat mood. As for me, well, I was doing all right. I'd spent the past four hours rocking back and forth to "Satellite," and tearing the dried urine-soaked paper towel into tinier and tinier pieces. So that was productive. I also wondered if I should try cutting myself a bit deeper with a knife this time, just to see what happened. Maybe for kicks I'd use a steak knife with an actual sharp edge this time. I was making plans for the future, which is generally a positive sign for a suicidally depressed person, except when said plans actually involve suicide. But at least I had goals.

Fake Happy-Time Mom Face smiled at me and asked, "You ready to go?"

"I was thinking," I began. "Maybe you could stay in a hotel room tonight and we could go tomorrow if I still feel bad. And if I don't, we could just have lunch, like a girls' weekend."

Fake Happy-Time Mom Face disappeared and was replaced by Actual Stop Fucking Around Mom Face. "Sara. It is not the weekend. It is Tuesday night—well, Wednesday morning. I took off work tomorrow so that I can bring you to the psychiatrist. We are not staying in a hotel room and I am not leaving you here. We are going home, now. Did you pack?"

"Pack? Uh—yeah. Yeah, I packed." I totally did not pack.

Fake Happy-Time Mom Face returned, smiling sweetly. "Great! Then get your stuff, and let's go."

"Uh . . . okay," I said. "Just uh . . . just give me a minute."

I puttered around the room, gathering a few important things: one unused Band-Aid, one copy of the August issue of *Yoga Journal,* and the Dave Matthews Band CD. I did not pack: any clothing, any schoolbooks, or any toiletries. I did put on shoes. I forgot to put on socks first.

"Ready to go," I said.

My mother, who had not ventured past my front door, pointed at a bowl of pee sitting on the kitchen counter and asked, "What is that?"

"Chicken soup," I said, and tipped it into the sink. I gave myself a mental high-five for being so clever.

At that point, I think my mom decided to drop any requests for me to take a shower, tidy up my room, pack a real suitcase, brush my teeth, or dress like a functional human adult. Clearly, getting me home was going to be task enough.

"Let's go," she said.

Alexandra had the advantage of surprise. My mother had the advantage of being the person whose job it had been to tell me what to do and what not to do for the first eighteen years of my life. When you've got nothing left, you revert to old programming. I did what my mother told me. I locked the door behind me and followed her down the stairs.

When I got to the car, the teddy bear was there, strapped into the front passenger seat. I guess it would've been a real tragedy if my mom had hit a pothole and the teddy bear had lurched forward into the dashboard or, God forbid, onto the floor. That's the kind of accident that haunts a person for the rest of her life. My mother was not going to have teddy blood on her hands.

I opened the door, unbuckled the bear, and got into the car, sitting bolt upright with my arms wrapped around my new stuffed buddy. I had the nagging feeling I'd forgotten something, and that was when my mother buckled me into the seat. She draped a blanket over me and offered me a bottle of water, a can of ginger ale, and one of those "nutritional" candy bars. Just looking at food made me feel nauseous, so I shook my head no and clutched the bear tighter.

Before I knew it, we were barreling down Newbury Street at an unprecedented speed for my mother in the city. We may have broken thirty-five miles per hour, an astonishing feat considering my mother's habit of crawling along at twenty miles per hour until an angry mob or a uniformed police officer commanded her to speed up already.

I closed my eyes and nearly dozed off for a few moments, until it fully hit me: I wasn't in my apartment. I wasn't near my apartment. I was speeding away from my apartment, and I couldn't turn the car around and go back. Yes, I was with my mother. But I was in a car, and I was not at home.

A flash of panic seared my chest. I knew that if I stayed in that car, I was going to die. I was away from my safe place, and I was going to go completely crazy, and they would have to put me away somewhere, and I would never feel safe or comfortable again, and why the hell was it so cold all of a sudden, and my heart was going to—

"Want to listen to some music?" my mom asked with a bright smile. It was a Fake Happy-Time Mom Face smile, but it was a smile nevertheless. Without waiting for a response, she popped in a Phil Collins CD (every mom has at least one).

The noise that issued forth from my being surprised even me. "NOOOOOOOOOO!" I roared, and hit the eject button. "Thisonethisonethisone," I chanted, jabbing the Dave Matthews Band CD at the disc player. Panicked, I tried to shove it in, but my fine motor skills had suffered somewhat. I kept missing the target, first shoving the CD up against the radio buttons, next nearly hurling it like a Frisbee over the dash. My mother caught my wrist and said, "Okay, I've got it, I've got it, I've got it," and gradually I lessened my death-grip on the CD.

She put the CD in, and I sprung forward again, punching the skip button until I got to the track I wanted, "Satellite." Only then did I sink back into my seat, close my eyes, and begin to breathe normally again. When the song ended, I lurched forward and hit the back button, restarting the song. My mother cast a sideways glance at me, but didn't say anything.

By the fourth time I jumped forward to hit the back button, we'd reached the toll booth for the Mass Pike. My mother turned to me and grinned with gritted teeth, a major Fake Happy-Time Mom Face if ever there was one.

"You know," she said, "there's a repeat button." She hit it, and left the song on repeat for the entire trip home. That's about four and a half hours of one sweet, mellow adult contemporary groove. Even the most diehard fan will tell you that's a fuckload of Dave Matthews Band.

So I sat, eyes closed, holding the white teddy bear, rocking gently back and forth to the same song for more than four hours. Here's what didn't happen: I didn't cry. I didn't vomit. I didn't open the car door and tumble out at sixty-five miles per hour. I considered doing all of these things, but I didn't. I didn't even set into motion my elaborate plot (conceived somewhere between Connecticut and New York) to claim I needed to use the bathroom and, at the rest stop, rig up an elaborate noose of paper towels to hang myself. It was a totally solid plan, but I put it on the back burner. I just sat there, with the music and the motion and my mother beside me, and all of it was a lullaby. But I didn't sleep. And she didn't tell me I was crazy, and she didn't turn off the music. She drove. I sat. The hours passed.

When the car came to a stop, I opened my eyes and blinked a few times. We were on the cracked driveway, the one I popped tar bubbles on in the heat of summer. Now it was edged with frost. The sun was just peeking over the edge of the hills. When my mother turned off the car, it sounded like a long exhale.

She got out of the car, walked around to my side, and opened the door. I tried to move, but she reminded me that I needed to unbuckle my belt first. I wasn't used to doing weight-bearing exercises like, you know, *standing,* so actually getting out of the car was a little hairy. But we got it done. After she shut the door, I leaned against it and breathed white steam into the air.

And somehow—I don't know what it was, the crumbling basketball hoop, the cracked vinyl siding near the garage, the nuclear New Jersey sunrise—somehow, in that moment, just for a tiny infinitesimal breath of time, I knew I was going to be okay. Not just a little okay, or "stable enough to live outside a psychiatric facility" okay, or "probably not going to kill myself today" okay. But really and truly *okay* okay, one day. Better than I'd ever been, even.

I looked at my mom, and smiled. She smiled back, a tired, half-assed smile, but a real one nonetheless.

"You know what, Ma," I said. "It's all gonna work out fine."

For the first time on our journey, she allowed her eyes to fill with tears. She looked away briefly and then back at me. I knew she was going to tell me she loved me.

Instead she said, "Do we have to bring the CD in the house?"

It was then that I noticed that her eyes seemed to have glazed over, and there was a sort of hollow darkness where her initial peppy fire had been. Four and a half hours of the same Dave Matthews Band song can do that to a woman.

"No, we can leave it here," I said reassuringly, and she exhaled until I thought she would deflate completely.

"For now," I added. Because already the bad thoughts were creeping back into my head, and I knew I needed some sound to block them out. But I figured my family could create noise enough for the next few hours, at least. Especially my younger brother, who loudly protested when awakened for breakfast each morning. It was about that time, anyway.

I can still remember how it smelled then, the cold air and the exhaust from the neighbor's car idling in his driveway and then, when my mother opened the door to the house, something else entirely. I wanted to throw up and I wanted to black out, but instead I walked into the kitchen and took off my shoes.

CHAPTER FOUR

Hairapy

Recovery is a peculiar thing. It doesn't happen on a set timeline. Some people claim to heal all in one revelatory flash. A man sees the face of God in his glass of gin and suddenly leaves the bar, never to return again. His taste for the sauce is miraculously lifted from him. He goes home to his family and apologizes for his missteps. He is a changed man from that moment forward—no need for therapy or twelve-step meetings. Like a medieval saint, he has experienced a full-scale spiritual transformation. And chances are that like many saints, he won't shut the fuck up about it. These are the people who become evangelists.

I hate evangelists.

Personally, I prefer the more common road to recovery. It's messy and it's slow, but I believe it has a far greater chance of lasting than does a sudden, ecstatic declaration of independence from one's demons. It generally begins with what addicts call a "qualifying event." My friend, the brilliant (and now sober) comedian Rob Delaney, had perhaps the most dramatic qualifying event I've ever heard of. Drunk one night, he drove his car over some parking meters and into a City of Los Angeles utility building. He spent the night in a hospital gown in jail, all four busted limbs wrapped in casts, sans underpants. Without the use of his limbs, and with a lot of alcohol still swirling around in his system, he lost his balance and slid down in his wheelchair so that his gown bunched up above his genitals and exposed him to the other prisoners. The guards pulled him back up and perched him on the chair again, adjusting his gown to hide his penis. And then it happened again.

Now that's one hell of a qualifying event.

Anyone who isn't taking care of him- or herself can have one of these terrible instances of bottoming out. Mine was certainly that urine-stained night with Alexandra and my mother. But everything doesn't magically get better once a sick person realizes he or she is in a bad way. For me, the real work began after I got home from Boston.

My father greeted me when I came through the door at sunrise. He was worried about me, but he would have been up anyway. This is a man who relishes the great fun of listening to Don Imus at the bum-crack of dawn while barreling down a road empty of other, more sensible commuters. His favorite way to relax is a luxuriously late seven thirty A.M. tee time at an inexpensive public golf course forty-five minutes from his home. He took a perverse joy in waking my night-owl brother Steve and me before school each day by knocking loudly on our bedroom doors and then flipping the light switch on. His "early to bed, early to rise" attitude did, in fact, make him healthy and even wealthy compared to a lot of folks, but I wouldn't say that antagonizing two grumpy teens at the start of each day was exactly wise. Thankfully, Steve was still asleep when I got home, so he didn't bear the burden of trying to keep groggy early-morning teen rage in check while greeting his unwell sister.

"Hey, Ra," my dad said, hugging me in the kitchen where I'd once tried to punch him a few years before. (It's an Irish tradition. My brother never did it, so I had to take up the cause.) "How you feeling?"

"Pretty shitty," I said. "I'm sorry."

"What are you sorry for?"

"I'm sorry about . . . this mess." I started to cry.

"Oh, honey, don't be sorry for that. Would you expect anyone else to apologize for being sick?"

"No," I sniffled, even though I probably would. I apologize a lot. It's more a reflex than a conscious decision. A Catholic upbringing left me with a perpetual sense of guilt as well as an enduring fondness for judgmental gays in dresses.

My parents put me to bed, and I slept for hours. They woke me at noon, long after Steve headed off to school, but I hid under the covers.

"Just give me a few minutes," I said. "I just need to psych myself up."

"Take your time," said my mom.

"Don't take too long," said my dad. "It's a beautiful day." I heard them walk away to do whatever parents do when their adult child is afraid to leave her bedroom.

"You are gonna do this," I told myself as the bright midday light filtered through the crocheted blanket. "You are gonna get up and feel the carpet under your bare feet. It's gonna feel nice and normal and homey, and you can just stand there and enjoy that feeling for as long as you want. And then you're gonna meditate, eat a good breakfast, maybe do some yoga in the living room, and then, to mix it up, write a short story at the dining-room table. After that, you can type it into your brother's computer in his room and print it out and send it off to a widely respected small literary magazine in the Midwest. They will accept it and you can send your professors back at school a copy of the magazine when it comes out in two years. 'I got into the *Frankenmuth Biennial Review,*' you'll write in a note. 'Looks like I didn't need college to be a literary success! Ha ha, just kidding, thanks for all the good times in The Art of the Personal Essay 302. Sorry I never handed in that final project.' "

By the time I got up, it was two P.M.

"We made an appointment with Dr. Morrison for you this afternoon," my mother said when I emerged from my room. She and my father were sitting at the kitchen table, and I could tell they'd been having A Serious Talk. Dr. Morrison was a shrink who had successfully treated two other people in my family—one for severe anxiety, the other for addiction. He had a great reputation among our clan, which is why my parents had decided that I would be the third member in fifteen years to enter his care. It might sound a little unorthodox to share a mental-health professional among family members, but I like to think of it as an ancient approach. I imagine several generations of my father's Celtic ancestors consulted the same shaman whenever young Arthywolgen was possessed by the tree-spirits or little Domnighailag expressed an interest in Christianity.

"Oh. Okay," I said. I'd heard only good things about this fellow, and I didn't regard the prospect of meeting him with any kind of dread. In fact, I thought it was particularly nice that he was going to make a house call.

"We need to leave in forty-five minutes, so you should take a shower and eat something," my mom added.

"Leave," I repeated. "Leave the house?"

"Yeah, you want me to make you a peanut butter sandwich to take with you?" my dad asked.

"Maybe I could go tomorrow," I said.

My father and mother had evidently prepared for this conversation.

"We think the best thing to do is to get you there as soon as possible," Mom said.

"It's better this way," Dad said. "You'll get it out of the way and start getting better. The holidays are coming up, and you don't want to be stuck at home."

Actually, I very much wanted to be stuck at home. My room was pretty and pink and smelled like the dried prom corsages that decorated my desk. That same desk also displayed a chunk of volcanic rock I'd brought home from Mt. Etna in Sicily. We had a fluffball of a young orange tomcat named Bing, so christened by my mother in honor of the Bada-Bing strip club on *The Sopranos* (my particularly warped brand of feminism is perhaps in part due to some things I learned at home). We had four television sets and loads of books. What more could life outside the house possibly offer me?

"Go on and take a shower, honey," Mom said. "It'll make you feel better."

Sometimes in the course of battle one needs to give up certain territory in order to achieve the greater goal of overall victory. It occurred to me that I might make a stronger case for staying in the house if I were scrupulously clean and pleasant-smelling. Emily Dickinson had probably been an impeccably tidy gal, and her family had let her crazy ass roam the home in white dresses for her entire life. I had lost the optimism I'd enjoyed for one brief moment on the icy driveway early that morning, and was again convinced of my incurable loserdom. Since I would probably live with my parents for the rest of my life, it made sense for me to accede to some of their unreasonable demands up front. With this in mind, I smiled and nodded and went into the bathroom.

There was nothing haunted about this particular powder room, which was one of two full bathrooms in our thirty-year-old, three-bedroom ranch. It smelled like a mix of Ivory soap and my brother's current department-store cologne of choice. It had a bright, cheery window and a bunch of clean, fluffy towels.

I turned on the shower and sat on the closed toilet, watching the water hit the floor of the tub. I wasn't really scared of being in the shower. I was afraid of coming out of the shower with a wet head. I'd had a monster panic attack immediately after a shower one time, which initiated an attack of stress-induced diarrhea. There are few experiences less pleasant than sobbing on the toilet, naked and shivering, as your heart pounds out of your chest and you piss out of your asshole. It's the kind of thing you might be hesitant to revisit.

My mother had always advised me to distract myself when I felt "jammed," which is how she described the state of being stressed out. She liked to take sudden solo drives to New York City in order to escape the sometimes-suffocating life of a working mother and wife in what she termed a "cupcake neighborhood." The other moms seemed content to watch television and throw dinner parties, but my mom needed a lot of multisensory stimulation in order to keep boredom and its twin, depression, at bay. Today, I follow her advice by juggling as many odd, fun, creative comedy projects as possible. But when I was twenty-one, I hadn't yet figured out how to devise the type of distraction plan (today I call it a "career") that produces such enjoyable results as additional income and sex-drenched e-mails from elderly gentlemen.

That's when I caught sight of the pair of scissors sitting in the catchall basket on the counter.

There are a few items that should never be left near a person in a state of nervous breakdown, including but not limited to: knives, guns, drugs, babies, credit cards, and scissors. When the afflicted individual in question is a woman, the scissors become even more dangerous. Sure, she may stab herself or a loved one, but she may do something even crazier: attempt to cut her own hair.

I'd recently seen the marvelous Jean-Pierre Jeunet film *Amélie,* a modern fairy tale and a truly wonderful work of art. In the film, lovestruck, socially anxious Amélie wanders around Paris in a fetching short bob with adorable blunt-cut bangs. It's the sort of look an adult woman should only attempt if she looks exactly like Audrey Hepburn, which the French actress Audrey Tautou does. It's also a strong argument for the predictive power of personal nomenclature. Tautou's parents named her after Hepburn, and so she grew up to look like Hepburn. My parents named me after a biblical character who laughed at God, and so I grew up to be a blasphemous jokester. And I was about to become a blasphemous jokester with a very unfortunate haircut.

My urge for hair modification may have had a genetic basis. I am the granddaughter of a former beauty parlor owner and, more important, a native-born child of New Jersey. Hair salons are my natural habitat. I grew up listening to my mother and her close friends Gee and Karen, a stylist and nail technician, tell raucous and raunchy stories in a hair salon on the first floor of a converted house in Central Jersey. I'd picked up a few tips there and in my own brief career as a Newbury Street salon receptionist in Boston. For example, I knew most stylists only cut wet hair, so it stood to reason that I would need to douse my thick, curly faux-reddish mane in water before I hacked it into a modern masterpiece. Since the shower was already on, I took the logical leap that it would be advantageous for me to get into said shower and use some shampoo and conditioner. Thus ended my fear of the shower. Vanity trumps anxiety.

I soaped, I loofahed, I shampooed, I conditioned, I conditioned again. I shaved while I conditioned. The hot water felt surprisingly good, and I reflected that the scent of coconut is really superior to the scent of dried urine and old sweat. When I emerged from the shower, I felt a sense of triumph at my ability to complete this basic human task. I didn't feel the least bit anxious. In fact, I felt rather delighted. If I were normal enough to start showering again, I probably didn't need to visit Dr. Morrison at all.

Then I dropped the towel and picked up the scissors.

All those years in hair salons had taught me that a short, curly haircut can go wildly wrong. In fifth grade, some older boys on the bus used to call me Medusa when I sported one unfortunate puffball short cut. This was both a nod to my coiled, serpentine locks and to my ugliness. Later, they added "Jewfro," though they knew I wasn't Jewish. Nothing confuses suburban white people so much as vaguely ethnic tresses on one of their own. When my hair grew long and more manageable, the jeers turned to fascination and admiration. A woman asked if she could touch it as I waited in line for the bathroom at a Dave Matthews Band concert at the Meadowlands. A drunk guy started playing with it while I sat at a Yankees game with my mother and brother. In high school, girls always wanted to know what kind of product I put in it, and if I used a blow-dryer, and if it looked like that all the time or just when I scrunched it after washing it. Strangers remarked on it at the mall. At the Newbury Street salon, the stylists admired its thickness.

"You've got a great head of hair, Sara," Alejandro said once.

"I love curly hair," the owner, Bruce, sighed. "Not too curly, but just curly enough that you can hide all your mistakes."

"Not, like, kinky-curly," Alejandro said.

"Oh God, no," Bruce said. "Sara's is about as far as I can go." I believed him. One of my jobs at the salon had been to intercept walk-in customers of African descent and politely direct them to a neighboring establishment that could better serve their particular follicular needs. I seemed to be the only one who worried about the ethical implications of this task.

Many civilians don't know that hair grows in identifiable sections. There is, for example, a triangle-shaped section near the ear that is tended to in quite a different fashion than the shorter hairs at the nape of the neck. Experienced stylists figure out their own way of dividing and conquering, but newbies adhere carefully to the diagrams distributed in cosmetology class. I had neither training nor talent. What I had was pure enthusiasm fueled by the euphoria of having successfully completed a basic hygiene task for the first time in several weeks.

First I combed my long, wet hair out, so that some of it hung straight down in front of my face. Then I cut a bang with one eager swoosh. And it looked cute, except that one side of my forehead seemed to have more hair hanging over it than the other. I snipped away with all the confidence of a seasoned pro and all the skill of a drunk five-year-old. Eventually the bang began to look a tad too short for my liking.

Oh well, I thought. *Hair always grows back.* And then I commenced hacking my long curls to my shoulders. All curly-haired girls know that layering is essential to a good curly haircut, so I set about chopping some hair shorter and some hair longer. It looked a little odd, so I kept cutting.

When I finished, the sink was covered in heavy, wet locks of hair. I sported something rather shorter than Amélie's bob, but again, *hair always grows back.* I sat down on the closed toilet seat and began merrily blow-drying it. The weight of my actions did not truly hit me until I stood up and looked at the wild, tangled, frizzy mushroom cloud that now graced my skull. It was an unholy marriage of Barbra Streisand's curly mop at the bittersweet yet ultimately uplifting conclusion of *The Way We Were* and Kid from Kid 'n' Play's flat-top in *House Party.*

"Uh-oh," I said aloud.

"What? What is it?" came a panicked voice from the other side of the door. Unbeknown to me, my parents had been keeping an ear on what was happening in the bathroom. My mother may have literally been keeping an ear to the actual door, listening for some telltale sound that I was opening a vein or performing an exorcism on the toilet bowl.

"Nothing," I said in the uneven voice that small children use when they lie. "It's fine. Everything's fine! Just doing my hair."

"Doing your hair?" A note of genuine fear crept into her voice. "Can I come in?"

"Why?"

"Just to talk." Translated, this meant *just to make sure you aren't doing exactly what you are actually doing.*

"Um . . ." I looked at my hair.

There was a long pause.

"You have to promise not to get mad," I said.

My mother's sigh seemed to last a lifetime.

"Okay," she said. "I promise I won't get mad. Just let me come inside."

I wrapped a towel around myself and gingerly opened the door. And I immediately watched Fake Happy-Time Mom Face crack.

Hair is important to Italians. We have a lot of it, and both men and women have to devote a substantial amount of time to its care and maintenance. The guido does not spend thirty minutes on his hair because he wants to; he does it because he must. Similarly, the guidette does not spend three hours at the salon out of joy, but out of duty. As the Italian daughter of an

Italian beautician, my mother had done her fair share of sweeping up Italian ladies' hair. The look that came over her face when I opened the door was primal in its agony, as if her anguish came from some deep, cellular level.

"Oh. My. God."

I went into my instinctive defensive mode: abrasive surliness.

"What?" I demanded. "It's my hair. I can do what I want with my hair."

"Oh my God. Oh my Gooooooood," she moaned.

"It's a pixie cut!" I said. "They're in right now." It was not a pixie cut, and we both knew it. I had committed the tonsorial equivalent of a partial-birth abortion, and my mother was the first person faced with my grievous sin.

"Jon!" she yelled. "Jon, she cut her hair!"

My father came running. His face registered shock and a tiny bit of fear. Unlike my mother, he hadn't actually seen my wretched apartment or borne witness to my Dave Matthews Band–induced trance. For him, this was the first tangible evidence that I'd lost my marbles.

"Ra, what'd you do that for?" he asked gently.

"I just wanted to," I said.

"Why?" my mother asked, and I got the sense that her question was not for me but for Jesus Christ himself. "Why now? Why this? Why?"

"Uh . . ." It was the first time I'd really considered the question myself. "I guess . . . I guess . . . I thought it would be fun?"

My mother took a deep breath and steeled herself.

"We're going to the salon after Dr. Morrison," my mother said evenly. "We're gonna see Gee. Gee is gonna fix it. Gee can fix anything." In addition to doing my mother's hair, Gee was responsible for the follicles belonging to my younger brother, my father's mother, and my father's father. I suppose you could say we choose our hair stylists the way we choose our shrinks: as a clan.

"I guess . . . I guess it'll grow back," my dad said. He put an arm around my mother. "Hair grows back."

"Hair grows back," she repeated, like a mantra. "Hair grows back."

"C'mon, Ra," my dad said. "Let's get going. Just . . . don't cut it anymore."

"Please," my mother said.

"I won't," I snapped. It may have been a disaster, but it was *my* disaster. I slammed the bathroom door and tried not to look at my reflection in the mirror as I dressed.

If I had needed a distraction to keep my mind off the possibility of diarrhea, a bladder explosion, a permanent maiming in a crash with a lumber truck, certain death, or an awkward first therapy session, my new 'do did the trick. When we got into the car, I sat in my customary spot in the front seat (I have a tendency toward motion sickness during car rides and during shaky-cam film shots, which is why I cannot watch the oeuvre of the great Paul Greengrass). I didn't need to put a towel or a blanket or a jacket over my head. I spent the majority of the car ride staring at my newly shorn head in the mirror behind the passenger-side sun visor. When I heard my mother's ragged sigh and caught her tortured reflection behind my head, I snapped the visor up and commenced slyly catching glimpses of my hair in the side mirror. We motored along to the soothing sounds of every New Jersey dad's favorite radio station, WFAN ("The FAN") then the home of "Mike and the Mad Dog" with Mike Francesa and Chris Russo. I'd grown up with their heavily accented voices as the soundtrack to my childhood car rides with my father. Years later, I would work at Sirius XM when Chris Russo left The FAN for bazillions of dollars and his own satellite channel, Mad Dog Radio. Whenever I saw Russo in the hallway and smiled shyly at him, I'd race to my office immediately afterward and text my dad.

Back then, however, Chris Russo was just the high-pitched, overexcited soundtrack to a ride to what my parents hoped would be a cure for whatever it was that so ailed me. If anyone had told any of us that I'd be a radio host and producer in New York City one day, it would've been a cause for considerable surprise. I felt like a newborn baby, tiny and defenseless, unaccustomed to the scents and sounds of the world. Even my hair looked like the sort of short, wild mop that sometimes grows in utero. It displayed about as much style, as well.

My mom took out her cell phone and dialed Gee's salon.

"Sara cut her hair," she said. "Yeah . . . yeah . . . I know. I know. Short . . . *really* short. Can you fit her in?" Gee could.

"I don't know if I'm gonna feel like it, Mom," I said. A little nauseous flare of panic bubbled up from my gut. I swallowed against it, as my mother made a tentative appointment for six P.M.

Dr. Morrison's office was located forty minutes from our house, immediately outside the painfully adorable town of Princeton, New Jersey. It was and remains one of my favorite places to visit. The drive there is pretty, passing by some of New Jersey's scenic preserved farmland and other notable sights.

"That's where they found the Lindbergh baby with his head crushed by a rock," I said, pointing.

"Put Flemington on the map," my dad said. It was true. The "Trial of the Century" brought throngs of reporters and onlookers to our little town—in 1934. It was still the most exciting thing to have happened in Flemington. The high school drama teacher directed a popular reenactment of the trial each summer at the old courthouse on Main Street. I smiled at the memory.

"You know his leg was missing?" I said as we passed trees dusted with snow. "And both hands."

"There are some sick people in the world," my dad said.

"Can we talk about something else, please?" my mom piped up, sounding enormously irritated. "Anything else."

"Lindbergh was into Nazi shit," I said.

"I said something else!"

"That *is* something else, *Mom*. It's not about his dead kid. It's about *Nazi shit*."

My mother sighed loudly and fell silent. My father turned up the volume on The FAN, his signal that whatever conversation had been taking place in the car was over. Under new coach Herman Edwards, the Jets were on their way to what would be a ten-and-six season, eventually qualifying for the Wild Card position in the AFC and losing to the Oakland Raiders. I'd learned long ago that the Jets would inevitably disappoint my father in the end, but at the moment, there was still hope.

We pulled into Dr. Morrison's parking lot twenty minutes before the scheduled appointment.

"You want to go in?" my mom asked.

"Nah," I said. "It can wait a few minutes."

The three of us sat in the car in silence and listened to two guys go back and forth about whether a team that showed such promise in its early years was going to live up to its potential or crash and burn, spectacularly, again.

CHAPTER FIVE

My Hero, My Cuisinart

When your daily routine includes repeatedly convincing yourself to not commit suicide, you probably don't have time left over to prepare haute cuisine. Personally, I've never been much of a cook anyway. I don't have the patience for the cleanup. But it's also generational. My mother worked full-time, and for a few years when I was young she went directly from work to Rutgers University, where she got her Master of Library Science. Between teaching elementary school, obtaining a graduate degree, caring for an increasingly ill mother, and managing two busy kids and a husband, she didn't have the energy to cook or to teach me how to do so.

What my mother did learn about cooking came largely from her grandmother and her aunt. I remember making pasta with all of them when I was quite small, how the dough fed into the hand-cranked metal apparatus that then slowly spit out neatly divided strings of spaghetti, linguine, or fettuccine. At Christmas, we would drop bow ties of dough into great vats of boiling oil and leave them to dry on paper towels. Later, they would get a celebratory coating of powdered sugar. Christmas also meant the flat, anisette-flavored waffle cookies called pizzelles, which sizzled in their own blazing-hot irons before cooling on a wire rack. (I keep telling myself I'm going to buy a pizzelle iron of my very own, but then I get distracted by shiny copper pots at Williams-Sonoma and forget about my culinary heritage.)

For a healthy eater, or for someone who gorges when he or she is depressed, it is perhaps difficult to imagine what it is like to view the act of eating as a terrible chore. It is even more far-fetched to imagine the feeling of abject revulsion that food inspires in those people who have committed themselves to shrinking until they disappear. I was one of those people for a short, painful time, and I don't know that I'll ever be able to forget those strange days when the ultimate act of nurturing became a nauseating torment. Quite plainly, the thought of eating made me want to vomit.

Such was the state in which I arrived home to New Jersey. In my first meeting with Dr. Morrison, the family shrink, I described my symptoms as he nodded intently and took careful notes.

"I feel sad all the time," I said, looking at the sky-blue wallpaper and the dark-blue rug. "But more than sad, I feel hopeless. It's kind of embarrassing because my life is really, really good. I feel like an asshole. I sleep all the time. I'm afraid to leave the house. I wake up and I just hear this . . ." I paused for a moment. He looked up.

"I'd really prefer not to be in an institution," I said suddenly. "I've seen movies and everything and I'm not, like, a danger to other people. And I probably won't die even though I want to."

Dr. Morrison looked at me over his glasses. "Sara, things are very different now than they used to be. It's quite difficult to have someone placed in an in-patient facility against her will, particularly when she is an adult. In fact, we try as professionals to do whatever we can to avoid that unless it is absolutely necessary for the person's safety and well-being. I have heard nothing so far that indicates to me you could benefit from that kind of care."

I sighed with relief.

"*Girl, Interrupted* just kind of freaked me out," I said.

"Well, this isn't *Girl, Interrupted,*" he said.

"So if I tell you these two things, are you going to change your mind?"

"I suppose it depends what two things, but I can almost guarantee you that my answer will be no."

I looked at the slate-blue lampshade behind him and 'fessed up.

"Sometimes I think about killing myself. Pretty much all the time. Like even now it's in the back of my head even though I'm not focusing on it. But it's there. I can hear it."

He seemed unmoved. "Well, have you made a plan to do it?"

"Is that the kind of thing people plan?"

"Sometimes."

"I gotta be honest with you. I'm not that big on plans these days."

"Okay, no plan. That's a good sign. Now, what's the other thing?"

"Um . . ." I had meant to tell him about the whole pissing-in-bowls habit, but I figured we could save that for another session. It didn't really seem like a first-date topic to me.

"Well, I really hate eating, lately."

"What kind of eating? Eating breakfast? Eating lunch? Eating in front of other people?"

"Just, um . . . pretty much any kind where you put food in

your mouth and then chew and swallow. Chewing and swallowing sort of freak me out."

He paused in the way that shrinks sometimes do. I hate that pause, because I never know what I'm supposed to do. Cry? Break eye contact? Say something else? I'm Italian. We don't do silence, except where murder is concerned.

"And also I have panic attacks," I added quickly. "And I'm afraid of cars and buses and trains and planes. I mean, I rode in a car today but I really didn't want to. And when I get anxious I have to use the bathroom. A lot."

He looked at me again.

"What?" I said defensively.

"I think it's safe to say you're on the wrong medication."

I left his office with a brand-new prescription, a couple of book recommendations and new breathing exercises, an appointment for later in the week, and the reassurance that I was going to be "just fine."

"But you'll get fine faster if you start eating regular meals again," he said. "Start small and go slowly. I have a feeling the new medication will start to help within the month."

"That's great!" my mother chirped when I relayed Dr. Morrison's pronouncement.

"Want to go to J. P. Winberries to celebrate?" my dad asked. Winberries was a tried-and-true Princeton pub that we'd gone to a few times a year since I was a little kid. It served my favorite childhood fare, including root beer, mozzarella sticks, and pasta. There were televisions in the bar where people could watch whatever station had the misfortune of broadcasting the latest Ivy League game. We always sat in the dining room, where the walls were covered in Princeton Tigers paraphernalia. You could dip your fried mozzarella in your root beer float while sitting beneath a black-and-white portrait of some antediluvian white dudes rowing a boat. In my youth, this was my idea of a great fucking time.

Now, though, the idea nauseated me. All the people, the noise, and the lights. I already felt guilty about not being able to finish the imaginary plate of food I would order.

"Nah," I said. "I'll find something at home."

"We don't have that much," said my mom, which was completely untrue. Most moms always have too much food in the house, not too little. "You wanna stop at the grocery store on the way home?"

"I don't think I'm up for that yet, Mom."

"How 'bout you make a list for us and we'll add it to our own shopping list." It wasn't really a question.

"Okay," I mumbled, and slunk low into the seat. I had to do some deep breathing when I pictured the harsh fluorescent lights and Technicolor packages in the supermarket.

At home, exhausted from the car ride, I went straight to my room. Before I fell into a soothing slumber, I dutifully made a list.

Food for Sara

Cheerios
Crackers
Peanut butter

"That's it?" Dad asked. "What kind of milk do you want with the Cheerios?"

"I just like them dry," I said, and hid under the covers. Dry Cheerios had been my snack of choice in day care when I was a toddler. Peanut butter on crackers had been a close second.

My parents returned from the supermarket with regular and multigrain Cheerios, Triscuits, Carr's Water Crackers, Wheat

Thins, chunky Skippy peanut butter, creamy Skippy peanut butter, a case of Canada Dry ginger ale, Smuckers raspberry jelly, a vat of baby carrots, rye bread, pumpernickel bread, whole-wheat bread, raisin-cinnamon swirl bread, skim milk, 1% milk, butter, I Can't Believe It's Not Butter, eggs, apples, bananas, Eggo waffles, maple syrup, Kix, Cap'n Crunch (a rare and beloved delicacy in my youth), Swiss Miss hot chocolate mix, and a jumbo pack of maxi pads.

"I don't know your cycle anymore," Mom explained cheerily, dropping the pads on the kitchen table. My brother, who had been home from school for a few hours and had emerged from his teen-cave to welcome me home, silently backed out of the room.

Things went on in this manner for about a week—Mom and Dad brought home more and more food, and it piled up, untouched. The fruits and vegetables and meats rotted. I did indulge in bananas, handfuls of dried Cheerios, and cups of water and ginger ale, though. One day I felt particularly hungry and had a packet of Lipton noodle soup. It was the same salty stuff my father's mother had served to me as a kid when I was home sick from school. It still tasted pretty good.

One night I sat up watching television, avoiding bed. Getting up in the morning was so hard, and I spent so long talking myself through the daily routine. I started to feel more alive in mid-afternoon. By the evening, I had hit my stride. I would practice walking outside around the perimeter of my mother's garden. Once, my parents stood on either side of me, each one holding a hand, and the three of us walked to the edge of the driveway and then down the street.

Sometimes my dad took me on a drive around the neighborhood just to keep me in the habit of riding in cars. My mom drove me to the pharmacy and to see Dr. Morrison. I rode along with them to St. Elizabeth Ann Seton Church and sat in the back so that I could leave and walk around in the giant narthex if I needed a break. I often needed a break during Mass. Plus, the word "narthex" sounded kind of dirty and always made me chuckle as I wandered over its cool stone tiles. And there were always fun pamphlets to read, like the ones advertising a "healing weeklong retreat for women suffering from the agonizing aftermath of an abortion." It was free, and happened somewhere in "the majestic rural hills of Pennsylvania, amidst God's natural splendor." It was called "Camp Rachel." I wondered if they had color wars.

By the time my parents went to bed each night, I felt almost normal again. I tried in vain to keep them awake so that I could have some company. I even crawled into bed with them a few times, brightly suggesting we all watch Conan or Letterman or just, y'know, chat about what we'd done that day.

MOM: I taught children to read.
DAD: I helped run a giant multinational corporation.
ME: I ate four whole crackers!

Aaaand *scene.*

Steve could usually be counted upon for some late-night companionship. But even he had a limit, and two A.M. was it. His school day began at seven thirty-five A.M., and he liked to sleep at least as much as I did, if not more.

Every night, after Steve retreated to his fortress of solitude for the evening, I was forced to confront the nasty reality that I, too, would need to crawl into bed and sleep. What really bothered me was the prospect of getting up in the morning and battling the demons all over again. I made so much progress by the end of the night, only to regress the following morning. I even took to writing myself little notes at night in an attempt to ease the transition. A Post-it on the wall beside my bed: "Good morning. I love you." A Post-it on the bedside table: "I believe in you." A Post-it near the doorknob: "You got up! I am so proud of you!" And so on and so forth, even in the bathroom I shared with my brother. I can't imagine what it was like for the kid to lift the lid on the toilet for a morning piss and find himself greeted by a yellow square of paper with a smiley face drawn in Sharpie, its mouth accompanied by a speech bubble that read, "You can do this!"

The notes helped a little bit. But after writing them each night, I still stalled before bedtime. Thank God my old friend TV was there to help me.

Like every other American kid who didn't have weird parents, I watched a lot of TV growing up. Early favorites included *Romper Room, Sesame Street, Fraggle Rock, The Muppet Show, Masters of the Universe,* and *She-Ra*. When I was in the sixth grade and he in the third, Steve and I would sneak downstairs and giggle hysterically at *Beavis and Butthead*. It goes without saying that Mike Judge's brilliant social satire went right over our heads. We just thought the word *bunghole* was hilarious. We still think that, actually.

By the time I was ten, I was watching *The Kids in the Hall* and the brilliant Nickelodeon series *The Adventures of Pete and Pete*. For one glorious season in seventh grade, there was *My So-Called Life*. My father always dug the more successful teen shows, like *Beverly Hills, 90210* and *Dawson's Creek*. The whole family watched *Ally McBeal* to find out what happened after one sassy unchecked eating disorder in a short skirt got a law degree. We watched *The X-Files* to scare the shit out of ourselves, and also because my mom and I totally wanted to tap Mulder's fine ass. But I'd never been much of a late-night fan. When I was twenty-one, I found myself flipping aimlessly past Letterman, Leno, and Conan to reruns of TV shows I never would have watched during the day. I quickly tired of those, and just kept flipping. I usually landed on Comedy Central. *South Park* was always pretty good.

I don't know if it was fate or chance that I accidentally reversed the numbers for Comedy Central one night and ended up on some channel high in the basic cable hinterlands. But I do know that what I saw instantly fascinated me.

A loud, jumpy man with a headset was extolling the virtues of a machine that he said would change the way everyone ate, forever. It would make you healthy, but more important, it would keep you slim and fit and desirable. It was fast and affordable and convenient. And it made things that were delicious.

I don't remember the name, although it was something like Zap-It Smoosh-It Smash-It Liquidification Smoothie System 3010. It was a blender. A really big, really shiny, really futuristic blender. It cost $250 in only four easy installments, and was guaranteed to last for sixty years!

You could throw an entire banana in there (peeled, of course) along with "the milk of your choice" and some peanut butter and honey, and boom! It was almost as if you were eating Elvis's favorite sandwich! If you wanted a Slurpee-like texture, you added ice first before putting in the solid ingredients and then the liquid ingredients. And there were plenty of other combinations. He had just about every kind of fruit imaginable out there on the butcher-block center island in his gleaming kitchen studio. And man, did the guy look excited about his invention.

There was something hypnotically soothing about the close-up shots of the strawberries, blueberries, raspberries, pineapple juice, and ice being smooshed and zapped into liquid. The mixture was red and then blue and then purple. The pitchman hoisted the machine's removable pitcher above a lovely big tumbler and tipped it. The smoothie glooped and glopped out of the pitcher magnificently until it thickly settled to the bottom of the fancy glass. The mushy pile looked like baby food for grown-ups. I padded off to bed, cradled my stuffed giraffe in my arms, and slept the blissful sleep of a grown-up baby.

When I woke up, I got out of bed extra early and walked into the kitchen, where my parents were scrambling to get ready for work. They both broke into smiles. Dr. Morrison and I had recently devised a checklist of daily goals for me to attempt. At the top of the list was "Get out of bed before noon." The other goals included "Take your medicine," "Go for a walk," "Call a friend," "Take a car ride," and "Write in your journal." I always hit at least four of the six daily goals, but "Get out of bed before noon" had never been one of them, until today.

"Well, look who's up with the rest of the world!" my dad said. "You want a bowl of dry Cheerios?" My mom was already pouring one for me.

"Thanks," I said. "Do we have a blender?"

My parents looked temporarily confused. We possessed a great number of cooking implements. We just didn't know what they were for, or how to use them, or why on earth our friends and family had thought to give them to us. These nice, useful stainless steel or ceramic or nonstick or copper instruments of culinary alchemy sat unused in our cabinets and drawers. On the rare occasion that someone made mashed potatoes or cookie dough, my mother's twenty-five-year-old yellow KitchenAid standing mixer did the trick nicely. It had been a wedding gift from my father's mother back in the seventies, and we all loved it. Even better, we all actually knew how to use it. Steve was the only one among us who displayed any hint of talent in the kitchen, and one Thanksgiving he had gone so far as to use the KitchenAid to make mashed *sweet* potatoes. He even added pecans. We still talked about that Thanksgiving in awed whispers.

But a blender? We'd never had cause to blend anything. A typical dinner consisted of Boston Market chicken with take-out cups of mashed potatoes. When we did cook, my father or mother put a bloody supermarket steak on a pan, sprinkled some salt over it, and put it in the oven. I emptied a can of asparagus into a dish and covered it with a sheet of waxed paper before heating it up in the microwave. Then I did the same thing with a can of creamed corn. Drinks were diet Coke for my dad and regular Coke for the rest of us. Occasionally, somebody mixed it up by drinking Newman's Own Lemonade or Arizona Iced Tea.

None of that required a blender.

"Steven!" my mother called. "Do we have a blender?"

"How the hell would I know?" came a tortured response from the next room. His voice was muffled by approximately seven quilts.

"Watch your tone," said my father.

My mother began rummaging through the lower cabinets.

"When was the last time we used a blender?" she wondered aloud, clanging pots and pans together.

"Never," said my father. "The last time was never."

"Aha!" she shouted in delight, pulling something out. "We have this!"

"That's a food processor," I said.

"Is that different from a blender?" she asked.

"It's on a different infomercial," I said. "We might just have to go buy one."

"Good chance for you to get out of the house, Ra," my dad said.

Early that evening, my mother and I drove over to our town's pride and joy, its outdoor shopping center. When my mother was a child in Catholic elementary school, her class visited a living-history educational village in Flemington. By the time she moved to Flemington with her husband and children, Liberty Village had been converted to a collection of name-brand clothing outlets. Busloads of tourists from all over the tri-state area poured into our town every weekend to get deep-discount, slightly damaged Calvin Klein underwear and "irregular" Maidenform bras. The Donna Karan store had great bargains if you didn't mind fucked-up hems. And most of the budget-conscious, unwashed masses tromping through the place didn't mind fucked-up hems (or haircuts, apparently).

Liberty Village had a Le Creuset outlet, and we made it our destination. It was the same place at which my mother had purchased the cereal bowls that met such an unfortunate end in my Boston apartment. I'd never actually entered the store before, but I'd had a job close by at Book Warehouse in high school. I remembered that it had looked nice enough, with pretty window displays full of objects I couldn't identify. I'd spent all day preparing for the trip, repeating to myself, "This will be fine. This will be fun. This will be fine. This will be fun." When the fear started to get too heavy, I reminded myself that Le Creuset was very close to the parking lot in case I needed a quick escape.

The drive to Liberty Village took us down Main Street, a place I loved. The trees, houses, and commercial buildings dated from the Victorian era. You couldn't look anywhere without catching sight of an adorable gable, trellis, awning, or bay window. In the spring, the tidy front lawns bloomed with pastels and every shade of green. In the winter, Main Street looked like a sleepy gingerbread village covered in very cold icing.

After school back in junior high, my friends and I had often walked into town to get a slice of pizza at Jack's and a box of candy at the newspaper shop. Sunday mornings after church, we picked up bagels at Bagelsmith. I liked mine with cream cheese and green Spanish olives. One old house was a requisite field-trip stop. It was canary-yellow and old and had Doric columns, so some imaginative local history buff had named it The Doric House.

Churches anchored the street on either end. One side had the big stone Presbyterian Church where I'd gone to nursery school (St. Elizabeth Ann Seton Roman Catholic Church hadn't had a nursery school). The other had the American Baptist Church. In between, there was a Methodist church and a Jewish Community Center.

The courthouse on Main Street was the focal point of a lot of Main Street tourism, especially during the summer. In high school, I'd briefly dated a boy whose father played the role of the district attorney in each summer's reenactment of the Lindbergh trial, where a jury sentenced German immigrant Bruno Hauptmann to death for the murder of Lindbergh's toddler son. It was generally agreed that Hauptmann had been wrongly accused and convicted, and that he had become a scapegoat due in part to anti-German sentiment in the United States. We never talked about the fact that Lindbergh later became a big fan of eugenics and believed that the survival of the white race was tantamount to peace and prosperity. We didn't learn that FDR had told J. Edgar Hoover that he was convinced Lindbergh was a Nazi. We just learned about Lindbergh the hero, and about the crush of reporters who stayed at the Union Hotel across the street from the big white courthouse. The trial had been the biggest thing to ever happen in Flemington.

Off Main Street was Flemington Furs, a yearly sponsor of the Miss USA Pageant. It was always exciting to watch the pageant and hear that the winner would receive, among other awards, a full-length mink coat from Flemington, New Jersey's own premiere furrier. The highways into and out of Manhattan had big billboards boasting of Flemington's fine furry establishment.

We rolled on down Main, took a right on Mine, and came to a stop in a giant parking lot designed to accommodate bargain hunters.

As we walked to Le Creuset, I prayed I wouldn't see anyone I knew from high school. Some people stay close to their entire passel of high school friends. I wasn't one of them. Not even three years out, I had abandoned contact with all but a few favorite friends—Gretchen and Rachel, and two others. To my mind, there was something pathetic about people who stayed all buddy-buddy with their high school pals. It was like they were afraid to grow up or something. I was glad I'd found Alexandra and Katherine, who kept in close touch with me even though I no longer lived in Boston. The rest of the crowd I'd run with in Boston didn't really seem to care that I'd left, or to understand why. That was okay, too. I figured I'd done with Emerson College what I'd done with Hunterdon Central: socialized a lot, read a few books, then gotten the hell out and cut all but a few ties. On to the next adventure. Which had seemed rather a grand idea when "the next adventure" was college, but not so fabulous when the next adventure was a bargain kitchenware outlet with deep-discount nicked pans and warped spatulas.

My mother and I walked into Le Creuset without running into anyone we knew. I stared at the mysterious and beautiful objects gleaming on every rack and shelf. I felt like a baby bird that had just opened its eyes and lifted its head to weakly greet a bright new world. A giant sign hanging from the ceiling boasted THE WORLD'S FINEST COOKWARE. MADE IN FRANCE SINCE 1925. I would later learn that the factory had taken a brief break from fine enameled cast-iron cookware in the 1940s, when the Nazis took over and began manufacturing grenades. They didn't put that on the sign in the Flemington store.

The outlet shop had everything one could possibly use in a kitchen: French ovens, braisers, skillets, grills, saucepans, roasters, woks, goose pots, crepe pans, pâté terrines, Moroccan tagines, fondue pots, grills, griddles, panini presses, trivets, canisters, butter dishes, spice jars, salt and pepper shakers, crocks, spoon rests (since when did spoons need to rest?), casserole dishes, tart dishes, au gratin dishes, pie dishes, cocottes, ramekins (what the fuck was a ramekin?), mortars with matching pestles, jugs, teapots, pitchers, serving bowls, salad bowls, French onion soup bowls, regular soup bowls, stockpots, frying pans, omelet pans (they made pans just for omelets?), pasta pots, pasta forks, pastry brushes, basting brushes, barbecue brushes, jar scrapers, spatulas, colanders, balloon whisks, handle mitts, potholders, chef's aprons, and something terrifying called a screwpull.

They did not sell blenders.

We drove across town to Bed, Bath and Beyond, where a clearance table greeted us as soon as we entered the store. I immediately grabbed the blender of my dreams. The saleswoman tried to interest us in a variety of fancier, more expensive models, but she was too late. I had fallen in love with the ice-crush function and the $30 clearance sale price. Five minutes later, it was mine.

As we walked to the parking lots, my mother asked, "So what are you going to make first?"

I stopped and thought of the enthusiastic man on TV, blending all those fruits into a frothy little vat of liquid health.

"Smoothies," I said. "So I guess I'd better go to the grocery store."

"Make me a list and I'll get it," my mom said automatically.

She was trained by now to not expect me to want to walk the aisles of commerce.

"No, it's okay," I said. "I'd like to go this time." I hadn't seen the inside of a grocery store in quite a while. We didn't say anything about it as we drove over to Basil Bandwagon, but this was something of a milestone.

Basil Bandwagon was the locally owned organic and natural foods store. It had opened nearly a decade before, but in 2002 Flemington was just beginning to wake up to the organic food movement. We were proud that the state had preserved some of our local farmland from developers, though McMansions continued to mushroom up all over our county. Farm stands were a frequent sight along the country roads that wound through the valley and up into the low, ancient mountains. But we didn't have what you might call a political food movement like the one you see today. If you wanted to see a big fancy organic foods store, you went to Wild Oats in Princeton or the brand-new Whole Foods shop in Manhattan. In Boston, we'd had Bread and Circus. But Flemington wasn't cosmopolitan like those places. Basil Bandwagon was still an anomaly, and most folks got their groceries at ShopRite.

We walked in and immediately inhaled the unfamiliar aroma of fresh, healthy food. Basil Bandwagon was the only place in town whose "deli" counter hawked lentil loaf, tofu with brown rice, gluten-free macaroni and cheese, quinoa with cranberries, and organic kosher matzoh ball soup. There was an entire aisle devoted to bottles of magical supplements that went way beyond the alphabetical vitamins. They sold odorless garlic capsules, wheatgrass tablets, echinacea pills, and some refrigerated bottles labeled FLAXSEED OIL and ACIDOPHILUS. They stocked powders and extracts of astralagus, eyebright, horny goat weed (I giggled out loud), dong quai (I giggled out loud again), reishi mushroom, calendula, milk thistle, feverfew, açai berry, skullcap, marshmallow root (sounded awesome), motherwort (sounded gross), and about seventy other things that sounded as if they ought to go into a good witch's brew.

I bought bananas and peanut butter. They were both organic, and I'm fairly certain the peanut butter was made by members of a back-to-earth Christian hippie cult. It was the type that separates naturally when it is in the jar, so it contains mostly a heap of peanut butter topped with half an inch of translucent oil. I'd never seen peanut butter like that before, but I'd read about it in Oprah's magazine.

Once home, I set about creating the kind of alchemical culinary masterpiece I'd witnessed on that infomercial: ice, bananas, skim milk, peanut butter. My father walked in as I was adding the latter. He started to laugh.

"What in the hell is that, Ra?" he said, pointing to the peanut butter jar. I turned it toward him so he could read the label. His expression of amusement changed to one of utter horror.

"You can't eat that!" he exclaimed. "It's gone bad."

"No, that's how *real* peanut butter is *supposed* to look, Dad," I said airily. "Your Skippy is full of artificial ingredients and it's going to give you Type II diabetes. Mine is natural."

"It looks horrible. How does it taste?"

"I don't know yet. I'm sure it's fantastic. There's no added sugar."

"So it's just . . . peanuts and oil?"

"It is just *peanuts*. Organic peanuts, from an organic peanut farm."

My father shuddered. "I think I'll stick with my Skippy."

He left me to my rudimentary cooking.

My first attempt at a smoothie was unsuccessful. There are a lot of reasons I could cite, but the primary one is that I didn't put the lid on the blender before turning it on. This resulted in a lacto-peanut-banana splatter show that resembled certain moments in the worst porn I've ever viewed. It took me a full hour to clean the wall, the counter, the rarely touched cookbooks on the nearby shelf, the kitchen telephone, the cabinetry, and the floor.

My second attempt went far better. I cautiously dipped a spoon into the mixture and sampled it. It tasted like a milkshake, but healthier. I poured myself a glass, sat down at the kitchen table, and toasted my own creativity. I downed it quickly, surprised at how hungry I suddenly was. I poured another glass and stuck a straw in it, slurping it up with all the delight of a (very simple) child. When I was done, I felt sated for the first time in a long time. It didn't even occur to me that I'd eaten real food, with real calories, real vitamins, real minerals, real fats, real proteins, real sugars, and real nutrition. If you could drink it, I thought, it wasn't food.

After I cleaned up my second, far less spectacular mess, I scanned the cookbooks. Mom had an ancient Betty Crocker tome, a few pretty gift cookbooks with photos of food no human would actually have time to make, and then some old healthy cookbook my Aunt Diane in San Francisco had sent my parents years ago. Unlike the other cookbooks, it was an oversize paperback that looked as if it had been stitched together by tiny, hemp-scented elves. It was filled with beautiful line drawings, and it had hardly any recipes with meat. It did, however, have an entire section full of "health drinks." I began making a shopping list.

The next day, we returned to Basil Bandwagon. I left the store with recycled paper bags full of avocados, lemons, pure pineapple juice, wheat germ, flaxseed oil, unsweetened cranberry juice, blueberries, raspberries, strawberries, more bananas, and plain fat-free yogurt with live "good" bacteria that had come from the milk of cows who did yoga or something. My mother cringed and paid $8 for a bag of crushed ice made from thrice-distilled spring water that burbled up at the base of some sacred mountain in upstate New York. I guess when you're glad that your daughter has decided to obsess over fruit instead of suicide, you'll spend big bucks on some Ulster County hippie's frozen tap water.

I experimented a lot over the next few weeks, and I learned a few important things. I'm pleased to share them with you now in a helpful list form. If you are recovering from a nervous breakdown or an eating disorder or just a bad day at tennis camp, these pieces of hard-won wisdom may inspire you.

1. Wheat germ makes you poop. A lot.

2. So does fruit.

3. Fruits are awesome for you and they're full of natural sugars. Natural sugars are way better than nasty-ass chemically processed sugars like the popular white stuff, but they're still sugars. So if you're susceptible to yeast infections, make sure you're not *just* eating fruit all day long for like two weeks. Which leads me to the following tip.

4. Unsweetened cranberry juice tastes like ass when you first try it. Also when you try it the second time, and the third time. But it's great at helping you avoid or clear up UTIs or yeast infec-

tions. It makes your piss crazy acidic, I guess. I don't know. I'm a comedian, not a doctor or a nutritionist. Anyway, it's good to have a bottle on hand just in case. But make sure it's 100 percent cranberry juice, not some bullshit cocktail from Ocean Spray.

5. If you add lemon juice to milk, it fucks the milk up real bad.

When you're building your smoothie, always put the ice in first. In order to go easy on your blender, make sure the cubes are small. You can also wrap a bunch of ice cubes lightly in a towel and then smash the shit out of it with a hammer and then put the crushed-up bits into the blender. This is also a great way to get out aggression and/or feelings of self-loathing!

After the ice, put your solids in. Again, make sure they're of a manageable size for your blender. And finally, add your liquid. Remember that the blender will kick everything up, so don't overfill the container. If you want a denser, chunkier smoothie, use less liquid.

Once you've got it all in there, pop the lid on and hold it down with your hand. It's tempting to think you can let that fucker do its thing alone, but I've been traumatized too many times by blender explosions (yes, even when I actually remembered to put the lid on).

I put together a few recipes of my very own. As you'll see, they're clearly too terrible for me to have stolen them from anywhere. Also, they don't use actual measurements. Feel free to use them and experience the magic of smooshed-up food for yourself. Think of me each time you tip a glass of delicious mush.

Lazy-Ass Lassi

Organic plain or vanilla nonfat yogurt with that good bacteria
Organic mango chunks (fresh or frozen)
Celtic sea salt
Ice

Instructions: Whir this shit up until it reaches sufficient levels of subcontinental Asian-tinged awesomeness. Feel free to break out in choreographed dance moves whilst singing at a super-high pitch. (Racism!)

Citricidal Tendencies

Organic orange juice
Organic pineapple chunks (fresh or frozen)
Organic lemon juice
Organic clementine segments (sans seeds, duh)
Organic lime juice
Whatever other citrus fruits you can find
Ice

Instructions: You know, blend it. This one has lots of vitamin C. You may be a depressed anorexic dancing on the edge of sanity, but at least you'll never develop scurvy.

The Sexy Mexican

Organic fresh tomato juice
Organic lime juice
Organic avocado chunks
Organic cilantro
Celtic sea salt

Instructions: Vroom, vroom, vroom. Puree the shit out of this liquid guacamole-like concoction. Did you know that avocado is a reputed aphrodisiac? Well, it is, you slut. This tasty concoction may just inspire you to lovingly fellate one of our kindly brethren from south of the border. Surprise! He's probably uncircumcised. I try to avoid fucking foreigners for exactly this reason.

Of note: You can substitute almond milk or rice milk for cow's milk in any smoothie recipe (not just my brilliant ones). Don't use soy milk. That shit is usually packed with weird, gross chemicals and tastes like the inside of a hamster's asshole. I mean, probably. That's probably what the inside of a hamster's asshole tastes like.

I invented these and other fine culinary delights every day in my parents' kitchen on their marble-top counter. It was the fanciest thing in the house. I liked to look at its swirling, irregular pattern every night when I set out the fruits, the cutting board, the knife, and the blender for the next morning. Knowing I had a new smoothie adventure on deck for the next morning gave me a reason to look forward to waking up.

The strange thing was that as I drank more of these liquid concoctions, I got my taste back for their solid counterparts. Soon enough, it was easy to down a peanut butter sandwich (with all-natural, organic, five-grain, sprouted bread from Basil Bandwagon, of course) accompanied by a glass of (all-natural, organic, free-range, grass-fed, reiki-treated, shiatsu-massaged) skim milk. I learned that you could spread ripe avocado on that same toast, then top it off with a (local organic heirloom) tomato, and the whole thing was pretty delicious. Every day brought a tasty new discovery, or a happy rediscovery. My efforts were tentative, but promising. Because I took tiny bites and chewed so cautiously, I savored my food in a way I never had time to do before.

"Food is actually pretty fucking awesome," I told Dr. Morrison.

"Most people seem to enjoy it," he replied. "The Prozac is helping, then?"

I leaned forward. "Totally. Sometimes I put it in my smoothie. It adds this really interesting texture. Peanut butter, milk, bananas, and emotional well-being."

He blinked.

"I'm just fucking with you," I said.

He actually laughed at that one. I really liked the way it sounded. His laughter was near-tangible proof that I'd said and done something right in that moment. For a moment, I felt all warm and glowy inside. I decided I could get used to that kind of feeling.

Then he asked, "So how is the driving coming along?"

"Driving?" I repeated. "Oh, I don't think so."

"You sound like you're doing pretty well. Have you thought about just practicing driving around your neighborhood?"

On to the next adventure.

CHAPTER SIX

Om Mani Padme Fuck You

While I was learning to eat solid foods and shit in a toilet and drive a car again, I read a lot of Zentastic, organic, free-range, fair-trade, sustainable, sage-scented self-help books, most of which were designed for postmenopausal ex-hippies with a fondness for moon worship and natural-fiber clothing. I wasn't rich enough to follow my dream of living among noble brown stereotypes, which is why this book isn't called *Eat, Pray, Love*. I just read books that similarly co-opted other people's cultural traditions and repackaged them with a neat, lily-white bow on top. I called this "spirituality."

My foray into the crunchier realm was not entirely without precedent. Flemington is about twenty minutes away from a lovely little riverside gay enclave called New Hope, across the Delaware River in Pennsylvania. When I was in junior high, I began spending free Saturdays and evenings there, taking in poetry readings and organic, locally sourced, artisanal snacks with equal reverence. After my mom dropped me off, secure in the knowledge that no adult male in that town had any designs on a young teen of the girl persuasion, I could get homemade rose petal ice cream at Gerenser's (it tasted like perfume, but it sure was more interesting than a cone from the Carvel back home) and walk right down the street to the two competing witch-supply stores. One was called Gypsy Heaven and was run by an actual witch with a shock of wild blond Stevie Nicks hair. The other was called the New Hope Magick Shoppe and offered tarot readings by an elderly, chain-smoking devout Catholic named Irene who taught catechism when she wasn't unspooling the mysteries of the Major Arcana.

Fresh from my Confirmation as a Roman Catholic adult, I saw no contradiction between what I learned in church and what I learned from the woman with the cards. Catholicism is steeped in mysticism, magic, and ritual anyway. And there was nothing in the cards to discourage my belief in the Ten Commandments, the Beatitudes, and the inherent evil of putting it in the butt. I figured Irene and I were safe from hellfire.

When I was thirteen, I loved nothing more than to scarf down my ice cream cone inside or just outside one of the witch stores (Irene didn't care if you brought your food inside, but Stevie Nicks wouldn't have it) and breathe in that mystical smell of Nag Champa incense, patchouli oil, and body odor. These stores stocked spell books, tarot cards, mini-gargoyles (to keep the bad vibes away), gemstones that could heal your physical and psychic illnesses, white sage smudge sticks to purify your home, and handmade candles that came with instructions for making wishes and visualizing one's ideal future. Stevie Nicks made her own magic(k)al herb blends that you could burn to attract love, calm an unruly pet, invite prosperity, and ease menstrual cramps. There was also a *Wild Womyn Mooncycle Jour-*

nal designed to help the fertile human goddess chart her sacred ovum's monthly journey.

Pantheistic earth hippies are obsessed with menstruation. A few years ago, my big gay bear friend Alan told me about some queer spring musical jamboree/fuckfest he attended on an organic farm in the hills of Tennessee to celebrate Beltane, May first. Before they could erect their giant maypole, there was a preparation ceremony. Alan, who was tripping on acid, can't remember exactly what the rationale behind all this was. Mostly he just remembers the intense, all-consuming fear that enveloped him when some of the organizers dug a hole for the pole. As he watched in horror, a couple of floppy-titted women took turns squatting over it and menstruating. After that, dudes were invited to jerk off into it. This happened during a sacred drum circle, *of course.* Only after the various effluvia had settled into the hole were the hippies ready to plant the giant ribbon pole in the ground. Everyone wondered why Alan stayed in his tent for the next two days.

Sadly, I've yet to attain that particular level of enlightenment. But when I was in junior high, I sometimes knelt and prayed in front of a little altar in my room, burning a blue candle (for masculine energy) and a pink candle (for feminine energy) while envisioning straight As and a really awesome date to the next dance.

When I entered Emerson College, I found myself with a pagan roommate. She told me ooky-spooky stories about passing an invisible ball of energy around with her friends, which I would later discover was a common beginner's level improv comedy game. This makes perfect sense, because Wicca and improv comedy are both packed with dorks who like to play pretend when they really ought to be learning a trade. Anyway, she was really nice and she encouraged me to read up on astrology, which I found at least as believable as the Catholic stuff I was beginning to disdain.

Emerson wasn't generally the sort of place where one worshipped any goddess other than Fame (and I'm pretty sure Fame might be a sparkly, glittery, fabulous he-god). Once again, my hippie inclinations fell by the wayside as I got caught up in more worldly pursuits, like finding a boy to date who preferred my company over that of cocaine and/or cock. School forced me to read a lot and write a lot, and the urban environment of Boston wasn't exactly conducive to meditation in nature or communing with a sacred grove of trees. I once passed a very pleasant morning communicating with fat squirrels in the Boston Public Garden, but I'm fairly certain they just hung around and listened to my boy troubles because I fed them a steady diet of leftover Cheetos.

When in the late fall of my junior year I went batty and went home, I found myself truly struggling for the first time with basic, day-to-day tasks. Even my trip to Sicily back in high school could be chalked up to the stress of being far away from home, if I ignored the fact that it had actually been a clear indicator of the mental illness to come. My first weeks in New Jersey were fraught with fear, stress, and strain, even though I was surrounded by familiar faces and places. The surroundings were cushy, but my mind was a minefield that kept exploding.

People in crisis often turn to religion and other drugs for comfort. I was ripe for some kind of new dependency. But instead of darkening the door of a church, I threw myself full-tilt boogie into the Holy Sacred and Apostolic Church of the Barnes and Noble New Age Section. Byron Katie, Stephen Mitchell, Pema Chödrön, Marianne Williamson, Eckhart Tolle, that dude who wrote *The Four Agreements* . . . I gobbled them all up. I accidentally stumbled upon actually helpful information in the form of a book about Dr. Jon Kabat-Zinn, Ph.D.'s, work at the University of Massachusetts Medical School. I credit *Full Catastrophe Living* and the Mindfulness-Based Stress Reduction Program with adding speed and sense to my recovery. Though he was a seemingly devout Buddhist, Kabat-Zinn dispensed with all the gobbledygook espoused by self-help charlatans and provided a workable program that incorporates cognitive behavioral techniques, good nutrition and exercise, and relaxation methods. And his book came with progress charts that you could photocopy. I love homework.

After a couple months of filling out weekly charts and downing all those organic smoothies and reading stories of gentle healing and sitting through marathon therapy sessions with Dr. Morrison, I felt a lot better. I wasn't totally healthy yet, but I was getting there. I'd learned a few breathing techniques and had begun doing slow, mindful walking meditation in the backyard at night. I saved the latter practice for after dark, when my deliberate perambulation was less likely to freak out the neighbors. I'd gained a little bit of weight and looked less bony. After some helpful reshaping by Gee, my hair was even growing back. As soon as I perceived that I was healing, I decided to start worrying about something else: money.

My parents, glad that I had re-mastered the use of the common bar of soap and ecstatic that I had begun to drive short distances on my own, gave generously without asking for any recompense. They covered the costs of my psychiatric appointments, my medication, my clothes, my groceries, the electricity I used at their house, the gas I put into the car they lent me, and the remaining rent on my old apartment in Boston, which my mother and my uncle Joe had cleaned out once and for all (kindly making no mention of any disgusting things they encountered therein). I couldn't shake the gnawing feeling that the closer I got to normal, the closer I got to freeloading. It was understandable that an insane, frail wretch of a daughter would restrict her activities to mooning about the house and making all her meals in a blender. In the early days, I had barely been able to generate a coherent thought, let alone an income. However, I was starting to resemble a reasonably sane human again. The new medication had kicked in full-blast, and my appetite improved all the time. I slept better, and it became a bit less difficult to talk myself out of bed, into the bathroom, and into the kitchen in the mornings. I even alternated showers with baths now, because you could read self-help books in the bath.

"You're doing well," said Dr. Morrison. "You might consider getting a part-time job. It would add some structure to your day, and you'd be around people. And saving some money is the first step to getting out on your own again."

"Also there's this thing called reiki I read about in *Sacred Living* magazine," I said. "It's like, someone puts their hands right above you and heals you? Like Jesus, but you have to pay and it's Japanese? I could save money and go get that done."

"Well yes," Dr. Morrison said. "You could also save to do that."

He suggested I make a list of what characteristics I wanted in a part-time job, in order to help me focus my search. I scribbled one in my journal that evening.

What I Want from a Job

Money
Happiness
Self-worth
Increased spiritual fulfillment
A boyfriend

It was a tall order, and not one I was sure a gig at BJ's Wholesale Club could fulfill. I decided to think outside the box.

I applied to a garden center, reasoning that the outdoor work would do my mood and my body good. During the phone interview, the owner asked me if I was familiar with the inspirational works of Dale Carnegie.

"Well, Mike, I can't say I've read any of his stuff," I said. "But I see his books in the section where I buy everything I read."

"What do you read?" Mike asked. He sounded maybe a decade older than me. His deep, manly voice betrayed his New Jersey upbringing, but only slightly. I'd never expected to be asked about my literary preferences during an interview for a job at a garden center. I pictured a tanned, well-muscled (but not steroid-fueled) outdoorsman who retired at the end of the day to a house he'd built himself. In my mind's eye, the house's primary feature was its giant library, with floor-to-ceiling bookshelves (just like in *Beauty and the Beast*). Of course Mike would have put those bookshelves in himself. My intellectual, overeducated side was intrigued. My salt-of-the-earth guidette Jersey girl side was turned on.

"I read a lot of books about . . . philosophy," I said. "I'm interested in self-improvement. And, um . . . nature. Horticulture. I'm taking a break from college because I'm considering changing career paths."

"Fantastic," he said, and it sounded like he meant it. "Well, you'd learn a lot about self-improvement *and* horticulture here. All my employees are required to read at least one of Mr. Carnegie's books. And my door is always open to discuss his philosophies about winning friends and influencing people."

"I'd like to do that with you. Talk, I mean. About friends. And people. And influencing."

"Sounds great to me, Sara. Why don't you come in for an interview?"

I went in for an interview. The grounds were spotless and immaculately organized. All the employees, clad in green T-shirts and cargo shorts, were as well-groomed as their workplace. A smiling young man directed me to the main office, which was housed in a lovely cedar cabin. As I walked down the hallway, I encountered a dozen framed posters, each emblazoned with a different inspirational message from Dale Carnegie.

I entered the office and saw the handsome, tastefully brawny man of my dreams sitting behind a desk. His olive skin had been gently browned by the sun, and the muscles in his forearms flexed gently as he typed at a computer.

"Hi," I said sweetly, sticking out my hand. "I'm Sara. I hope you're ready to talk about books!"

"You're looking for Mike," the guy said, ignoring my hand. "He's in there." He cocked his thumb in the direction of another door.

Mike was portly, middle-aged, and visibly disappointed by my appearance. He thanked me for coming in, but told me he needed to hire an employee capable of lifting something heavier than a watering can.

"That's not very inspirational, Mike," I said.

"I'm sorry," he said. "You sounded like a bigger girl on the phone."

I left with a sourpuss expression and the secret desire to steal a ficus.

Next, I applied to a recently opened New Age bookstore in a nearby town. The owner informed me that he specialized in the books and "inspirational products" of Louise Hay, a wealthy snake-oil purveyor who claims to have cured herself of vaginal cancer through positive thinking. She has made bullshit-loads of cash telling others that they've brought their own diseases upon themselves. Even in my twenty-one-year-old fruity daze, I couldn't see myself convincing cancer sufferers to buy a book telling them that if they'd only thought more about unicorns and rainbows, their ovarian tumors wouldn't have metastasized. Nor could I see myself explaining to the parents of dead children that their kids would've made it out of St. Jude's if they'd worked harder at generating happy thoughts while puking after chemo.

Years later, when I thumbed through that nuclear disaster of a book called *The Secret,* I recognized a lot of Louise Hay's influence. My favorite part was when Rhonda Byrne effectively laid the blame for all disasters, tragedies, and crimes at the feet of the victims, basically claiming they'd brought it on themselves via "the law of attraction" and too much negative thinking. I hope they have pens in Hell so that all those stupid, frowny-face Jews, Rwandans, Cambodians, Congolese, Sudanese, and Native Americans can belatedly take a note.

Anyway, I wouldn't have lasted long in that bookshop. When the owner called me for a second interview, I politely declined. Then I went back to the classifieds section of the local newspaper and resumed my hunt.

Hippies love to say, "When the student is ready, the teacher appears." They stole it from the Japanese Zen Buddhists, or the Chinese Taoists, or some other set of brownish-yellow people upon whom they projected all their Orientalist fantasies in the 60s and 70s. It pops up in many of their books and pamphlets and on their T-shirts and bumper stickers. These days, they like to put it on their blogs. I took it to heart and asked the heavens for a teacher. And then he appeared, right there on my computer screen.

It happened in the third week of my job search. I wondered if maybe a yoga studio would hire me as a receptionist, and I could get in touch with my body through free classes and weekly *kirtan* sessions. *Kirtan* is a Sanskrit word that means "unwashed persons with liberal arts degrees chanting atonally at loud volume." I searched online for yoga studios, then retreat centers, then ashrams, and that's how I found Edgar.

Edgar ran the Blessed Sanctuary, a fifty-acre spread in the low, softly rolling mountains of eastern Pennsylvania, near New Hope. Its elaborate website advertised a "center for learning and growth founded in the classical tradition, with modern influences drawn from all great world cultures." I wasn't sure what constituted a classical tradition of learning and growth, but I was positive I wanted to be a part of it. The homepage displayed a gorgeous photograph of the sun setting behind a beautiful stone hut. The caption on the photograph read, "The Blessed Sanctuary has been blessed with contributions from many benefactors and thus was able to construct its own sweat lodge in 1989. The building of a sweat lodge is considered meritorious and karmically beneficial." I still wasn't quite sure what karma was, exactly, but I figured it was probably better for a sweat lodge to be karmically beneficial than karmically, you know, shitty.

According to the site, the Blessed Sanctuary was founded by a spiritual teacher of some appropriately exotic extraction. Precisely why he chose Pennsylvania as the site of his American mission was unclear. Perhaps he thought the local Amish community's horses and buggies would raise the spiritual vibration. Maybe he was just really into their amazing hot pretzels. He soon attracted the attention of local evangelical Protestants, some of whom wanted to convert him to Christ. Thankfully, his proximity to both Philadelphia and New York put him within toking distance of a variety of disaffected American youths and their robust trust funds. Some of these disheveled-by-design artsy types began coming to his fledgling center in order to learn the mystical ways of the Far East, the Southwest, and other mysterious places. Among these wide-eyed, well-heeled seekers were Arthur and Edgar. Eagerly, I read that the two "fell in love during a monthlong silent meditation."

"How romantic," I whispered, sighing dreamily. According to the website, Arthur and Edgar had been at the center ever since, doing a brisk business in workshops and daylong conferences on all sorts of fascinating subjects, like yoga, ayurveda, and therapeutic Scandinavian dance. In addition to the sweat lodge, they'd built a white "contemplation house" that resembled a small church. Arthur himself traveled frequently to lead spiritual retreats "around the globe." He was also available for "partnership ceremonies" and corporate events.

It was just about the most exciting thing I'd ever heard of, and I couldn't believe I hadn't known about this place when I was growing up. Had something happened at the PA-NJ border to stop the flow of information? Why hadn't I been notified during my early adolescent Wiccan phase that there were actual practicing spiritual gurus *with their own sweat lodge* only sixty minutes away from where my middle school baton-twirling team rehearsed?

The website offered information on internships and volunteer opportunities, but there were no job ads. Undeterred, I decided to send a prayer to the universe and an e-mail to Edgar. Nothing ventured, nothing gained, right? I dug out my two old Wiccan candles, abandoned when I decided student council was more interesting than drawing down the power of the moon. They had melted into stubs, but the wicks remained perky. I lit the blue one on the left side of the family computer and the pink one on the right side. I took a deep breath, and began typing.

Dear Edgar:

Hello. It is an honor to meet you via correspondence. I seek employment with an organization that combines practical work with the spiritual journey. I am taking a break from my college education because it was interfering with my search for divine enlightenment. My last job was as an assistant at a high-end hair salon in Boston's most fashionable district, where I interacted with many individuals of great import and also sold nail polish. I can type upwards of 60 wpm. I would love to work with you to further your goal of lifting up the community. I hope to hear from you soon.

Respectfully yours,
Sara

I hit "send" and took a moment to envision the ideal outcome of the situation. Edgar was somewhere deep in meditation, maybe in the sweat lodge thing. The whole place probably smelled like sage and lavender and green tea. Suddenly, in the midst of Edgar's meditation, he was struck by the conviction that he needed a good worker, pure of heart and intention, to whom he would pay $20 an hour to make tea for fascinating teachers and students from around the world.

To my shock and delight, Edgar e-mailed me back the very next day.

Dear Sara:

Thank you so much for your letter! You may be the answer to our prayers. We're very busy this year with a host of projects at the Blessed Sanctuary. In particular, we've got a big annual conference coming up that will bring 200 visitors and three renowned speakers to the site. I could really use a personal assistant to help me with recycling, correspondence, and the upkeep of our large organic garden, where we grow most of our own food.

Would you be interested in driving up later this week in order to meet with me?

Blessed be,
Edgar

Would I be *interested*? In driving up to a place where spiritual teachers grew their own *food*? Um, duh. These people sounded like magical elves from another dimension. Edgar and Arthur were clearly way more evolved than anybody else I'd ever met. I knew this meeting was going to change my life forever.

I hadn't spent an hour in a car in months, and hadn't driven myself that far in—jeez, I couldn't remember how long it had been. But thanks to counseling, Prozac, and all those books, my enthusiasm far outweighed my anxiety. I prepared an inspirational mix tape for the journey—a lovely combination of Enya and Gregorian chanting, interspersed with soothing interludes of my own voice saying things like "You have enough. You do enough. You are enough" and "Everything in your life has led you to this one place. You are on the right journey."

I drove the hour in a state of great excitement. I was driving a longish distance, just like a normal person! I was going to a job interview, just like a real adult! I felt so good that I even shut the tape off at one point in order to listen to some plain old-fashioned rock and roll on the radio.

The driveway to the Blessed Sanctuary was a long, winding gravel one. It twisted and turned through woods for about a half-mile until it broke into a clearing. I could see the contemplation house plain as day about a hundred yards from my car. It gleamed bright and beautiful in the sunlight, a mystical beacon of hope. Up on the wooded hill behind the contemplation house was a gorgeous little stone edifice, which I recognized as the sweat lodge, shiny with a freshly stained cedar roof.

I followed the driveway up to the contemplation house and saw hidden behind it another building—a drab, gray 1960s ranch-style house with a sign out front that read RESIDENCE. I was a little disappointed, as I'd hoped Edgar and Arthur dwelt in something resembling Yoda's hut, or perhaps a Rudolf Steiner–inspired hobbit-house with a round door in the side of a hill. This place just looked so normal and unexciting. At least it had a little garden out front, still frozen in the winter chill. All magical, fairy-tale places should have a garden, like the Garden of Eden or the one the witch owned beside Rapunzel's parents' house.

Edgar came out of the house to greet me before I'd even turned my car off. He wore loose black pants and a heavy wool sweater. He had gray-flecked brown hair and a neat mustache. He was short like me, and he looked around forty even though I knew he must have been in his late fifties. His lively brown eyes were as active and curious as those of a handsome ferret. His pale skin glowed and betrayed no trace of acid peels or face-lifts. But when he smiled and waved, a patchwork of fine lines and tiny wrinkles showed up around his eyes and across his nose. That was natural and kind of nice, actually. I figured all those years of clean, peaceful living had made him look the way he did. He was really rather striking.

"Welcome to the Blessed Sanctuary!" he exclaimed when I

got out of the car, and immediately enveloped me in an enthusiastic, powdery-scented hug. "Let me have a look at you." I smiled shyly as he stepped back a foot and surveyed me from head to toe.

"What a beauty you are," he said. "And a good, kind spirit. I can see it. A spirit full of the love of service. You've had some hard times, but you are recovering nicely. A heart full of love."

I felt a delicious chill run down my spine. I hadn't even told him anything about why I'd *really* dropped out of college. He was obviously super-intuitive and probably some kind of bodhisattva. I wasn't positive what a bodhisattva was, exactly, but I'd come across the term several times during my scramble to bone up on spiritual stuff before the interview. I had a vague idea that it meant "good spirit" or "saint" or "someone who is sort of like a holy person, maybe."

"Thank you," I said humbly, bowing my head. "I am so deeply pleased to be here. It is an honor."

"It is," he agreed. "Now come on inside and meet Arthur and our intern, Jason. I can't tell you how nice it'll be to have a woman around after being cooped up with these alpha males for months." He let out a dry laugh that ended in a cough. "I'm sorry. Still fighting off a cold Jason brought with him. Maybe I can send you down to town for some echinacea later in the day. We've got one decent grocery store that stocks what I need."

"Of course! I'd love to help." He used herbs for healing, just like the Stevie Nicks witch had done! I finally understood what people meant when they said that life comes full circle. This was so cool.

We went into the house, which had all the trappings of a normal abode—floors, walls, windows—but was obviously a gathering place for humans from this world and spirits from the great beyond. First, it smelled like delicious tea and soothing incense. Second, I'd never seen so many religious icons in my life. Every available inch of the interior was adorned with special spiritual knickknacks. Edgar helpfully explained as we went along.

"Here's a framed original poster by our friend James, who is a famous artist. You may have heard of him. He has his own gallery in Chelsea. He took the Four Noble Truths and painted images of four Hollywood celebrities who epitomize each truth. The first one, 'Life means suffering'—that's Marilyn Monroe, over here on the lotus. She was so beautiful and she suffered so much for it. Men used her like a towel, and once she was dirtied up they threw her away." Edgar shook his head and sighed. I sighed to match him.

" 'The origin of suffering is attachment'—that's Jim Morrison, on the mountaintop. He was attached to drugs and alcohol, and he suffered terribly for it. He visited us once here before he died. He wrote a poem for me. All the other folks here were very jealous. I found him insufferable."

My mouth hung open in shock. "Jim Morrison was *here*? And he wrote a poem for you?"

He nodded solemnly. "I was quite gorgeous when I was younger." He smiled gently. "Stevie Nicks visited us, and we connected on such a deep level. She really considered me a dear friend for a time. And here she is as the third noble truth, riding the unicorn. I've always liked how the white fringe on her scarf matches the unicorn's mane."

This was just too much. There was Stevie Nicks, looking just like the Stevie Nicks witch *and* the actual Stevie Nicks.

"The third noble truth teaches us that the cessation of suffering is attainable." Edgar gazed at the painting and smiled softly. "Sometimes, of course, you have to break free of controlling men in order to do it. And Stevie did. She finally, finally did."

"Steve Nicks was the sound track to my youth," I said reverently. I'd listened to Fleetwood Mac's live reunion album all through the summer between eleventh and twelfth grades.

Edgar smiled benevolently. "She was the sound track to mine, too," he said.

"Does she still visit?"

"Oh, no," Edgar said, laughing. "I can't stand her."

"Um. Oh."

"Now, the fourth noble truth is the cessation of suffering," he said. "And of course the only true cessation of suffering is death. So here we have Audrey Hepburn, who became a living saint at the end of her life. But before that, she endured the deprivations of the Holocaust and, even worse, the emotional abuse of several husbands. At least one of them cheated on her. Can you imagine anyone cheating on Audrey Hepburn?"

I was aghast. "But she was so pretty!"

Edgar suddenly looked very angry. "Yes, she was pretty, Sara!" he snapped. "But more than that, she was a human being with feelings. And there is nothing people hate so much as a kind spirit who knows who she is and will not apologize for it. She was too nice. They walked all over her. Are you going to let them walk all over you, Sara? Are you?" I shrank back. He looked irritated almost to the point of genuine anger.

Then, as if someone had flipped a switch, he softened and smiled. "So that's the painting by James. He's lovely. Gay, of course. A really nice guy. He'd love you. He adores me."

The storm appeared to be over. I relaxed.

"He's very talented," I said tentatively, and he nodded with great enthusiasm.

"I knew you and I would get along. I see so much of myself in you." He stared deep into my eyes, and I met his gaze and beamed. I was too flattered to point out that we'd met less than ten minutes prior and that I wasn't even sure he knew my surname yet.

It took nearly an hour just to get through what might have been called the living room in a normal house. I had no idea that so many things could be carved from soapstone. Gold was also well-represented, as were silver, brass, copper, paper, yarn, and cloth. That room alone contained a gift appropriate for every imaginable wedding anniversary.

We went through the rest of the house, including Edgar and Arthur's meditation room, their bedroom, the spare bedroom, the upstairs bathroom, the downstairs bathroom, the playroom ("Sometimes guests bring children, though I discourage it"), Arthur's office ("His inner sanctum—I'm barely allowed in here"), and the mudroom, where a mouse rattled about inside a cage trap ("It's a compassionate trap. We don't kill animals here. We'll let him out in a field later."). By the time we reached the kitchen, my mind swam with beads, statues, and tie-dye. It was as if the CEO of Pier 1 Imports or Bombay Company had entered the house and exploded.

"And now to meet the manly men of the house," he said as we entered the kitchen. "Boys, meet Sara."

Two men—one my age, one about sixty—looked up from steaming mugs of tea at the kitchen table. The younger man was cute enough, with thick black hair and mournful blue eyes. The older one had clearly once been quite handsome. He remained good-looking, albeit in a creased, faded way. He looked a bit like a fancy, sturdy boat that has been battered by wind and waves over the years. His expression was slightly dazed, but gentle and welcoming.

The young man offered his hand. "Hi, I'm Jason," he said. "I'm the intern."

"We have one every semester," Edgar said. "Jason is a student at NYU. He helps Arthur with his work for part of the day, and he's been doing some projects for me around the house, haven't you, Jason?"

A look of terror briefly flickered across Jason's face. He looked down into his tea and murmured, "Yup."

An awkward moment of silence passed.

"Well, say something, Arthur!" Edgar said cheerfully. "Aren't you excited to meet my new assistant?"

I looked at Edgar with surprise. I hadn't even shown him my résumé yet, much less interviewed for the position. He grinned at me. Clearly, I had the job.

Arthur peered at me in kind confusion. "Assistant?" he repeated. "Well . . . that sounds very nice. Welcome, Sara. Would you like a cup of tea?"

"I'll offer the tea around here, thank you," Edgar said quickly. "Sara, sit down and I'll give you some tea."

I thanked him and sat.

Edgar rattled around the kitchen, chattering nonstop about the upcoming annual conference, his plans for the garden, future celebrity guest speakers, and some facts I'd already picked up from the Blessed Sanctuary website. Throughout Edgar's monologue, Arthur nodded on occasion, blinking very slowly and offering a word or two. My impression was of a brilliant man who had at one time done a lot of acid. Like, a *lot.* Jason said nothing, and stared into space or into his cup of tea. When Arthur rose slowly and creakily from his chair, Jason looked enormously relieved. He stood up so fast he nearly knocked over his teacup, which was still mostly full. He didn't exactly run out of the room, but he speed-walked toward Arthur's office.

When the other men were safely out of earshot, Edgar heaved a great sigh of relief and plunked down in the chair beside me.

"Isn't it better with them gone?" he asked. I had no idea how to answer that question, so I sipped my tea.

"Some male energy is so disruptive," he continued. "You'll see soon enough who really runs this place, and it isn't my partner. And it certainly isn't the intern." He shook his head and looked at me with a level gaze. "Take my advice: don't fall in love with him. He's trouble."

I nearly spat out my tea.

"I don't think he's really my type," I said, even though he was.

"Good," Edgar said, and smiled. "Now let's tour the grounds and I'll tell you about all the things I want you to work on with me."

By the end of the day, I'd gotten a closer look at the contemplation house, though we didn't enter it. It was designed specifically for whatever celebrity spiritual teacher happened to be in residence at the time. This building, like all the others, was funded by wealthy donors. We walked around the house, but didn't go inside. Edgar explained that the construction of the contemplation house had kicked up so much dust that he couldn't sleep for a year (I didn't ask what dust had to do with his slumber), and that while it was quite pretty, he avoided entering it unless he absolutely had to. Apparently the sight of the interior triggered a kind of PTSD. He hated psychiatrists ("Crooks, all of them!") so he was praying on it. We visited the organic garden, for which he had grand plans, as well as the forest that took up most of the property. We finished our journey in the mudroom, where Edgar picked up the cage that housed the mouse.

"We're going down the road a mile to let it out on a farm," he informed me as the terrified creature shook in the corner.

"Poor little guy," he said, cooing at him. "I chant to soothe them. Do you know 'Om mani padme hum'?"

"Yes," I said.

"Let's chant it together then. Om mani padme hum om mani padme hum . . ."

"Om mani padme hum," I joined in whisper. I have a terrible singing voice, and chanting is too close to singing for my comfort.

"Om mani padme hum," he intoned, poking his finger in the cage and waggling it at the creature. "Om mani padme hum om mani padme hum om mani padme—FUCK YOU!" He shrieked and dropped the cage. The mouse squealed.

"Oh my God!" I gasped. "Are you okay?"

"The fucker bit me! I'm bleeding. I'm fucking bleeding!" He held up his finger, which showed no trace of blood.

"Go let it out in the forest!" he screamed. "Let it out in the forest behind the house!" He took off down the hall, yelling for Arthur.

I looked at the mouse and the mouse looked at me. I picked up the cage, left the house, and walked about fifty yards up the forested hillside. Everything grew very quiet except for the occasional rustling of a small animal in the brush. It was cold there, but the air was crisp. From my vantage point, I could see into the valley below. The sun shone through the bare winter trees, and the sky was very blue. I had driven here, all by myself. I hadn't panicked. My belly didn't hurt. My head didn't throb. I felt a cool peace wash over me. I could do this—all of it.

I knelt down on the near-frozen ground and released the mouse. He skittered away, free of compassionate traps and sacred chants. As I walked back down the hill to the house, I looked up. A hawk was circling overhead, eyeing something. It dove, slicing soundlessly through the frigid air. I turned my eyes back to the house and walked through the mudroom and into the kitchen.

Jason the intern was sitting alone in a chair at the table. When I entered, he rose quickly.

"He's gone to bed for the day," he said in a low tone. "But he says to come back tomorrow the same time if you want the job." His eyes seemed to flash something at me, but I couldn't understand what, exactly.

I hesitated.

"He'll pay you twenty dollars an hour," he said. "Cash."

"I'll be back tomorrow," I said.

Driving home, I turned over the events of the afternoon in my mind. Edgar had certainly behaved in an unusual fashion, but maybe that was just how professional spiritual gurus were. Arthur was odd in his own way, and the intern seemed scared. Maybe Jason was just intimidated by the people who had the power to write the evaluation for his college course. Maybe Jason was shy. Or maybe Jason was the weird one, and Edgar and Arthur were quite normal.

I figured I wasn't really the authority on what was normal and what wasn't, seeing as I was about two months out from a daily routine that included peeing in bowls. It was hard enough to get a decent job, much less one that involved the spiritual stuff that so fascinated me. And what an awesome wage! I'd be lucky to make half that much anywhere else. I knew I would go back the next day.

And go back I did. The next day was less dramatic, with no real or imagined bloodshed. Mostly I followed Edgar around and helped him with chores around the main house. As he showed me the proper way to iron Arthur's shirts, he told me about his upbringing in a "spiritually bereft" family in Orange County, California. He had tennis lessons and Boy Scouts, but his parents always favored his older sister "because she was pretty." Edgar turned his attention to more important matters, marching with various student and community groups during the 1960s.

"Arthur," he called into the hallway. "Arthur, who's the black guy I marched with? The famous one?"

"Martin Luther King Jr.!" Arthur called back in his low, pleasant voice.

"No, the other one!" Edgar yelled. "The one who got killed."

"Martin Luther King was killed!"

"I know that, do you think I'm stupid?! The other one who got killed!"

"Malcolm X?" I ventured timidly.

"Was he the one in the driveway?" Edgar asked, impatiently tapping his foot.

"That was Medgar Evers," I said. "I think."

"Okay, then it was Malcolm X. I know it was him because the black guy I marched with didn't die in a driveway."

"I can't believe you marched with Malcolm X," I said, some of the first day's excitement returning to my voice. "I mean, you've met everybody!"

He nodded solemnly.

"And they were all egotistical bastards," he said. "Every last one of them."

I stared intently at a batik-print cotton shirt and resumed ironing.

Days at the Blessed Sanctuary were pretty similar. I helped Edgar complete some menial task, like organizing receipts, cleaning windows, or returning phone calls from people interested in registering for the big upcoming conference. He told me stories from his life, pausing frequently to tell me exactly how I was screwing up the task at hand. I took direction well, and when I corrected my techniques, he'd resume his tale. His stories usually featured a male villain of some sort—the mailman, the building inspector, a professor back in his school days, his father, Arthur.

For his part, Arthur stayed mostly out of the way. He was apparently quite a gifted teacher and was much in demand at yoga conferences and sweat lodges around the country. Edgar grumbled frequently about how he could have used more construction work around the house, but Jason stuck close to Arthur's side. We exchanged few words, but I noticed him peering at me carefully when we passed in the hallway.

Then one day, about three weeks after I began working at the Blessed Sanctuary, Jason disappeared. He wasn't at lunch in the kitchen, or the afternoon tea break. Edgar wasn't usually interested in answering my questions about anything, but I got up the courage to inquire as to Jason's whereabouts.

"He hated work," Edgar spat, pounding his fist on the kitchen table. "We had to get rid of him." Arthur blanched slightly before regaining his usual dazed composure.

"Oh," I said, and busied myself collecting everyone's empty teacups.

And that was it. No explanation of why, exactly, Jason hated work—or how—or when. His internship, meant to last for the entire second semester of his junior year in college, had been suddenly curtailed. I wondered what that meant for his credits and his progress toward graduation from NYU. I'd been thinking of that kind of thing a lot since I dropped out of Emerson.

When Jason was axed, I had to wonder when Edgar's rage would refocus itself on me. I didn't have to wait long to find out.

One day, Edgar declared that we must load up the back of the pickup truck with junk from the basement—old furniture, out-of-date electronics, broken toys—and drive it all to the dump. He had me add boxes full of old glassware to the load—glass candlesticks, glass vases, ugly glass figurines he didn't want.

On the way to the dump, we stopped at a gas station. He commented to the attendant that the price of gas seemed unreasonably high. (Actually, he said, "Jesus, you're charging me an arm and a leg here! Are you trying to bankrupt me?!")

"Well," the man said, "I hear you, sir. But the price of oil these days is pretty crazy. I get a little discount here, and I can barely afford to fill up my own truck. And I've got four kids at home, so we're pinching every penny."

"I do church work," Edgar announced, apropos of nothing. "I don't make a lot of money either." Soon, we roared off.

Edgar was fuming. "I don't need to hear him tell me about his stupid family," he muttered. "It's not my fucking fault he decided to have four kids. *Four kids!* I don't need to hear his sob story. If he can't manage his money, that's his problem. What am I, a goddamned therapist?"

"No," I said. "You're certainly not that." I had told Dr. Morrison about the job, but had spared him some of the wackier details of Edgar's character. Similarly, I hadn't filled my family in on exactly what went on at the Blessed Sanctuary. My parents would've told me I ought to get a more normal job, and my brother would've laughed and laughed.

When we arrived at the dump, Edgar backed the truck up to a giant Dumpster into which he instructed me to throw everything.

"You're not doing it fast enough," he complained as I slowly and gingerly removed a rattan chair from the Tetris-like configuration of junk. "We don't have all day. You need to work harder if you're going to get anywhere. Faster and harder! I didn't hire you to be slow!" Nervously, I sped up, pulling things out at a slightly quicker pace.

"Be careful!" he warned me. "Don't break anything near us. But hurry up while you do it!" Again, I quickened my pace, heaving old record players and VCRs into the abyss of that giant metal trashcan. Exasperated, he began pulling items out, too.

"Watch what you're doing!" he shouted as we each grabbed a leg of the same stool. Startled, I whipped my hand back and accidentally jostled the box of glassware. It tipped over, and an old glass vase smashed on the ground beneath us.

I knew instantly that I had committed an unforgivable sin. Frightened, I apologized over and over as I bent down to pick up the larger shards with my bare hands. It was going in the trash anyway, but Edgar's face was red with the kind of rage one might reserve for an insubordinate servant who purposely smashes the entire contents of the cherished family china cabinet.

"I'm so sorry, Edgar," I said again. "It was an accident. I'm really, really sorry."

He was so angry that the bristles of his mustache trembled with rage.

"YOU COULD HAVE BLINDED ME!" he screamed, loud enough for the sanitation workers at the dump to peer at us from twenty yards away. "I could be BLIND now! And it would be your fault, and we would sue you, do you know that? We would sue you, and your family would never be able to pay for you to go back to college! I am not paying you to BLIND ME!" He got right in my face, like a badass Southern California high school *chola* girl spoiling for a fight.

"YOU COULD HAVE BLINDED ME!" he screamed again. "What the hell is wrong with you? Are you a fucking idiot?"

For a moment, some of my old spunk flared up, and I nearly glared at him.

"Actually, Edgar, I could have blinded both of us," I said. "I was standing here too. It. Was. An. Accident."

I thought he was going to hit me.

"Get in the car," he said through gritted teeth. "And do not speak to me for the rest of the day. I will drive us back and then you will drive home."

Whatever fightin' Irish or scrappin' Sicilian spirit I'd summoned quickly dissipated as I sat in the passenger seat and contemplated getting fired. This gig was my chance to show people—my parents, my friends, Dr. Morrison, myself—that I was capable of holding down a job just like a real adult. Having this job meant that I was getting better, that I had a future outside of my parents' house, that I might even be able to make it back to finish my college degree one day. This job meant I wasn't a loser anymore, or at least not as big a loser as I'd been when I was afraid to leave my one-room apartment. How would I explain the loss of my job in a way that wouldn't make me sound like a completely incompetent fool?

Edgar unloaded the rest of the crap on his own and then got into the car. He stared straight ahead as we drove the twenty minutes back to the Blessed Sanctuary. When we parked outside the main house, he turned to me and said simply, "I will see you here at the usual time tomorrow." Then he went into the mudroom.

I had prepared myself to be fired right on the spot, so I was a bit confused. Did he want me to return the next day just so he could fire me? If he didn't get rid of me, would a letter still go in my permanent file? Would Stevie Nicks be notified, and if so, would this preclude my attendance at all future Fleetwood Mac reunion concerts?

The next day, I walked with great trepidation through the mudroom and into the kitchen. There I found Edgar with a bright smile on his face. The table was set with a pitcher of milk, a jar of honey, a bowl of raisins, and a pot of tea. Two matching breakfast bowls sat beside two matching teacups.

"Sara!" he exclaimed when I entered, clapping his hands and grinning. "We have so much to do today! Come, eat up! We need our strength for the tasks ahead. Can you believe it's only two weeks until the annual conference?" Warily, I sank into a chair. He ladled a steaming pile of oatmeal into my bowl and handed me a spoon.

"I slow-cook it, the way it's meant to be done," he told me as he poured me a cup of tea. "Steel-cut Irish oats. Only takes thirty minutes on the stove. I don't know why people can't be bothered with it. I find it meditative. Chop wood, carry water, make oatmeal!" He laughed a high-pitched, tinkling laugh. I realized then that while I hadn't heard Edgar laugh often, I'd never heard him laugh in the same way twice. Something about that really freaked me out.

Soon enough, I was too busy to worry much about Edgar's laughter. Edgar was preoccupied with the logistical preparations of getting three guest speakers to the Blessed Sanctuary from points all over the country. He also had to figure out how much food to buy for the two hundred donors who would come to the conference for learning and worship. He gave me a list of tasks and basically left me to my own devices for the next two weeks. Early spring was upon us, so I had some weeding to do. I also had to sweep, vacuum, dust, mop, shine, alphabetize, iron, polish, and fold all manner of things in the main house, the contemplation house, and the sweat lodge. I finally got inside the sweat lodge, which proved rather annoying to clean because I had to individually dust all the nooks and crannies of every sacred ritual object (and there were hundreds of them). The mystical thrill of holding a genuine sacred eagle feather really fades when you have to clean forty of those fuckers in an hour.

I spent so little time with Edgar in those weeks that I might have almost forgotten how disturbingly unbalanced he was. But in case my memory had grown dim, he saw fit to remind me on the day of the big conference. At least this time his rage was mostly reserved for someone else.

My workday usually began at ten A.M. and ended at six P.M. But on the morning of the big conference, I arrived at seven A.M. in order help Edgar set up. When I turned onto the long driveway, I saw that the trees around the property were festooned with bright, brand-new cloth peace symbol flags fluttering in the early-spring breeze. Unlit tiki torches were set on either side of the drive. I assumed these were either a nod to some mysterious hippie-Hawaiian religious connection or else a cheap way to get the party started.

I pulled up to the house and saw Arthur puttering in the garden. This was rather unusual, as he didn't often leave his office.

"Hey, Arthur!" I called as I got out of the car. "You ready for all these people?" He was a kind guy, and my impression of him as a sweetly befuddled ex-hippie hadn't changed.

He looked up slowly and blinked in the dim morning light. It seemed to take him a few moments to recognize me. When he did, he smiled his gentle smile.

"Hello, Sara," he said. "I am so glad you are here to help." There was deep relief in his voice. I walked over to take a look at the garden.

"Shoots are finally coming up," I said. "You'll have fresh vegetables every day."

He stared at one particular plant for a long time, seemingly mesmerized.

"Yes," he said finally. "Maybe Edgar will like that." When he said Edgar's name, we both shivered a little.

"I guess I'd better get inside and help him out."

"Oh yes, please, Sara." There was that immense relief again. "He's in . . . he's . . ."

"Oh, I bet I know how he is." Arthur looked at me in surprise, and I grinned at him.

I left him there, wandering peacefully among the quietest living things in the world. I felt sorry for the guy. Oh, he wasn't exactly a henpecked husband. Edgar seemed to treat his partner with more care and dignity than he afforded most people. He capably managed the day-to-day aspects of life with Arthur. I'd seen Edgar pay the bills on time, make healthful and nutritious meals, and keep an eagle eye on his partner's physical health and work deadlines. I don't think Arthur was necessarily capable of managing the details on his own, and in Edgar he had an able and energetic partner. They obviously loved each other, and their mutual loyalty was evident. It might even have been a happy union, in its way. But Edgar resented Arthur, and I can't imagine Arthur didn't know it. And while I knew Edgar could be overwhelming one on one, I had a feeling he also wasn't the most adept at coping with large groups of humans.

This last bit was reinforced as soon as I stepped into the kitchen. Edgar rushed about the room in a tizzy, his usually perfect hair frizzy and unkempt. I could tell he'd been up much longer than I had, and I'd risen at five thirty A.M.

"Good morning," I said. "Tell me what to do."

"It is a terrible morning, and I will gladly tell you what to do," Edgar snapped. "I wish you had been here earlier. I should've had you sleep over and get up with me at three. We're hours behind. Hours!"

It was ten after seven.

"The downstairs bathroom needs to be completely cleaned," he said.

"In the basement? Are you letting people go down there?"

"They'll go all over, Sara! They don't care that this is our house, that this is our life. They think they paid to have access to everything. They'll go in our bedroom if I don't put up a sign. And that's the next thing I'll have you do. Cordon off the hallway with tape and put up a sign that says PRIVATE QUARTERS. NO ACCESS! Put an exclamation point at the end. No, put three. Now do the bathroom."

I descended the stairs to the basement, glad to be out of his way. As I disposed of dead flies, dirt, and dried toothpaste, I heard his little feet pounding the floorboards overhead.

When I came upstairs thirty minutes later, he'd already put up the tape and the sign. "You took too long!" he said by way of explanation. "Now go to Arthur's office and photocopy and fold the leaflets up there."

He kept me busy with various tasks all morning. As with all the other work I did for him, none of it was inherently difficult or unpleasant. But as usual, everything I produced wasn't quite up to his standards. If I folded napkins into triangles, I ought to have folded them into rectangles. If I defrosted frozen fruit in the steel bowl, I ought to have defrosted it in the ceramic bowl. If I greased a pan with olive oil, I ought to have used canola oil. The little criticisms seemed as necessary to his daily routine as the tasks he had assigned me. He inspected the basement bathroom and redid all my work. I wanted to point out that none of the guests were likely to use the shower, but kept mum as he scrubbed the grout I'd already attacked with an old toothbrush.

The day's program was set to begin at noon, but the guest speakers were to show up at ten A.M. There arrived in due course a local rabbi, a local minister, and a writer named Elizabeth. She edited the religion section of a well-regarded newspaper and made not-infrequent appearances on television to discuss the ways in which Eastern spirituality had penetrated the mainstream American consciousness. What intrigued me the most was that she was a product of the 1960s-era Blessed Sanctuary where Arthur and Edgar had fallen in love. She had lived with them, eaten with them, and worked with them for a couple of years. Her sister Mary had also stayed at the place for a time, and Edgar had wondered aloud in passing if Mary would also return for this year's conference. It was hard for me to imagine that Edgar had existed in any form other than his current one, and I longed to hear stories of his youth from a surviving witness. Was it possible that he'd actually *mellowed* over the years?

I was out in the woods stringing extra peace symbol flags between trees when I distantly heard a car's tires crunch over the loose gravel near the house. By the time I emerged near the back of the house, the guests were out of the car, laughing warmly and greeting Arthur.

I rounded the corner of the house and saw an attractive, hippie-chic older woman with well-maintained silver hair that shone in the midmorning sun. She wore a nicely tailored gray suit accessorized with some sort of ethnic-print lavender scarf and tasteful chunky silver jewelry, and her makeup was subtle but perfect. Her companion was similarly attired and resembled her too strongly not to be her sister.

What I found the most remarkable was Arthur, who stood chatting amiably with the two women. He wasn't animated, exactly, but he certainly showed more energy than the slow-moving fellow I was used to watching sip tea each morning at the kitchen table.

When I got close enough, Arthur introduced me to Elizabeth and her sister Mary as "Edgar's assistant."

"Well, that must be quite a job," Elizabeth said dryly.

I was shocked and sort of delighted to see Arthur laugh. I hadn't even considered the possibility that he was capable of laughter.

"You can imagine," he said. "Edgar works very hard."

"Yes, of course," Elizabeth said faintly, looking past us. Arthur and I turned around to see Edgar barreling down the front lawn at a near-run. His face wore a smile so forced it nearly qualified as a grimace.

"Elizabeth! Mary! You're finally here!" Now Edgar was upon us, and Arthur had shrunk back into himself. He seemed to find a nearby butterfly utterly captivating.

"We were beginning to wonder if you'd forgotten about us," Edgar added, putting his hands on his hips and forcing that smile even wider.

"Oh no, are the others here already?" Mary said apologetically.

"Not yet," Edgar said. "You're all late!"

"So we're first," Elizabeth said.

"Well, yes," Edgar conceded. He paused and then looked at me. "Elizabeth, this is my assistant, Sara," he announced.

"We've met," I said. I caught Mary looking at me with great sympathy.

"Yes," Elizabeth said. "Now Edgar, dear, did you want me to set up inside the contemplation house? Mary is here to help. She may be a businesswoman today, but she's still got some of that Blessed Sanctuary spirit in her." Unexpectedly, Edgar linked his arm through Elizabeth's and led her away, chattering eighteen miles a minute about the plans for the day. The two got about ten feet toward the temple before Edgar halted and turned.

"You too, Mary!" he called. "I don't want my personal assistant telling you stories about what a horrible boss I am!" He let loose one of his unsettling laughs. This time it took the form of a cackle. Some things are funny because they're true. Perhaps in Edgar's head this was one of those, but I doubt it. He was smart, but he didn't possess sufficient self-awareness to realize that he was a tiny gay nightmare. I certainly didn't give him any indication that I was unhappy. Twenty dollars an hour bought a lot of my tolerance. I even laughed gamely as Mary crept away.

The rabbi and the minister arrived in a car together, and they were as jolly as Elizabeth had been reserved. They wanted a tour of the grounds in order to see the improvements Edgar and Arthur had made since last year, and I took them around quickly, pointing out the expanded garden, the newly painted contemplation house, and all the new peace symbol flags. Edgar returned from the contemplation house with Elizabeth and Mary in tow. He embraced the rabbi and the minister with an enthusiasm that had been lacking in his greeting of the two women. Arthur wandered outside and immediately plunged into deep conversation with the new visitors and Edgar.

Elizabeth approached me with a folder in hand.

"Sara, do you think you might be able to photocopy these for me?" she asked politely. "I need two hundred copies for the visitors." I looked up into her sparkling blue eyes and found myself immediately eager to please. This woman had an intimidating charm and an undeniable magnetism. I could see why she was such a successful figure in her field. There was just something about her that made you want to pay attention. And she smelled like the slightest dab of some wonderful, expensive perfume.

"I'd be glad to help," I said. "I can copy them in Arthur's office."

"Oh, thank you *so* much," she said, and a genuine smile broke over her face. It was like the sudden emergence of the sun on a cool, pleasantly quiet gray day. I hurried into the house.

It takes a bit of time to make two hundred copies on a small, antiquated photocopy machine in a home office. I was only halfway through the task when I heard the first paying guests arrive. Immediately after I noted the car sounds, I noted a much louder, much nearer sound. It was getting closer, and closer, and closer and—BOOM!

Edgar flung open the door. His face was redder than I'd ever seen it, and he looked angrier even than the day I'd dropped the vase at the dump.

Oh, fuck, I thought. *He is so going to fire me this time. How am I gonna explain this to my parents? They're gonna think I can't hold down a job. They're gonna think I'm still crazy and a baby.* I didn't know what the reason would be, but Edgar didn't really need a reason to scream at anybody. Rage was his default setting.

Instead of screaming, he hissed.

"What the fuck *are you doing up here?"*

"Making copies for Elizabeth." My voice was very small. Unconsciously, I braced for an actual physical attack.

"Making copies for Elizabeth?" Instead of getting louder as I'd expected, his voice got lower and lower. *"And who the* fuck *told you to do that?"*

"She did."

"She did!"

I gulped. Edgar's face remained frozen in a kind of immovable fury. I scrambled to explain my apparent sin.

"I'm sorry. I thought it was part of my job, to help you out by doing little things for the guest speakers. So you wouldn't have to be bothered with them." Outside, the voices of visitors grew louder. More cars were pulling into the driveway each minute.

Edgar looked hard at me.

"I want you to understand that I am not angry with you," he said very carefully, as if he were afraid he'd choke on the words. "I am not upset with you. This is what she does. This is how she operates. She manipulated you into thinking you were helping me, because you love me." I wasn't about to object to that last bit, so I nodded and he went on.

"Elizabeth must be the center of attention at all times. She must feel that everyone worships her." Edgar was pacing now, slightly bent at the waist, with his hands grasped together behind his back. "She was the same way when we all lived together thirty-five years ago. She was Queen Elizabeth, and her sister was Queen Mary, and we were their worthless subjects. Arthur was patient with Elizabeth because she was very beautiful, and even gay men are easily controlled by beautiful women. I don't mean to imply that anything happened between them. He was captivated by me. Utterly captivated. And he hasn't been with a woman since college." I nodded again.

"But that is just the way women like Elizabeth work. They pretend to be feminists and peaceniks and Buddhists or whatever you want to call them, but they're actually weak and selfish creatures. They cannot abide another person having any power. She saw that I was a successful businessman and nonprofit director with my own personal assistant, and she wanted to co-opt you for her own needs. To show me that I'm still beneath her. To show me that she is the queen. Well, would you like to hear something, Sara?" I nodded for the third time, as if I were in a trance.

Edgar rose up with all his might and gazed at me with the fury of Kali, Mother-Destroyer (if Kali wore Birkenstocks with thick gray socks).

"I am the queen of this kingdom," he declared, throwing his chin up and squaring his shoulders. "*Princess* Elizabeth will never take that from me." He kept staring at me. I searched desperately for a proper response.

"Well, you look much younger than she does," I offered weakly.

"Sara, don't be superficial," Edgar said. "That's your generation's greatest weakness. You only care about what's on the exterior. In the sixties, we concerned ourselves with greater things."

"I'm sorry."

"Don't apologize. You apologize all the time. It's the mark of a woman who doesn't know who she is."

"Well, you're right about that," I agreed pleasantly. "Would you like me to start the coffee for the guests?"

"You haven't started the coffee yet? What am I paying you for? Go do it, now!"

I abandoned Elizabeth's photocopies and scurried down to the kitchen, where I hid for most of the remainder of the day. I churned out more tea and coffee than an entire kingdom could consume. The two hundred now-enlightened middle-aged white people who filed through at lunch left more caffeinated than was probably legal. I served them with an obsequious manner, taking care to offer them an array of vegetarian snacks and, controversially, roasted chicken drumsticks ("People need fucking protein," Edgar had snapped when I timidly ventured that most of the attendees would be vegetarians).

As I cleaned up and the guests began to depart, I heard a woman in a flowing purple dress thank Edgar for the event.

"That girl you've got working for you is just lovely," said the purple lady.

"She's my personal assistant," Edgar said. "But she's more like a daughter to me. I'm teaching her so much."

"I wish I'd had a mentor like you when I was her age," the woman said.

"So do I," Edgar said. "I had to teach myself everything I know."

"To be quite frank," the woman said, dropping her voice, "I wasn't very impressed with that writer woman's workshop. Arthur, the rabbi, and the minister were lovely. Perhaps next year you can give a lecture instead."

"Oh, I'm no public speaker," Edgar said. I looked over and saw him actually blush with happiness.

As I squeezed more organic dish liquid on another Pottery Barn plate, I knew I wasn't going to come back to the Blessed Sanctuary. And in that moment, for the first time since I'd begun working there, I felt something that might be described as inner peace.

At dusk, I went outside to ask Edgar's permission to leave for the day. He nodded, barely seeming to notice me. He and Arthur were standing together with arms slung around each other's waists, laughing gently at something Elizabeth was saying. Elizabeth's sister Mary was laughing, too. All traces of anger had left Edgar's face. He and Arthur looked like an older couple enjoying themselves immensely at a high school reunion. Or maybe they looked like a pair of medieval royals, grateful to dispense for a moment with the duties of state and simply enjoy themselves with members of their inner circle at court. I left them there, King Arthur and Queen Edgar, and drove out of their kingdom and into the real world.

The next day, I called Edgar and told him I'd decided to enroll full-time at the local community college. I asked if he'd like two weeks' notice. He said it wasn't necessary, and without a trace of anger in his voice wished me well. I returned his good wishes in kind.

The community college thing was a lie. I went out on the job hunt again and found a gig back home in Flemington at a "health bar" inside a twenty-thousand-square-foot mega-gym. My primary job was to make smoothies, a task at which I excelled. I also served espresso shots to juiced-up Jersey muscle-heads and wheatgrass shots to anorexic, farty, "vegan" trophy wives. My favorite customers were the cardiac rehab patients who met their physical therapists in the special mini-gym for medical cases and then stopped by my bar for a bagel with cream cheese and a mocha latte with whole milk.

A couple of months later, while I was filling out new college applications (some schools actually let you apply in May for the next semester), I got an e-mail from Jason, the intern who had mysteriously disappeared. He asked how I was doing, and if I was still working at "that place." He said he'd wanted to get to talk to me more, but he'd done his best to avoid Edgar at all costs, and that meant avoiding me, too. I wrote back that I was doing well, and that I'd, thankfully, left the Blessed Sanctuary behind. We exchanged a few more e-mails, and he invited me to meet him in New York for the day.

I hadn't had a meaningful interaction with a boy in nearly six months. This fact alone was enough to make my brain circuits override my trepidation about New York City. I told Jason I'd see him that weekend.

I took out the cassette tape I'd used for the first time I drove to the Blessed Sanctuary, the one with Enya and Gregorian chanting and me saying soothing inspirational things. It didn't seem quite right for this trip. It seemed a little too . . . cheesy. And boring. And like it was designed for someone I didn't relate to as much anymore. So I made a mix tape of Liz Phair songs interspersed with my voice. "This is fucking awesome!" I said into the tape recorder. "Look, you're on the train! Look around. Look at the windows. You can see outside. You're safe. You can get off the train at any stop and then take the train back home. You could call a local taxi service anywhere and have them drive you to Flemington. You took your medicine today. You've got your journal with you. Did you bring your giraffe, Mary? Of course you did. See, you're fine. I'm so proud of you." It meshed rather well with Liz Phair's expletive-laced lyrics. I rode the train listening to the cassette player on headphones. And I made it in just fine.

Jason met me at Penn Station. He was cuter than I remembered, and looked way more relaxed. We greeted each other enthusiastically, and began walking down to Union Square. He was going to show me the L train, which would take us to a neighborhood in Brooklyn called Williamsburg.

"It's where all the punks and artists live now," he told me as we wandered past rainbow flags and leather boys in Chelsea. "Manhattan's too expensive. Even the Lower East Side. Everybody's moving out there."

On the L train, he asked me why I'd dropped out of school.

"I went kind of nuts, I guess," I said. "I got really depressed, and I just didn't want to leave my house ever. I had all these panic attacks."

"That happened to me in high school," he said. "It sucked."

"Yeah," I said.

"Is it okay that we're on the train? We can get off anytime you want and just walk." He was looking at me in such a matter-of-fact way, it was as if he'd just asked, "Do you want to grab some lunch?" There was no pity, no fear, no concern. I'd never seen someone look at me like that when I first talked about my weird mental problems. He looked at me like I was normal.

"I'm okay, actually," I said. "But thank you."

We got to Williamsburg pretty quickly. It was a neighborhood of warehouses and humble row houses. Here and there we passed an open garage that had been turned into an art studio or a ramshackle bar. We walked past a bread factory with a Dumpster outside, where a vat of discarded dough rose in the hot late-spring sun. The smell of yeast mingled with the exhaust from the delivery trucks and the odor of tacos from a nearby cart. Men dressed like nineteenth-century Polish villagers strode by, yammering on cell phones. Women in ankle-length skirts and wigs pushed baby carriages down the sidewalk. Punk kids with liberty spikes on their heads and jagged black tattoos on their arms rode past us on souped-up bicycles. Girls with short hair and chunky-rimmed granny glasses drank cans of beer on their front stoops.

What shocked me the most about Williamsburg was the sky. It was enormous. It was almost as wide and bright as the sky back home in Flemington. I'd grown up a Manhattan tourist, rarely venturing beyond the Metropolitan Museum of Art to the north and Times Square to the south. We never went farther east than Park Avenue. I hadn't known you could be in New York City and see this much sky. I could breathe here.

We climbed up a ladder to the top of this warehouse he knew about and sat drinking iced teas in the sun.

"So Edgar is awful," Jason blurted out, as if he'd been waiting the whole time to say it. "You know that, right? I'm not, like, a homophobe."

"Totally fucking wacky," I said. "He flipped out on me so many times."

"You know why I had to leave?"

"Why?"

"He said I didn't make enough eye contact when I spoke to him. He said I didn't talk to him as much as I talked to Arthur. I was there to talk to Arthur. I had an internship for credit, and my job was to help Arthur with his lecture business—booking, events planning, scheduling, writing, all that stuff. I planned to be there for four months. Edgar kicked me out after one. Every day, it was something else about how I didn't look at him enough or talk to him enough or offer to help him enough. I didn't know I was supposed to help him. I'm not good at building things. I'm a nerd." He was speaking in a rush, barely stopping to breathe.

"I had a bicycle there. I brought it with me. He wouldn't let me use it. I had to ask him to drive me every time I wanted anything from town. He would spend the whole time telling me about how I had problems with authority, and how my generation was selfish and I was a perfect example, and how he knew I just wanted to use friends and throw them aside and I couldn't deal with a boss." He cringed at the memory. "It was so scary. It was seriously really scary every day."

"And Arthur didn't do anything?"

"Dude, that guy is nice but he did so much acid back in the day. I don't think he's all there."

"I know," I said, and sighed. "Jesus. I thought Edgar was weird to *me*."

"No, he liked you. But I felt so bad when you got there. I wanted to warn you, because I knew he'd be crazy to you, too. I called my dad and told him what was going on, and Edgar caught me and freaked out. He said, 'Ooh, you really get off on criticizing people, don't you, you little asshole?' It was so fucked up!"

I felt bad for the guy. He clearly had some kind of Edgar-induced PTSD.

"My dad said he was shocked. He said I could come back and get an internship in the city. I got out of there. I would've just ridden my bike away with my stuff on my back, but Edgar drove me to the bus station. And he said the craziest shit to me the whole time. It was like he wasn't even talking to me. It was like he thought I was someone else." He twisted his hands nervously.

I put my hand on his back.

"Jason," I said. "You're free now. And he's still back there, and you never have to go there again. Neither do I."

"I'm so glad you left," he said.

"Me, too. I learned some stuff, though. Like how to make coffee for two hundred pretentious hippie fucks."

We laughed together, and fell into a companionable silence. I looked at the Manhattan skyline, with the new, big empty space downtown like a gap where two front teeth used to be. The view was still beautiful, maybe even more so because you were acutely conscious of what was missing and it made you appreciate what was still there. The Chrysler Building shone in all its Art Deco glory, and the Empire State Building, and the bridges and the tugboats.

"I could maybe live here," I said, breaking the silence.

"You should come to NYU," Jason said with an eagerness that warmed something inside me. "You'd love it."

"My grades aren't good enough," I said.

"You should try anyway. We could hang out. My friends would like you and I bet you'd like them."

"I'll think about it," I said.

We ate dinner at a Malaysian place in what used to be a lamp factory. He took me back to Penn Station, and I hugged him good-bye.

"We should do this again," he said.

"Definitely," I said.

I walked down to my train, and rode all the way home without listening to my tape. I never saw him again.

CHAPTER SEVEN

Best Little Psych Ward in Carolina

I ended up in Asheville, North Carolina, the way a lot of people have historically ended up in Asheville, North Carolina: I went crazy. Because of its various rehabilitation institutions, Asheville has long been a destination for the addicted, the depressed, and the clinically insane. In 1936, author F. Scott Fitzgerald placed his reportedly delusional wife, Zelda, in Highland Mental Hospital in the Montford section of town. In the early days of her residence there, he famously stayed at the luxurious Grove Park Inn and chased young tail all over the hills. She spent time in and out of Highland over the next several years. One night in the spring of 1948, she was locked into a room where she was scheduled to receive electroshock treatment. A fire broke out in the kitchen and spread throughout the building, and she burned to death, as did eight other women.

Before it became a mental-health oasis, Asheville's real claim to fame was tuberculosis treatment. By 1912, when famed osteopath Dr. William Banks Meacham built the popular Ottari Sanitarium, Asheville was already known as a "health resort" for the TB-afflicted. The Ottari was more like a hotel than anything else. It had mahogany furniture and fancy Persian rugs, and the whole place was built in the Spanish–mission style. Meacham lost everything during the Great Crash of 1929, and the building was sold and converted into apartments. I once visited my favorite professor from Warren Wilson College there. She was a hot lesbian with an equally hot pro soccer player for a girlfriend.

I'd always wanted to go to college in North Carolina. For one thing, it was right next to South Carolina, where we spent a week's vacation each summer. For another, it was packed full of history and pretty scenery and friendly people. Those academically competitive New Jersey teens who do not get into good schools in New England often end up at Chapel Hill or Duke. We'd visited Duke and Chapel Hill when I was in the ninth grade. Duke just seemed like a younger version of Princeton, in a shittier town. (Durham has come a long way since the mid-nineties, when I first visited. It's now home to some of the hottest restaurants in the South.) By contrast, Chapel Hill seemed fun and exciting, and there were handsome boys everywhere. But back in high school, my grades hadn't been good enough for Chapel Hill's rigorous admissions standards for out-of-state students. After Emerson, they still weren't good enough. I set about looking for another North Carolina school that appealed to me, and found one five hours west of Chapel Hill, up in the Blue Ridge section of the Appalachian Mountains.

The college was called Warren Wilson, and its advertising materials read, "We're not for everyone . . . but then, maybe you're not everyone." That was enough to get me interested. It appealed directly to my twenty-one-year-old narcissism. *I'm* not *everyone,* I thought. *I'm me. I'm special. They* already get that *and I haven't even applied yet!*

Surprisingly, that tagline was actually correct. Wilson wasn't for everyone. Sure, it had a hippie aesthetic like Hampshire or any one of those crunchy schools, but at Wilson you had to work. Not necessarily academically—I learned a lot when I was there, but I wouldn't call the curriculum rigorous. No, you had to literally *work.* Like, with your hands. Everyone on campus was assigned to a work crew, and if you didn't work at least fifteen hours per week, you risked getting booted out of school.

The work crews were numerous, and I read through the list with a combination of excitement and confusion: Auto Shop (what kind of college had an auto shop?), Plumbing, Painting, Blacksmith Shop (was this some Colonial Williamsburg shit?), Maintenance, Carpentry (ooh, Jesus-y), Locksmith Shop, Landscaping, Chapel (ooh, extra Jesus-y), Farm (farm? They had a fucking farm?), and dozens more.

Not only did you have to work on one of those eighteen thousand crews, you also had to complete a hundred hours of community service in order to graduate. This was about as different from Emerson College as you could get. Back there, "community service" was about as popular a concept as discount shopping. Emerson College was full of people who focused with laser-like intensity on only one thing: their outfits. Even with all its hippie trappings, this college Down South seemed like a place where you could actually learn applicable life skills. Plus, it cost about 40 percent less than Emerson did. I applied and got in. I even did a solo road trip to visit Asheville, and I immediately fell in love.

When I met with the admissions counselor, it was on the porch of an old farmhouse in a rocking chair. She told me that the school had originally been founded as a Presbyterian mission school for poor farm boys in rural Appalachia, and had later expanded to include girls. It eventually became a college for aspiring teachers, and then added other courses of study. In 1952, it quietly desegregated, two years before *Brown v. Board of Education*. It was one of the first undergraduate colleges in the South to do so.

I enjoyed hearing about the school's history. I'd like to say it made more of an impression on me than the pickup trucks with the shirtless farm boys in the back, or the swimming hole with the rope swing and the naked hot girls and guys sunning themselves. I'd like to say that, but I can't.

I came back brimming with stories of how awesome my new school was going to be. I left out the parts about the hot naked people and left in the parts about history and work and all those other buzzwords parents like.

My mom and dad were excited but nervous. Asheville was eleven hours away by car, and a middle-of-the-night emergency call would be a bit more difficult to handle. I assured them that wouldn't happen. With the advance assistance of the Warren Wilson Counseling Office, Dr. Morrison, and a lovely female talk therapist I'd been seeing, I located a psychiatrist in Asheville (there seemed to be thousands) as well as a psychologist (there seemed to be tens of thousands). I also found a pharmacy where I could pick up my prescriptions.

"I'll be fine," I told my parents as I loaded up my car one early August morning. "Really. I promise."

"We know," said my dad.

"Just call us every day this time," said my mom.

"Okay," I lied.

The school turned out to be just as fun as I'd hoped. On the downside, I got assigned to the maintenance crew. I quickly established myself as the worst dormitory bathroom cleaner on campus, if not the entire world. I could devote an entire book to the colonies of shower-curtain bacteria I nurtured through neglect, but I'm not sure there's a market for that sort of thing. The live experiment didn't test particularly well among my dormmates.

On the upside, the campus was gorgeous. I had the run of thirteen hundred acres of organic garden, farm, woods, and landscaped grounds. A river bordered campus, and the students kayaked down it in nearly all weather. There were miles of hiking trails. We ate fresh food from the garden, and even beef and pork from cattle and hogs raised on the farm. The classes were interesting, and the 750 students were a mix of international students of color and domestic white kids. Some of the latter bore unfortunate dreadlocks and had been kicked out of boarding school. Others had been raised on small family farms all over the South. Others were post-rehab sober kids. Some were angry anarchist punks. Some were quietly devoted to a life of service as teachers or social workers. Nearly all the students were weird in one way or another, and many were broken little birds on the mend, just like me. Even though I didn't drink or smoke pot, I fit right in.

The first year passed largely without incident, aside from one of the dormitories burning down (only one person was hurt—she busted her knee when she jumped out of her first-floor window). I formed friendships, some of which solidified into strong bonds. I slept with a few guys. I read cool books. I hiked on the trails. I drank a lot of tea. I went to my new therapist and my new psychiatrist regularly. It was all so relaxing that I only had two or three panic attacks the whole year. And I didn't feel depressed at all, not even when the recovering crack addict I liked started banging my friend instead of me. There were plenty of moments when I felt genuinely happy. Inexplicably, I didn't go through a lesbian phase.

I spent much of the summer in Kentucky, completing my service requirement by volunteering at a migrant outreach center run by nuns. One of the nuns had definitely gone through a lesbian phase, and was inarguably still going through it. The fact seemed to make her angry, and she was even more short-tempered than Edgar the angry peacenik. Thankfully, she was not my only boss. The other two nuns in charge were marvelous, smart, capable women who took the edge off Sister Bitchface. That trio of alleged virgins did a bang-up job of running a free health clinic, free food pantry, and free clothing closet. My time with them remains one of my most pleasant memories. I even left with some respect for Sister Rage-a-lot. She wasn't nice, but she worked her ass off. I saw in those women the best of what the Roman Catholic Church provides today. I spend a lot of time thinking about the bad the Church does in this world, but those women showed me some of the good.

I returned to Warren Wilson in August and began my second year at the school. I had moved my way over to the Writing Center crew, so I tutored students instead of occasionally pushing a mop around their bathrooms. I was also an R.A. for freshmen, and distinguished myself by only hooking up with two of them. (Not at the *same time.* I'm a class act.) I was twenty-three and they were eighteen, which sounds really gross in retrospect but was highly entertaining at the time.

Once, I was away for my childhood best-friend Gretchen's wedding and couldn't do my R.A. shift. Another one of the R.A.s helpfully took over. When I was on my way back to Asheville, I had a brief stop at the Charlotte Airport. A funny feeling tickled the back of my brain, and I sensed that I ought to check in with my supervisors and dear friends, Karen and

Chauncey. Karen was a badass blond social worker and recent Warren Wilson graduate. Chauncey was a gay, bearded Atlanta-born bear who was still figuring out what he wanted to do with his life. All he was sure about was that he really liked books. As it turned out, his bibliophilic inclinations were correct, and he'd eventually become the head librarian at a hyper-conservative Christian college in a neighboring state. But that was a few years away. Today, he was dealing with another issue entirely.

"Hey, Chauncey," I said when he picked up the phone. "Is everything okay back at school?"

"Oh God," he said, sounding exhausted. "Oh God. Shit went nuts as soon as you left."

Karen got on the other extension, and demanded, "Sara, you didn't sleep with Brett Ferris, did you?" Brett was one of our eighteen-year-old charges. He was the tall, handsome, athletic scion of a well-connected Southern family. He would've gone to USC, UNC, or Duke, but he was the family fuck-up. A lot of the kids at Wilson were the family fuck-ups (ahem).

"Enough with the freshmen-fucking jokes!" I said. Karen, Chauncey, and our friend Dylan loved to make fun of me for hooking up with two frosh. And to be perfectly fair, I didn't actually have actual, you know, *sex* with either of them. It was just oral sex, which as a lapsed Catholic I simply considered a very entertaining abomination against Christ.

"He just got kicked out," Chauncey said.

I had trouble keeping up with the story as both of them jabbered excitedly over one another. The gist was that Brett had gotten incredibly intoxicated, hardly an unusual experience for him. What was unusual, however, was his reaction. High on a combination of mushrooms, acid, and booze, Brett stripped off all his clothes and ran naked and screaming through the dorm at three A.M. He ripped open an unlocked door on my floor.

Thankfully, the girls who lived there were out at a drum circle summoning Gaia or whomever one summons during drum circles. He emptied all their drawers into the hallway, threw their mattresses across the room, and peed on just about everything. He ran back out into the hallway and slammed the fire alarm before returning to their room to hide. When Karen found him, he was incoherent. The fire department arrived along with an ambulance. Brett managed to punch a firefighter before being strapped down to a gurney and hauled off to the hospital. When he sobered up hours later, he denied taking any drugs. Unsurprisingly, blood tests said otherwise.

"I miss all the good stuff," I said, genuinely disappointed. "Why did Gretchen's wedding have to be *this* weekend?"

"It was actually kind of awful," Karen said.

"God, I wish I'd been there," I said wistfully.

And no, by the way—I never had hooked up with Brett Ferris. In fact, once I'd gotten the young gents out of my system, I fell in love with a more age-appropriate fellow. His name was Carl, and we soon became attached at the hip.

I'd never loved someone so much. Back at Emerson, most of the straight guys were consumed with writing the perfect haiku or making the next great underappreciated black-and-white shaky-cam opus. This guy was into literature, but he was also into manly stuff. He was strong and smart and funny, and he knew how to do lots of cool things. He could change a tire, and the oil in his car. He could build things. I met his parents and his older sister. We even talked about having children, or anal sex. It was a real deep kind of love.

Eventually, it soured in the way that these things do. We just weren't right for each other. We didn't fit. He drank a lot, and I didn't drink at all. He exercised a lot, and I didn't exercise at all. He worked hard at school, and I didn't work hard at all. He was a saver, and I was a spender. He was a partier, and I was a napper. These things and more were cause for frequent disagreements. I called him to break up with him, but I got his voice mail. So I broke up with his voice mail. It wasn't the most sophisticated use of communications skills, but I wasn't the most sophisticated gal. He appeared at my door after he got the message, drunk and sad. I didn't change my mind. He went to get drunker.

That night, I tried to go to sleep. I had the ne plus ultra of college dwelling-places, a dorm with its own private bathroom. I'd decorated the place with swaths of brightly printed fabric, art prints I'd salvaged from the recycling bin, and loads of books. It was a peaceful little sanctuary, and I loved it. Yet I couldn't fall asleep.

I miss Carl, I thought. *I really, really miss Carl.* I meant it. But why did it hurt so much? After all, he and I had gotten on each other's nerves a lot. Karen, Chauncey, and Dylan thought we were awful for one another. And quite frankly, they had a point.

Still, I couldn't stop thinking it. *I miss Carl. I miss Carl. I miss Carl. I miss Carl and I want to die.*

Whoa! I sat bolt-upright in bed. Where had *that* old thought come from? I didn't want to die! I had a nice life. I had good friends. I loved my school. My family was healthy and reasonably happy.

I want to die. I want to die. I want to die. There it was, over and over again. I turned on music to block it out. I'd gotten into bluegrass since moving to Asheville, and if anything could cure this little funk, it was banjo.

I want to die. I want to die. I want to die. It wouldn't let up. I spent a solid four hours trying to get that bad old thought out of my head. I took a shower. I did jumping jacks. I cracked open a textbook for once. Nothing helped. If I'd been a drinker, I might have drunk the pain away. Maybe I would have passed out and woken up the next day with an awful headache and the strong conviction that liquor and Carl were both bad news. That might have been a tidier conclusion to this story. But that's not what happened.

As time wore on, I felt as though my heart had been ripped out and pounded. I felt lonely and frightened. What if I'd made the wrong choice? What if nobody else would ever love me? What if Carl got together with another girl? *I want to die. I want to die. I want to die.*

I guess I'd never felt real heartbreak before, or at least not since high school—and that had been over five years ago, more than enough time for a heart to un-learn how to deal with the end of a romantic relationship. Sure, I had done the dumping, but that somehow made it more confusing. Why did I feel so bad if I was the one who had ended things? I must be going crazy. Was I going crazy again? Oh, no. I couldn't go crazy again. I just couldn't. Things were working out so well. *I want to die. I want to die. I want to die.*

Finally, at four A.M., I dug up the R.A. manual we'd all been given at training a couple of weeks before the school year started. I flipped to the part about mental health emergencies.

"If a student expresses a persistent desire to hurt him- or herself, or a desire to commit suicide, notify the Dean of Students and take the student to Mission Hospital's St. Joseph Campus. Doctors there will be able to determine whether to admit the student to the Copestone mental health care unit. The Dean of Students will immediately notify the student's parents or guardians."

If I were my own R.A., what would I do? In this case, the student (me) didn't express a desire to commit suicide, exactly. But some crazy voice in her brain sure was expressing a strong desire to die. Was it worth splitting hairs over terminology, considering the student's history of mental health crises? I decided it wasn't, and called Karen.

"Hello?" Her voice sounded sleepy and muffled.

"Hey, Karen, it's Sara. I think I need to go to the emergency room. I think I'm going crazy again. I can't stop thinking about dying."

"Okay," Karen said simply. "I'll be up in a sec." She knew about my history and why I'd dropped out of my old college, but I think she would have reacted the same way if anyone had called her with that announcement. Karen just had that kind of cool head under pressure. You could tell her that a giant carnivorous dinosaur was eating all the cattle down on the farm, and she would've casually picked up the phone to call Animal Control. And she would've already had the phone number memorized, too, just in case something like this ever came up. She was always prepared. Today she has two master's degrees and a sweet job as some kind of grand social work queen. Back then, she already displayed the right attitude for that kind of high-stress job.

She got to my room and said, "So you want to go to the ER now?"

"Sure," I said.

"You should probably pack some stuff."

"Like what? Clothes?"

"I mean, bring a change of underwear in case they put you in a gown. Your toothbrush, a wallet, any prescriptions you have. Bring the phone numbers of the people you'll need to contact, like your shrink."

"That's a good idea," I said. I threw a few things in a bag, and then she drove me to the ER in her lipstick-red, biodiesel-fueled pickup truck.

We put my name on the list and sat down. Even the hospital waiting rooms in this town had comfy rocking chairs, apparently. Karen read a *Southern Living* magazine. After I filled out and handed in my medical history chart, I found the inevitable *Highlights* issue hiding beneath the grown-up periodicals. It turned out Goofus and Gallant had been up to pretty much the same shtick since I'd last made their acquaintance. I was partway through a pretty awesome maze when the intake nurse called my name.

She was a thin middle-aged woman with big, curly, dyed-blond hair, a thick mountain accent, and those permanent lines chain-smokers get around their lips from all the years of pursing, sucking, and blowing. Her nametag read MAYBELLE S., I assume to distinguish her from the other Maybelles wandering round the place.

"Okay, Sara," Nurse Maybelle S. said. "You been taking your Prozac on schedule?"

"Yes, ma'am," I said. Two years of living in the South had taught me that "ma'am" wasn't just for female police officers and complaint-line staffers.

"You feeling good physically? No cold, no nausea, no fever, no nothing?"

"Yes, ma'am."

"Your period's normal. You don't think you're pregnant. You have a history of depression, panic attacks, and suicidal thoughts."

"That's right, ma'am." She made a few notes and then looked me square in the eye.

"Now baby, what's going on this morning?" she asked. "You just tell me how you're feeling, and we'll do our best to sort it right out."

I told her everything, starting with the breakup ("Well, you can't be with a man who just isn't right for you. Believe me, I been to that rodeo about as many times as they'd let me go") and ending with the whole wanting-to-die thing.

When I finished, she took a big bag of gummy bears out from her desk. Then she shook several out into a tissue and gave it to me.

"We'll have you see the doctor, just in case," she said. "But honey, brokenhearted and crazy are two different things. I've been both, and if we had more time I'd tell you tales to make your toes curl. And I'm glad you came in to be safe, but I'm thinking what we have here is a heart that needs mending."

"Well, that's a relief," I said. Nurse Maybelle S. nodded emphatically and popped a gummy bear into her mouth. Then she told me about her third divorce, which in her opinion bore certain resemblances to my situation with Carl. We had a real nice time sharing her gummy bears and talking about guys until the next sick person showed up and she had to excuse herself to do her job.

I sat back down with Karen until Nurse Maybelle S. came over and told us we could go back to wait for the doctor in an exam room. We were met at the door by a social worker, who walked us into a little private room that I guess they kept for potential psych patients. She said apologetically that she'd be by in a few minutes, but had to complete an evaluation with another patient next door.

Karen and I sat and talked shit about some of our teenage residents for about thirty minutes. Our foxy, tattooed friend Talia showed up to join the party, with food she'd smuggled from the school cafeteria. Karen left to start her shift at her day job, and Talia and I had a fine time reading old magazines and listening to the other potential psych patients freak out.

My next-door neighbor, the one who was taking up the social worker's time, was a girl around my age. I saw her briefly when she ran out of her little waiting room and past the open door of mine. She was a brunette like me, and short, but her hair was messy and her clothes were rumpled. The social worker went after her and then gently walked her back to her little room.

"They're trying to kill me!" the girl shouted.

"You're safe here," the social worker said reassuringly.

"That girl is seriously nuts," Talia whispered. "I think that's why they're taking so long to get to you. She's higher on their list of priorities."

"I guess the squeaky wheel gets the lithium around here," I said. We giggled.

"Do you want to die anymore?" Talia asked.

I paused. I actually hadn't thought about dying for at least an hour.

"I don't think so," I said. "But I think I have to stay now and, like, explain that to them."

Being friendly types, Talia and I commenced getting to know the nurses and orderlies on the floor. Apparently Talia frequented the same bar as two of the male nurses, and they got into a long discussion about whether or not the bartender was actually on the run from the mob. I gave one of the female nurses the Cosmo Sex Quiz of the Month and we cackled at how stupid it was.

The dean of students, my psychiatrist, and my psychologist called to check on me. I spoke to each of them in turn, assuring them that I was going to be okay, and apologizing for waking them up. Then came the call I'd been dreading.

"Hey, Sara," said one of the nurses. "It's your mom and dad."

"Are they freaking out?" I asked.

"They sound fine," she said. "Don't worry."

I got on the phone, more nervous than I'd been in forever.

"Heeeey, guys," I said uneasily. "I guess school called you."

"We think you should come home today," Mom said. "We'll get you a ticket. Can your friend drive you to the airport?" She didn't sound fake-happy. She sounded sort of normal, with a tinge of worry. I started to cry.

"Are you mad?" I asked, sniffling.

"Why would we be mad?" my dad asked.

"I don't know. I just feel like I'm backsliding."

"Honey," my mom said. "Breakups suck."

"But they shouldn't land you in the hospital. I just feel like a crazy person, or a loser, or something. I shouldn't even be here. I just got scared when I couldn't stop thinking those bad thoughts again."

"We're glad you went to the hospital," my dad said. "Hey, it was the middle of the night. If it was during the day, you would've just gone to your doctor or your therapist. But you were scared and you didn't want something bad to happen, so you went. That's a good thing. That's smart."

I started crying harder.

"Sweetie, why are you crying?" my mom asked.

"Because you're being so nice to me," I sobbed, gulping down air.

"We can be assholes if you want," my dad said.

"No, thank you," I said.

I blubbered some more before getting off the phone.

Talia was having such a good time that she decided to skip class and stay.

"I mean I'm here to support you, but also this is kind of fun," she said.

"Thanks," I said.

The social worker finally got to me after I'd been at the hospital for about three hours. She was joined by a tall, strikingly handsome doctor with a square jaw and an odd resemblance to a generic Disney prince. Except, you know, not a cartoon.

"Hello, Sara," he said in a deep, manly, superhero voice. "I want to thank you for coming in. You did the right thing. Have you made a plan to do yourself any harm?"

I looked at Talia, who was stifling a snort and miming a blow job behind his back.

"No, sir," I said.

"Excellent," he said. "Marla here will put together a plan for self-care with you. We'll have you sign it, and then you'll be released."

"Totally awesome," I said, and Talia made a sound somewhere between a cough and a squeak.

"Good luck," he said, and swept out of the room to save some other damsel in distress.

Marla the social worker and I worked out an agreement that I handwrote and signed. I found it in an old shoe-box last year.

> I agree to call a friend, a family member, or a mental health professional if I have a future mental health crisis. My plan of care is as follows:
>
> 1. Continue to take Prozac as directed.
>
> 2. Continue to take Xanax as directed on an as-needed basis.
>
> 3. Go home to New Jersey today to see my family.
>
> 4. Drink chicken soup.

We added the last one when Nurse Maybelle S. stopped by to see how I was doing.

"Baby, you need to go home and let your mama take care of you," she said. "And get you some chicken soup. Just take care of yourself the same way you would if you had the flu. Lots of liquids, lots of rest." Marla and Talia both nodded emphatically.

"That sounds good to me," I said.

"Don't you forget the chicken soup, now," Nurse Maybelle S. said before she returned to her post.

"I won't."

It took us awhile to get out of there, because we had so many new friends to alert that we were leaving. Talia told the guys she'd see them at the bar. On the way out, we passed my neighbor's waiting room. The door was slightly ajar. She was still inside, crumpled up in a heap beneath a blue blanket. I wondered what she'd think if she knew I used to pee in bowls. I imagined she probably would've thought I was a real freak.

An orderly buzzed Talia and me out, and the doors opened with a great *whoosh* as we stepped into the Carolina sunshine.

"You wanna go to Waffle House before I drop you at the airport?" Talia asked.

"They got chicken soup? I never tried to order it there."

"Yup, they do. Plus waffles."

"Shut the fuck up. Waffle House has waffles?"

"Come on, my little rejected mental patient," Talia said, opening the car door for me. "We're gonna have us a fancy celebration lunch."

We blasted Liz Phair's "Fuck and Run" all the way out of the parking lot and down the highway. It was that kind of day.

CHAPTER EIGHT

Billy Has a Boner

Billy's boner was big and hard, and it was stealing the attention of my entire ninth-grade writing class. They were cracking up, but when he tried to join in he winced in pain.

"It hurts!" he moaned. "Don't make me laugh, you guys!"

No one was doing anything about it, and I knew that the job had fallen to me. I had to handle it. Well, not *handle* it, but—you know.

I had not moved to Texas to deal with a fourteen-year-old's unruly erection. And yet, there it was, straining against his baggy jeans, challenging me to prove that I was an adult who could weather any crisis. I had a feeling even Billy's boner could tell I had no idea what the fuck I was doing.

Billy's boner was just the latest in a series of problems that had plagued me since the summer. I hadn't graduated from Warren Wilson at the expected time, because one of my professors had flunked me. This was partly his fault for being unsympathetic to my particular needs as a crazy person and partly my fault for not showing up to class very often. My friends all graduated in a big, beautiful ceremony on the lawn right outside my dorm window, while I hid my head under my pillows in an effort to drown out the amplified sound. All my Emerson friends had graduated on time the previous year. I couldn't even manage to graduate from my second-chance school.

I felt enormously guilty that I had wasted even more of my parents' money on my never-ending quest for a college degree. Exactly how many loans was I going to ask these people to take out before I actually had a degree to show for it? And now my brother was in college, too. He'd chosen a five-year program up in Boston, and it was just as expensive as my Emerson tuition had been.

After my failure to graduate, I moved out of the dorm and into an $800-a-month two-bedroom house with Chauncey and our pals Donnie and Belinda. I stayed in the tiniest bedroom, which had just enough room for my queen-size bed and a little bookshelf. Donnie, who was gay, shared a big bed in the big bedroom with Belinda, who was straight. Chauncey slept in the laundry room. We couldn't afford to put in a washer or dryer, so he had plenty of space. Unfortunately, we also couldn't afford to put in a door. Chauncey tacked up a big rainbow flag over the open doorway.

Asheville's economic engine ran almost entirely on tourism, and year-round jobs were hard to come by. I found work as a cashier at Earth Fare, the local branch of a Southern natural-foods chain. It had somehow resisted absorption into the Whole Foods brand, which made it acceptable in the eyes of my punk-anarchist-farmer pals. They would've preferred I work on a co-operative collective utopian farm, but I enjoyed air-conditioning and paychecks. Earth Fare offered an array of "natural" anti-anxiety agents and antidepressants. I tried a few, even though I was doing just fine on the higher dosage of Prozac my Asheville psychiatrist had prescribed after my hospital adventure several months prior. Someone recommended valerian root as an effective deterrent for panic attacks, but after spending a day with the stinky bottle at my cashier station, I decided I'd stick with odorless Xanax.

The ultimate cashier job in Asheville was at the French Broad Food Co-op. The place was not named for Catherine Deneuve or Brigitte Bardot. Its unique moniker came from the French Broad River, which wound through town and was a favorite spot for rafters and kayakers. The Co-op was much smaller than Earth Fare, but it was way cooler. Its employees were called "worker-owners" and they got amazing discounts and *actual health insurance.* To get a job there, you had to be like some kind of master Jedi of cashiering. I was past the Padawan learner stage, but I didn't exactly qualify for Obi-Wan levels of greatness. I mean, I didn't memorize barcodes or anything like that.

I liked Earth Fare, and managed to do a decent job. I suppose a well-trained monkey could have operated the computerized cash register, provided said monkey were duly devoted to fresh local produce and fast, efficient customer service. I spent a great deal of my wages on the lunch buffet, which cost two arms and sixteen legs even with my 15 percent discount. My boyfriend at the time was a carpenter named Tom, and after I got done with work, sometimes we'd drive over to the cheap supermarket and buy the fixings for a kickass barbecue. I kept hoping he'd propose, just so I could protest, "But Thomas! We haven't been together long enough!" and then, with tears of joy, accept his offer. If I couldn't be a college graduate, I might as well be somebody's fiancée. But the proposal never came.

Before un-graduating, I had applied for the world's most

useful degree, the Master of Fine Arts, at a variety of schools. I got wait-listed at the University of Virginia, and an enthusiastic professor wrote to tell me he felt sure they'd be able to find a spot for me. They didn't, and I had been sorely disappointed until I found out I wasn't graduating. Then I was relieved. I couldn't imagine how embarrassing it would be to have to renege on an agreement to attend a big fancy MFA in writing program because I'd flunked part of my final undergraduate semester.

I had also applied to the AmeriCorps program in the winter, back when I'd foolishly assumed I would graduate on time. AmeriCorps, a government-funded program started under the Clinton administration, functions as a confederacy of nonprofit organizations. It's the Peace Corps for pussies, public service for people who don't want to take malaria pills. In fact, I'd first learned about it way back in high school at the New Jersey Governor's School on Public Issues and the Future of the State. It sounded like a fine, respectable way to spend a gap year between college graduation and actual adulthood.

By the time *everyone in the whole entire world but me* graduated, I still hadn't heard from any of the AmeriCorps programs to which I had applied. I figured I hadn't gotten in. I would later hear that hardly anyone gets rejected by AmeriCorps. Makes sense, too. When your big draw is offering approximately $10,000 a year (before taxes) plus crappy health insurance and a $4,700 scholarship (before taxes) as an exit reward, you probably take anybody who is willing to fill out the application.

One day, on my extremely expensive in-house organic lunch break at Earth Fare, I heard from a program in Texas at a brand-new public high school for the arts. They wanted to interview me for a position as an artist-in-residence. I would have studio space in which to write, and I would get to design and teach my very own elective courses. I would also assist in the classroom of a regular teacher, perhaps in English or Social Studies.

"I'm sorry," I said to the personnel director. "I'm really quite interested, but I didn't end up graduating on time from college. So I don't have a college degree."

"Oh, that's not a problem," the personnel director said.

That should have been my first clue.

The initial interview went well, and so did the one after that. When they called to offer me the job, I was shocked. I'd never really considered moving to Texas before. The Southwest held no attraction for me. And I didn't want to be a high school teacher.

But really, what else was I going to do? Hang around Asheville, go back to Warren Wilson in the fall, and pass my smirking professor on campus while I walked to and from my two required courses? I hated feeling like a loser and seeing all the classmates who had graduated come through my line at the grocery store. I'd ask them what they planned to do, and they had so many ideas, so many possibilities. I didn't. With the aggravated narcissism of a woman in the thick of an extended adolescence, I imagined they were all staring at me and feeling sorry for me. I needed to do something big and significant to prove to everybody (read: myself) that I wasn't a failure. Moving two thousand miles away seemed pretty big and significant. I took the job.

"Do they have psychiatrists out there?" my mother asked when I told her.

"Of course they do, Mom!" I snapped. "It's a completely normal state with normal things like shrinks and Prozac."

"You were just in the hospital eight months ago," she said.

"I wasn't *in* the hospital. I was in the ER, and I went there by my own choice. I was *rejected* by the hospital for not being *crazy* enough." I was huffily shoving clothes in duffel bags and wondering how I was going to convince Tom to fly out to Texas every weekend to visit me.

"What are the roads like?" she asked. "Do they have direct flights from Newark? What if you need me and I can't get to you?"

"I'm twenty-three years old, Mom!" I shouted. "I haven't had a panic attack in three months! I'm totally fine!"

"Just make sure they have Xanax in Texas," she said.

They definitely had Xanax in Texas. And thanks to its proximity to Mexico, they also had every other kind of drug imaginable, legal or illegal. My brother and I drove out to Texas, found me an apartment within a day, and walked over the border to notoriously violent Ciudad Juarez shortly thereafter. We ate some great Chinese food and wandered among the sex tourists and rifle-toting *federales*. I came back with enough cut-rate prescription drugs to last me for months, at a fraction of what I would have spent at Walgreens. I also hauled a large Virgin of Guadalupe statue back over the border, and plopped her down in the corner of my bedroom. I figured I'd probably need her help. I was right.

The school turned out to operate in a manner very similar to community theater. Someone in town said, "Let's put on a school!" and decided to do it. Thanks to the Bush administration's enthusiasm for throwing money at anyone who wanted to start a charter school, the state of Texas's historically awful public school system was flush with cash for just this purpose. The founder, teachers, and administrative staff were enormously enthusiastic, and their good intentions were evident. But in that first year, upward of 40 percent of the staff quit or was fired. It was hard to know how to follow the rules when the rule-makers kept disappearing.

On the upside, the school was small. Only about eighty-four students enrolled that first year, so there was no question that each student would get lots more individual attention than would be possible at the four other large public high schools in the district. The school provided a safe haven for the gays, goths, and other weirdos who'd been endlessly tormented by the vicious popular kids and wannabe thugs that populate the halls of every American public high school. It also served as a last-chance school for gang members who'd been kicked out of all the other schools. And then there were the religious homeschooled kids who'd never been socialized in human society. Their parents decided our school was the place for them, in the thick of awkward adolescence, to learn how to behave in public. Among the latter group was a sweet Jew for Jesus who had a messianic bat mitzvah instead of the traditional Mexican *quinceañera* when she turned fifteen. The Christly bat mitzvah still featured a mariachi band, though.

Thankfully, I had a team to bond with over this odd, strange, wonderful, insane, stressful new job. There were eight AmeriCorps artists-in-residence from all over the country, ranging in ages from twenty to fifty. Some had experience working in classrooms, and some (like me) didn't. None of us had teaching licenses. A couple of us didn't even have college degrees. Eventually I enrolled in a weekend class at the local university and transferred the credits back to Warren Wilson. They shipped my diploma from North Carolina to Texas. But by that time, I'd already logged nine months in the teaching trenches.

We designed our own courses, wrote our own lesson plans to comply with state-mandated standards and benchmarks, ordered our own supplies, graded our own students—all with little supervision. Two of the AmeriCorps artists mysteriously disappeared before the end of the first semester. One was said to have quit, while the other was rumored to have been fired—for what, we never knew. I'm pretty sure we weren't supposed to teach in a classroom without a licensed teacher watching over us. But that's what happened, every single day. And the results were predictably a mix of great success and great disaster. Which brings me back to Billy's boner.

I didn't actually notice it myself (I mean, it wasn't *that* big). What I noticed was the tittering and giggling that arose as soon as I entered my classroom that afternoon.

I looked around suspiciously. My initial thought was that they must be laughing at me. I knew my dyed-red hair looked a little odd with bright pink streaks, but it had been that way for weeks and they ought to have been accustomed to it by now. Was it my thrift-store skirt? My dangly plastic earrings? The other gaudy accoutrements that marked me as a stereotypically wacky, unconventional, artsy-fartsy teacher? Or had the sad joke of my complete and utter incompetence as an educator (and human being) finally dawned on them?

We were reading *Romeo and Juliet,* because that's what I had learned in ninth grade and I figured it was their turn to be tormented by it. I found Shakespeare's language just as boring as they did, but when I'd taken this job I had agreed to play the role of an Adult, and Adults make Children do boring things for their own good. I'd wanted to liven it up by assigning the kids *Sandman* by Neil Gaiman, but had gotten called up in front of the principal when ex-homeschooler Miguel Sanchez's evangelical Christian father had complained about a panel depicting a nearly nude woman. ("*Technically,* she's a goddess, so it's not even *human* nudity," I had protested when the school director scolded me.) Years later, I would interview Gaiman and his rock-star girlfriend, Amanda Palmer, in a bathtub at the Maritime Hotel in Manhattan's Chelsea neighborhood. Neil wore a business suit, and Amanda was completely naked. I wore a short skirt, a push-up bra, and a T-shirt that read, THIS IS WHAT A FEMINIST LOOKS LIKE. During a break in taping, I found my mind wandering back to Miguel's father. This was probably exactly how he had imagined I spent my free time.

Being a teacher was difficult because of all the lying that was required of me on a daily basis. I had to pretend I actually cared if my students came into the room smelling of pot smoke, or if they cursed aloud in class. Mostly, I just wanted them to have a good time, learn how to write a complete sentence, and avoid shooting heroin between their toes while inside my classroom. I had an idealistic streak when I started. I wanted to show them the poetry and novels and art and music that inspired me, in the hope that it would inspire them. But a lot of times it seemed the stuff that inspired me wasn't considered appropriate for the classroom. And then I got in trouble for using *Sandman*. Thus, *Romeo and Juliet*.

On the day that Billy's boner hijacked my classroom, we were supposed to talk about Mercutio. We were supposed to talk about his friendship with Romeo, and what it means to be a good friend, and whether your friends are always obligated to take your side in arguments. I had a lesson plan. I had designed it to conform with Texas State Board of Education standards and benchmarks. I had a short, interactive lecture. I had a quiz game. I had small-group assignments. I had discussion questions. On paper, it looked like the perfect lesson. If you'd read it, you would almost think I had actually graduated from college. You might even think I was a real teacher with some actual training, maybe a license. You might believe I had the right to stand in that classroom and wield authority. When I strode into that classroom that day, even I believed it.

And then Billy's boner proved me wrong.

Terribly, terribly wrong.

The class was a giggly, squirming mess. I stood in front of them and cocked an eyebrow.

"All right, guys," I said in a booming voice. "Settle down." This was my I Mean Business Voice—louder, deeper, and more confident than my natural voice. I thought it gave me an added air of authority, but I actually just sounded like a chain-smoking drag queen.

The kids obeyed briefly, if only because they liked me most of the time and I liked them most of the time. I was easy on them, grading more for effort than for excellence. I laughed at their jokes. I let them write whatever they wanted in their required class journals, so long as they wrote a full page for me each day. I'd given them a speech about not writing anything incriminating that would force me to contact their parents, but my version of "incriminating" seemed to exclude tales of smoking weed, drinking beer, and fucking their significant others. They picked up on that quickly. One day Octavio Gomez asked me about it in class.

"Miss, I wrote about what I did this weekend," he said, a mischievous glint in his eye. "I broke, like, six laws."

"Did you put anyone in the hospital or the morgue?" I asked. This made the whole class crack up.

"Naw, miss, I didn't kill nobody," he said, laughing.

"Then I hope you had a good weekend," I said, and went back to drawing Freytag's Pyramid on the board. They laughed when I explained the concepts of rising action and climax to them ("Yo miss, I always climax after my rising action!") but they got what I was saying. They even understood *denouement*. That day felt like a victory.

Today, though, the victory would go to someone else. Well, some*thing* else. Something that was stuck somewhere between rising action and climax.

We got into *Romeo and Juliet,* and the Mercutio discussion evoked a few intelligent comments from the usual suspects who always had smart things to say. Everybody else seemed to be struggling to contain smirks. Even the do-gooder kids stifled snorts of laughter when they weren't answering my questions. I followed their eyes across the room, and that's when I realized they were laughing at Billy.

Billy was different from the rest of the students. Most of my students were either Mexican (which meant they had some drop of Mexican blood) or Anglo (which meant they didn't). When it comes to categorizing local human specimens, southwest Texans are not unlike the Amish in their charmingly quaint simplicity. The Amish refer to all non–Amish Americans as "the English," even if the folks in question are, say, American-born with Russian or Italian ancestry. You're either one of the bonnet-and-beard set or you're English. Southwest Texans use three categories: Mexican, Anglo, and Indian. Blacks or Asians are Anglos, because they're not Indian and they're certainly not Mexican. This does not come up often, because there aren't a lot of blacks or Asians in southwest Texas.

It was universally agreed that blue-eyed, blond Pablo, who sat next to Billy, was Mexican. His mother was Anglo, but his father was Mexican. Pablo had a Mexican name, knew Spanglish, and had recently been jumped into a gang. Pablo had done time in juvenile detention for stabbing a kid at his old high school with a switchblade. Pablo drove a low-rider and only hung around with Mexican kids. Pablo was rumored to possess a gun. Pablo was Mexican.

But dark-haired, dark-eyed Billy was harder to pinpoint. First of all, his name was Billy, which clearly wasn't a Mexican name. His mother was most definitely Anglo. But his father was Spanish, from Spain. Billy spoke fluent Castilian Spanish, an entirely different dialect than what the other kids heard at home. Did that maybe make him kind of Mexican?

It wasn't just about racial stuff, either. Billy wasn't in a gang, so he wasn't a thug. But he hadn't been homeschooled, so he wasn't one of those bright-eyed innocents newly released into the wild. He had been known to buy some of his clothes at Hot Topic, but he wasn't one of the mall goths who thought shopping at a corporate chain made them rebels. He didn't wear dark makeup around his eyes or write songs about death. He wasn't one of the gay artsy refugees from the other big schools. He skated around the parking lots in town with some friends after school. He listened to rock music and he had an eyebrow piercing. Sometimes he clowned around in school and got in trouble, but usually he was pretty obedient.

You couldn't put Billy into a category. And that was his biggest problem, really. In high school, you've got to pick a category and stick with it. In certain cases, you can make lateral moves across categories, or even jump up to a whole new level if you get your braces off or lose a bunch of weight one summer. But the one thing you cannot do is stay undefined. Billy was an undefined entity. He upset the natural order of things. And because no one knew what to do with him, they made fun of him sometimes. Typically, the kids seized on his appearance: he was slightly doughy, and his hair was often wild and unkempt. He took the teasing well, and knew how to be self-deprecating, so he didn't get beaten up. You might even say he was well-liked. But he didn't *belong* anywhere.

When I saw that the kids were laughing at Billy, a sense of righteous indignation rose up within me. I hated bullies.

"You guys!" I snapped in my own voice. "What the hell are you doing? Focus unless you want vocabulary quizzes all period.

With *no extra credit.*" This was met with groans, and I smiled with satisfaction. Extra credit was the only thing that kept most of these kids' grades above water. My extra-credit questions were always adorable queries like, "Who is the most inspiring person you know?" and "What emotions does your favorite song evoke in you?"

They quieted down, and I looked more closely at Billy. He sat in his usual chair, but his books were on his lap instead of on the table. He was slightly hunched over, and his face was pale. Beads of sweat dotted his forehead, and his eyes were closed in what looked like pain.

"Billy, are you okay?" I asked gently.

At this, the class roared. I turned on them with a fury.

"Cut the shit!" I used profanity in the classroom on rare occasions, and it generally shocked the students into silence. "You guys are acting like jerks! How can you laugh when someone obviously doesn't feel well?"

They were silent, but I could tell they were struggling to contain themselves. I rolled my eyes and walked over to Billy.

"Hey, do you need to go down to the director's office, maybe call your parents?" I asked. We didn't have a nurse's office. We also didn't have a full-time guidance counselor, which was unfortunate since half the kids and most of the teachers were out of their fucking minds.

Billy shook his head, and whispered, "No. No, I'm fine."

I looked at him doubtfully. He looked as if he were about to throw up.

"Are you sure? You look really pale."

Pablo the gangsta blond could no longer contain himself. "That's because all the blood in his head rushed to his—"

"SHUT THE FUCK UP, PABLO!" Billy shouted. We all

jumped a little. Billy never showed anger, certainly not toward one of the toughest kids in school. But Pablo shut his mouth and didn't seem offended in the least.

"Billy, you gotta calm down," I said. "And try not to actually yell 'fuck' in my classroom. I'm not mad, I'm just saying another teacher would probably throw you out."

"I'm sorry," he said in a pained whisper. "I'm seriously sorry, miss. I'll be fine if I just . . . wait it out."

"You sure you don't wanna get up and—"

"No, no, I don't want to get up! I don't want to get up, okay?" He was nervous and irritable. He clutched his books protectively.

"Okay, no worries, I won't make you get up."

As I turned and slowly walked away, everyone heard Billy mutter to Pablo, "I'm gonna go to the bathroom and just deal with this." The other students burst into laughter once again.

I didn't lose my temper often, but I had actually put some effort into this lesson plan. They were going to learn some Shakespeare if I had to fucking kill them. And I was getting to the point where I might actually consider doing that in order to shut them up.

"That's it!" I shouted, much louder than before. "What the hell is happening right now? Somebody tell me so we can just deal with it and move on. Write me a note or some shit. I don't care. Just do it now."

Pablo looked pleadingly at Billy. A glance passed between them in which permission was conferred.

"Miss, don't you know?" Pablo demanded excitedly, bouncing up and down. "Everybody in the school knows Billy took Viagra!" The students fell immediately into what I can only describe as a joyful silence.

I paused and took a moment to let the information sink in. Meanwhile, twenty pairs of eyes watched eagerly for my reaction. Once I was fairly certain I'd actually heard what I thought I'd heard, I looked at Billy.

"Billy," I said slowly, enunciating each syllable perfectly. "Is this true?"

"Yes," he groaned, cringing.

"And why . . . exactly . . . did you take Viagra?"

"It was a bet, miss. It was a bet."

Pablo jumped in. "Jorge Jimenez had it in his *abuelito*'s medicine cabinet, and Jorge dared him to try it, and Billy said it only works on old guys, and Jorge bet him fifty dollars it would work on young guys too."

"Jorge was right," Billy moaned. "It wasn't worth the money."

Slowly and deliberately, I placed my copy of *Romeo and Juliet* on the table. I tried to make it to my chair, but couldn't. My legs were about to give out. I sat down on the floor and burst out laughing.

"That—that is—" I sputtered, trying to get the words out. "That is seriously—I mean, seriously—the stupidest fucking thing I have ever heard." Then Billy was laughing, and then the whole class was laughing. We nearly rattled the windows.

"Holy shit, miss, don't make me laugh," Billy groaned in between giggles. "It hurts when I laugh."

"Billy," I said, trying to regain my composure. "Dude. You're so much smarter than this. You're probably the smartest person in this class. Sorry, you guys, but he is." I had lost the ability to feign that they were all unique and special flowers.

"Yo, that's true, though," Pablo said reflectively. "You are, bro. I'm sorry about your dick, yo. Like, it's funny? But I bet it hurts."

"Thanks, man," Billy wheezed. "Ouch. Shit."

"How could—why would—okay. Okay. Okay." I took several deep breaths in a row, and the class quieted down. I think they were afraid I was actually going to pass out.

"I—I have no idea what to do," I said, standing up and dusting myself off. "Can you guys just, like, talk amongst yourselves for a minute quietly? Don't laugh too loud or the director will come in here and get on my ass about it."

"Shit, miss, we don't want her up here neither," Pablo said. "We'll talk quiet."

"Thank you, Pablo," I said.

I sat down in my chair and thought. On the one hand, the rules dictated that if any child in the school was found to be under the influence of an illegal drug, it must be immediately reported to the school director. On the other hand, Viagra wasn't an illegal drug, although it was certainly illegal for Billy and Jorge to steal someone else's prescription medication. On the third hand, no one in this school followed the rules—not the kids, not the teachers, and certainly not the ever-rotating cast of administrators. On the fourth and most important hand, I had a pretty good idea of what Billy's Old World father would do if he found out that his son had ingested Viagra on a dare, and it would probably involve the use of a belt. The kid had enough to deal with at school on a daily basis. And I sincerely doubted there was any chance at all that he'd repeat this particular episode in future.

So with that, I made a decision. It had taken me approximately sixty seconds to arrive at it, but once I made it, I knew I would stick to it.

"Billy," I said. "I need you to come into the hallway for a talk."

"Miss, he can't get up!" Pablo protested. "For reals, miss, you're a girl, you don't know what it's like. It's mad awkward and shit." I squatted down beside him and lowered my voice.

"Pablo," I said. "You are in charge while I'm outside. I gotta take care of this situation so nobody gets in trouble, you understand?" He nodded sagely. Pablo was well-versed in the art of dodging The Man.

"I got this, miss," he said.

"I want everybody to write a full page for me—don't worry about paragraphs or proper punctuation—on what makes a good friend versus what makes a bad friend. Can you get them to do that?"

He sat up straighter. "No problem."

"Thanks," I said. I stood up and looked at Billy. He rolled his eyes at me.

"Can I at least keep my books over my—"

"Yes!" I said quickly. "Yes, of course. C'mon. Outside, now."

He stood up, hunched over like an osteoporosis-riddled old man, and shuffled out the door with his books over his crotch. I raised my eyebrow at Pablo, who nodded and stood up.

"Yo, everybody, she wants us to write a page about friendship. You don't gotta give a fuck about commas and shit. Just write what you think makes a good friend, and what you think makes a bad friend. Like a good friend don't snitch, and a bad friend sells you out so he don't have to do no time."

When I went into the hallway, they were all writing quietly. They kept at it the whole time I remained outside the door.

"Billy," I said, facing him. "Seriously. What the fuck?"

"I know," he sighed. "I know."

"I'm supposed to send you to the school director."

"I know."

"And then she'll call your parents."

"Fuck."

"Yeah, fuck is right. You can't take other people's prescriptions, ever. Ever ever ever. Especially not on a dare. Especially not Viagra."

"I know that *now*."

"All right. How long has this—situation been going on?"

"It's been hard for—"

"Billy! Don't use words like that. This is like sixteen different kinds of inappropriate. How long has this situation—"

"—I get it, miss. This situation has been going on for three hours."

"Okay. And, um . . . what are your other symptoms?"

Billy looked confused.

"I'm trying to figure out if your life is in danger or something. You're young and healthy, so I doubt it, but do you have a fever? Is your pulse racing? Do you feel nauseous? Are you dizzy?"

He shook his head. "No, I feel fine except it hurts. It's like, never been this way in my whole life. You know how the skin on a drum is stretched really—"

"Aaaaagh! Don't finish that sentence!" I looked nervously up and down the hallway, then glanced into the classroom again. You could've heard a pin drop. Everyone was scribbling away quietly. Pablo walked slowly around the classroom with his hands clasped behind his back, nodding in approval as he looked over different students' shoulders.

"Look, Billy," I said. "I think this is an inappropriate and very silly joke you and your friends came up with."

He looked startled. "What?"

"This joke, about the Viagra. That's inappropriate and very silly." I looked at him meaningfully. "It is a very silly story to make up to tell your teacher."

"Miss, it's not fake!" he exclaimed, looking wildly befuddled.

"No, Billy, it is fake. And you just admitted to me that it was fake. And I just told you that it was a silly waste of classroom time and that I know you're a funny guy, but pranks like this are not okay. And you just said you were sorry, and I said just don't do it again. And then you promised you wouldn't. And then you asked if you could use the bathroom because you had a stomachache, and I said you could." I saw the light of comprehension dawn in Billy's fearful eyes. An expression of relief came over his face.

"Now, Billy," I said. "I give you permission to go to the bathroom for as long as you need to go."

"Thank you, miss," he said almost reverently. "Oh, miss, thank you so much."

"And Billy?"

"Yes?"

"Do not come back into my classroom until you . . ." I paused, searching for the right words. Then it occurred to me that in this situation, there were no right words.

"Until you *feel better,*" I said, looking at him meaningfully.

"I won't, miss, I promise," he said happily.

"One more thing."

"Yes, miss?"

"If you tell anyone about this, I will get fired. If you tell anyone I told you not to tell anyone about this, I will get fired. I don't want to get fired, Billy. I need to not get fired, Billy."

"Miss, I promise," he said solemnly. "I will never forget you for this."

"No," I said. "No, I don't suppose you will. Now I'm going in there and I'm telling everyone about how this is all just a big silly prank. And later you can tell them that's how you got out of trouble, and I fell for your cover story because I'm so gullible."

"What's 'gullible,' miss?"

"It's on your next vocabulary quiz. I gave you the words last Mon— you know what? It doesn't matter, Billy. It really doesn't matter." He was nearly giddy as he shuffled rapidly off in the direction of the boys' room.

I looked down at my feet, then up at the ceiling. Then down

at my feet again. If I'd had the choice, I wouldn't have reentered my classroom. There was something about covertly ordering a fourteen-year-old boy to jerk off that really took the idealistic wind out of my professional sails. Besides, Pablo clearly had the class under more control than I ever would.

I looked in through the glass in the door and saw the students sitting up and paying rapt attention to Pablo. He was speaking with authority, gesticulating to make points, and pausing to answer questions. He carried himself with the regal bearing that comes naturally to those who are doers and winners, those who set goals and accomplish them. As he captivated that audience of his fellow ninth-graders, Pablo seemed much older than a fourteen-year-old freshman. Which made sense, because he was a seventeen-year-old freshman.

I shifted my gaze to the board and saw that he had drawn detailed, labeled diagrams of the Glock 29 and the Glock 36 semiautomatic pistols. He had even spelled "sub-compact" correctly. I smiled proudly and stayed in the hallway for another few moments, watching a truly gifted educator at work.

CHAPTER NINE

Maybe, Baby

As my year teaching high school in Texas drew to a close, I knew I had to devise a plan. To my deep disappointment, I realized I would never be properly compensated for my favorite pastime: sitting in the local Middle Eastern restaurant/hookah bar/grocery store, scribbling my feelings in a black-and-white mottled notebook and sipping very sweet Moroccan mint tea. I hated most things about teaching, except for the standing-in-front-of-a-crowd part. The only other profit-generating occupation I could think of that would employ an audience was stripping, and I am neither a confident nor a talented dancer. And while I could entertain a crowd of teenagers with relative ease, I had no other discernible skill. Changing children's lives, it seemed, was my best option. I decided to apply to graduate programs in teaching, figuring I could always write "on the side." I conveniently ignored the truth I knew so well: teaching high school leaves room for absolutely nothing "on the side" beyond exhausted stabs at dilettantism, and drinking.

I got an A in the course I took in Texas to make up my missing credits, and I knew my diploma from Warren Wilson was forthcoming. Because I couldn't wait to resume my old life, I applied to Western Carolina University's master's program in teaching. I maintained the fantasy that I would move into an adorable rented Victorian house in Asheville with my long-distance carpenter boyfriend Tom, a place he'd fix up in exchange for a discount on the rent. I'd go to WCU, get my degree, and get a nice job teaching nice students at a nice private school, something without too much Christ in the curriculum (a *little* Christ was okay). I'd have an organic garden (even though I couldn't even keep a spider plant alive) and we'd get a puppy and I'd cook all the time (even though I didn't know the difference between baking powder and baking soda) and he'd propose to me and give me a gorgeous vintage ring with a non-bloody gem (ooh! Maybe a sapphire!), and then we'd buy a cute gingerbread cupcake house together and start a new garden and the puppy would run around in the yard and I'd get pregnant and deliver painlessly via a C-section from which I'd immediately recover, and I'd lose all the pregnancy weight plus some, because I'd breastfeed, like a proper back-to-nature hippie, and we'd have the sweetest little family in the whole wide world and when the baby was napping I'd write a bestselling novel and we'd be totally rich.

But I also harbored another fantasy of what my future might hold. I'd nurtured the dream since childhood, tucking it into the very tiny corner of my mind where all things were possible. This was also the corner where a sense of adventure and freedom reigned, an itty-bitty infinitesimal space where risk seemed like a reward rather than a death sentence. In this wee little nook, which was too small and insignificant for Fear or Doubt to ever notice, I folded up and tucked away a very big plan that I knew would never come to fruition. If you visited this secret hideaway in my mind (you would have to crawl in, as the ceiling was too low for standing), you would have found a degree from Columbia University in the City of New York. That's what I wanted. And that's what I knew I would never get.

Still, it didn't hurt to dream. I'd been wondering what life was like at that particular overpriced institution of higher learning since I was in the seventh grade. That was the year I took the SATs for the first time (my parents and I agreed it was excellent practice). I got a high score for a thirteen-year-old, and this was significant enough to fill my parents with the hope that in a few years, I'd nab a full ride to . . . to . . . well, it didn't really matter where.

When I was fourteen, I read an article in *Sassy* magazine, for which the admissions committee at Columbia University inexplicably allowed a reporter to sit in on the meeting in which the powers-that-be decide who gets in and who gets a polite "no thank you" letter. It was fascinating to read how the different officers decided who was worthy and who wasn't. There were the obvious measures of success—test scores, GPAs, academic awards—but then there were the less tangible aspects of a student's value. Did he or she write a moving or funny essay? Had he or she overcome a disability or personal tragedy? Was he or she a curious, motivated learner? I read that *Sassy* article over and over, combing it for clues that would help me get into this mythical place where everyone read really impressive books all day and played Frisbee on something called a "quad."

Then my mother suggested we visit the actual campus, and I became the happiest eighth-grader in the world. Though my usual queasy/nauseous/terror-of-death combo was present during the ride into the city, the actual campus tour was a blissful marvel. All those columns! All that brick! All those cute boys on the quad, which turned out to be a green rectangle of grass in front of the majestic Low Library, where they filmed *Ghostbusters!* Later, I learned that Low was now just an administration building, but it had the famous Alma Mater statue and those beautiful, oft-photographed steps. I felt like I'd stepped into an enchanted world, a world full of people just as fascinated by literature and art as I was, a world where nerds were safe from ridicule and where sophisticated intellectual discourse took place twenty-four hours a day, seven days a week. Most important, it was a world without parents.

Unfortunately, it became clear within a few years that I was not Columbia material, academically at least. And by the time I was twenty-four and applying to graduate schools, I knew for sure I'd never get into my childhood dream school.

Among the many reasons my attending Columbia was an impossibility, a few stood out. First, my grades weren't high enough. In high school, I'd gotten mostly As and Bs, but those were hardly the stellar marks expected of an Ivy League student. And college . . . well, that hadn't gone so smoothly.

Second, there was the whole terrified-of-living-in-a-city thing. Specifically, there was the lifetime-fear-of-Manhattan thing. While I'd managed to adjust enough to be able to enjoy day trips and even the occasional overnight stay at Alexandra's aunt and uncle's apartment in the big city, I still didn't greet the idea of life in New York with excitement. It was too big, and too hot in the summer, and too cold in the winter, and too bright at night, and too busy, and too gray, and too smooshed-together. I wasn't thin enough or glamorous enough or hip enough to make a splash there. I'd get lost in the crowd, and I'd freak out and choke on my own terror and go crazy all over again.

Besides, what did people in New York City do when they waited for the subway and had to pee? I thought about this frequently. I also wondered what happened if they got stuck on the subway, and what happened if the air-conditioning on the subway broke on one of those face-melting, humid, hundred-degree Manhattan summer days. Terrorist bombings didn't enter my mind, but the thought of not being able to get to a proper bathroom gave me nightmares.

Besides, a teaching degree from Columbia would take me away from Tom. We'd been together for almost two years, which to me meant that we were destined for the altar. What started in Asheville became a long-distance relationship when I moved to Texas. Early in my desert adventure, he drove all the way out to see me, carrying scrap lumber in the back of his van so that he could build me a bed when he got to my new apartment. This genuinely generous and romantic feat distracted us both from the fact that we made each other miserable. He criticized me constantly out of a misplaced desire to save me from myself; I cried jealously to him over the phone when he did anything remotely fun or interesting without me. I called him each night from the bed he built for me, and our conversations usually ended with one or both of us in a bad mood.

Yet I was sublimely happy to have him in my life, because what frightened me even more than the prospect of being trapped in a bathroom-less, A/C-free subway was the prospect of a life spent alone. A few years earlier, my spectacular breakdown in Boston had left me with the conviction that my mind was too volatile a thing to be left unoccupied. A relationship gave me something to focus on, obsessively, all of the time. And it gave me the chance to take care of someone else's whims and worries, which I did religiously, whether he wanted me to or not. This in turn provided the alluring option of feigning martyrdom whenever he got angry with me. Truly, dating me must have been a party and a half for the guy. I loved him desperately, and couldn't wait to get back to Asheville.

Still, there was nothing wrong with dreaming about a school I'd never actually attend. I might as well apply to Columbia, just for the fun of it, just so I could say I'd finally gotten the chance to fill out that powder-blue application and mail it off to New York City. So I printed it out, and while pondering whether to write in black or bubblegum-pink ink, I called Tom.

"Hey," he said, and my heart bounced in the way it always did when I first heard his voice. I still idolized him, even though I sometimes fantasized about setting his tool belt on fire.

"Guess what I'm doing?" I said, in the worst possible way in which a woman can pronounce those words. "Guesssssss what *I'm* do-inggggggggg?" with a chirpy trill at the end.

"I can't imagine," he said.

I paused and grinned at my reflection in the mirror.

"Filling out my application for Columbia!"

Silence.

Oh my God, I thought. *He's upset. Oh my God oh my God. He's upset. Oh, that's—that's—that's awesome! He doesn't want me to go to Columbia! He wants me to go to WCU so we can live together and do that thing with the garden and the puppy and the baby and the vintage fair-trade non-diamond ring! It's sort of like I told him I was kind of maybe interested in another guy, and it made him value me more! Awwww.*

"Oh honey," I said. "Don't be scared. Even if I got in, I wouldn't go. I just wanted to see if I could get in. It's this dream I've had since I was a little girl. But you're bigger than that dream. I want to come home to you, and that's exactly what I'm going to do."

More silence.

"Are you mad?" I asked, a familiar note of anxiety creeping into my voice. "I hate getting you mad. I'm so sorry, I shouldn't have said anything. I feel so bad. I didn't mean to worry you. I'm really totally one hundred percent committed to us and to our future together, I promise. I really, really, really—"

"How much did you spend on the application?" His voice was stern.

I was taken aback.

"I'm spending . . . I'll send a check for seventy-five dollars with the application."

He sighed loudly.

"Baby?" Now I wasn't sure exactly what I had done wrong, but I knew I could apologize for it repeatedly, until my apologies annoyed him into forgiving me.

"Why would you waste money on an application for a school that'll never take you?" he said irritably. "You can't get into Columbia."

Everything got very quiet then, on both ends of the call. I felt something bumping against my ear and realized with a start that my hand was shaking. At the same time, a feeling I couldn't identify rose in my stomach. I immediately wondered if I were having some kind of stroke, or if I'd suffered irreparable nerve damage while printing my name on the application.

Then I looked at my other hand. It was clenched. And I realized, to my shock, that I was angry.

Angry. I didn't get angry, or at least I tried not to. Whenever I started to get mad, I took deep breaths and stuffed the feeling down into some box deep inside me. Anger was something men displayed, and women were the ones who soothed them. Only cunts got angry and showed it, and I wasn't a cunt. I was a nice person. I was a very, very, very, very, *very* nice person.

And he was just looking out for me. Tom was being protective, really. He knew sometimes I spent too much money on silly things, and he was trying to instill good habits in me for our financial future together. And besides, he was right, wasn't he? Sure I'd done well in the class I'd taken in Texas, and those credits would enable me to finally graduate from Warren Wilson. But I still had those two Fs on my transcript, and my graduating GPA was barely a B. Plus, I'd taken six years to finish college. I didn't go to any good schools, either. I didn't win any impressive awards or do anything spectacular other than drop out that one time and go to the hospital that other time, and you didn't get bonus points with Ivy League admissions officers for being a recovering mental case with a history of "episodes."

I opened my mouth, and what I meant to say was, "You're right, Tom." But to my surprise what came out was, "I'm gonna get in."

"Sara," Tom said in the tone he used when I was being childish. "You're basically throwing seventy-five bucks away."

I looked at the black pen and the bubblegum-pink pen and realized I had a third option resting on the floor near my foot. Purple. The favored color of royalty, like Queen Elizabeth I, and Prince. Yes. I was going to use my purple pen. And maybe draw a picture of myself in pink, in the margin, to be funny. Admissions officers had to slog through a kabillion of those applications, right? Must get boring after a while. I could probably make somebody laugh if I drew something really goofy. And I could probably make them laugh even harder if I wrote a really funny essay. How many times a day did admissions officers get to laugh? Probably not many. They had to read transcripts all day, and everyone knew transcripts were just lists of numbers and letters that totally didn't represent the actual worth and awesomeness of the prospective students who had earned said numbers and letters.

"You're being irrational," he added.

I thought, *You stupid fucking fuck, I'm going to make you eat your words, shit them out, smear them on your face and walk naked through the center of Asheville. I will fucking destroy you. I hate you so goddamned much! I hope you fucking die!*

"I love you," I said. "Gotta go." And I hung up the phone.

The next morning, bleary-eyed and queasy, I walked into my first-period class and collapsed into a chair.

"Damn, miss," a girl with tattooed eyebrows said with a whistle. "You look busted today."

"Yes, Teresa," I said faintly. "Yes, I suppose I do."

"You out partying or what, miss?"

"No," I said, struggling to sit upright. "I was applying to Columbia University. I spent six hours writing an essay. Just mailed the whole thing out this morning."

"Miss, didn't you already go to college?"

"Yeah, but that was undergraduate college. This is grad school."

"Grad school?" Teresa looked horrified. "What the fuck is that?"

"It's for an advanced degree, like a master's degree," I said, trying to remember if I'd put on deodorant. "It's not required. It's just . . . you can go if you want to."

"I do not fucking want to," Teresa said. "Like, for reals? No fucking way, miss. I'm doing an associate's in fashion merchandising and that is fucking *it*."

"That's cool that you're going to Colombia, though," a boy said. "They make coffee down there, eh? They speak Spanish but I heard it's like nothing you can understand. Plus there's mad cocaine down there."

"That is true, Manuel," I said, thinking of the trust fund babies who regularly flood Ivy League universities with entitlement and nose candy each fall. "Now who actually did their homework?"

Months passed, and I got my acceptance letter from Western Carolina University. It came in a big, lovely envelope stuffed with various letters of congratulations, as well as a request that I phone the departmental office when I received the letter. I did, and was bowled over with excitement when a honey-voiced official offered me a full ride plus a paid teaching assistantship that would cover many of my outside expenses for the year.

"Can you believe it?" I squealed to Tom over the phone. "A full ride *plus* a teaching assistantship!"

"I knew it," Tom said with what I told myself was pride. "I'm not surprised at all. Congratulations, baby. You deserve it."

"Oh, Tom, you believed in me that much?"

"Well, it is *Western Carolina* University," he said, laughing. "Did you really think there was a chance they wouldn't take you?"

I was so excited by the good news that I didn't feel bad about the inevitable rejection letter that I knew would arrive from Columbia any day. The point had been to say I'd applied. I could always be proud that I'd tried.

A week or two later, I opened my mailbox and saw something powder-blue poking out from beneath some bills and magazines. "About time," I said to the rejection letter. I touched the blue corner, and realized to my surprise that it wasn't the thin business-size envelope I'd expected. And then I pulled a big blue packet out of the mailbox.

I stared at it in shock. Were the admissions people particularly cruel? Didn't they know that a short, polite rejection letter was kinder than some big envelope full of reasons why you didn't get in? Unless . . .

I left the rest of the mail in the mailbox and rushed inside. I sat in the middle of my sunny kitchen floor and opened it.

"Dear Sara: We are pleased to inform you . . ." And that was all I needed to read.

"Oh my God!" I shrieked, as if I'd won a sweepstakes. I jumped up and down on the floor, on my couch, on my bed. I performed a series of awkward yet enthusiastic high kicks. I considered doing a back-flip but remembered I had never done one previously, and that didn't seem like the sort of skill one spontaneously exhibited on command. And then I called Tom.

"Hey, what's up?" he said in the way he always did, and I almost burst with happiness.

"I got into Columbia," I said.

"What?" he said, his voice rising an octave and squeaking at the end.

"I did. I got in."

"How?"

"I don't know, because *I'm fucking smart*?" I was shocked at myself for actually saying the words that had leaped to mind.

He was quiet for a moment.

"I'm sorry," I said. "I didn't mean to jump on you like that." *Oh, no. Now he'll be angry. I'm sorry I'm sorry I'm sorry. Please don't leave me. Please don't ever leave me.*

"No," he said. "You're right. I deserved that."

What?

"Congratulations," he said. "That's amazing." He sounded wistful and sad and actually proud.

"I'm not going, or anything," I assured him. "I just wanted to see if I could get in. And I did, so now I can always say I got into Columbia. We can frame the acceptance letter and put it up in our bedroom!"

"If I were you," he said, "I'd really think about what the best choice is for you. Not for me or for us, but for you."

Something was wrong. Everything was right, but somehow something was wrong. He never spoke to me like this. Like an equal.

"Oh, I want to come home," I said, fighting the rising anxiety inside me. "Columbia would be too expensive, anyway. I mean, I can't afford that."

"Yes, you can," he said in the same weird, quiet way. "You can take out loans."

"Well, I'm not going," I said resolutely. "I'm really not. Besides, I've already asked you to do a year with me living far away. I promise I'll never move far away from you again."

The next day, I e-mailed the department head at Teachers College at Columbia and offered my thanks, but explained that I wouldn't be coming to school in the fall. The day after that, Tom broke up with me.

"Why are you doing this?" I sobbed, even though I knew there were a million reasons why.

"Because this isn't working," he said. "You and me. We're not good for each other. It hasn't been good for a long time. You know it, too. And now you're going to give up your dream to come back here and live with me, even though we make each other unhappy? No way. You can't." He was crying, too.

Alongside the pain, I felt an enormous surge of relief. I ignored it.

"But we were going to get married," I wailed. "And have a house, and a dog, and a kid. And now I don't even know what I'm going to do."

"You're going to move to New York City," he said. "And your dream is finally going to come true."

The next day, puffy-eyed and weak, I called Columbia and asked if I could please come to their school anyway. They kindly said yes, and advised me that I'd better move quickly if I wanted to get those $60,000 in loans. I said I'd see them in a couple of months. Then I called Western Carolina University and politely un-accepted their offer of admission. As I spoke to the woman from WCU, my voice cracked a little.

"You okay, honey?" she asked.

"I'm just going to miss Asheville," I said, sniffling. "I've missed it all year out here and I thought I was gonna be home in a couple months, but now it turns out I'm not."

"Well, honey," she said. "We'll still be here. You can always come and visit, you know. But if I were your age and I got the chance, I'd give New York City a try. You only get one shot at this kinda thing."

I thanked her and hung up.

The last couple of months in Texas were a whirlwind of preparations. I thoroughly enjoyed my drive back East, stopping in Asheville to stay with friends for a few days before I made it up to New York. I managed to avoid Tom, which wasn't hard at all because he wasn't exactly trying to hang out with me. I moved into an apartment with two women I met through Craigslist, and delighted in the two dogs and the cat with whom I also shared my new place. They didn't belong to me, so I didn't have to do anything other than cuddle them, which was ideal.

Then there was Teachers College, the most obviously-named graduate school in the world. It sat just north of Columbia's main campus, a labyrinthine pile of bricks and stone. I busied myself with selecting courses, buying books, and learning the geography of the Upper West Side. Night classes began, as did my daily student-teaching assignment at a public middle school in Manhattan. And sometime in mid-September, I realized with a start that I hadn't had a panic attack in . . . in . . . I couldn't remember how long. Not when Tom had dumped me, not when I'd said good-bye to my colleagues, not when I'd driven alone through midnight summer storms in Texas, not when I'd sat in the front passenger seat of my mom's car and barreled through the Lincoln Tunnel, not when I'd discovered my apartment of choice was a rather steep walk-up. I hadn't even panicked on the day I met my perpetually disapproving cooperating teacher, the woman charged with mentoring me while educating thirty-five precocious New York City seventh-graders. She had the bitterness one only finds in certain older teachers, the ones who've been in the system far too long and who still nurture a wish that they'd done something else. She watched my lessons with a sour expression on her face, but somehow it didn't throw me.

No matter how stressed or tired or uninspired I felt, I didn't panic. I was too busy to panic. If I wasn't downtown at middle school, I was uptown at grad school. If I wasn't uptown at grad school, I was doing homework in my bedroom. And if I wasn't actually at one of these three sites, I was on the subway en route from one to another. I had discovered that subway trains generally didn't get stuck in one place for over four minutes, and that in New York City there was always a Starbucks with a bathroom when I needed it. I might have to wait in the store while a drunk woman took a shit on the floor beside the toilet, but I *would* eventually get access to that toilet.

To my enormous surprise, I found the strange manic pace of life in New York oddly soothing. Perhaps my anxiety was not only crowded out by my daily obligations but by the wild quirks of my fellow New Yorkers. On any given block in New York, I was bound to be, if not the sanest individual, at least not one of the craziest. And there were more of "the craziest" than any other type.

I did not, for example, shit on any floors in public or private spaces. I did not walk down the street screaming about the coming of the Messiah, the Devil, or the ice-cream truck. I did not engage in fisticuffs with an imaginary pugilist beside the strawberry stand at Union Square Farmers' Market. For the first time in my life, I was too busy to worry about anything unrelated to lesson plans, adolescent social development, and the New York City Board of Education's benchmarks and statistics for success in English, grades seven through twelve.

One night in September, I went out to a pub near Columbia with some new friends. During the dinner, Tom called me and promptly apologized for everything he'd ever done wrong in our relationship. He was almost certainly drunk, but I enjoyed the moment nevertheless—at first.

"Oh, we both made mistakes," I said magnanimously, out on the street where I wouldn't interrupt my friends' heated debate about charter school funding. "And you really did me a lovely favor by breaking up with me. Now we've both moved on to better things. I'm living in the world's greatest metropolis and making a difference each day in the lives of little children, and you—what exactly are *you* doing, Tom?"

"Just working, you know," he said. "Seeing a nice girl. Playing touch football with my buddies. Man, I'm happy to hear you're doing so well, Sara."

"Good to hear," I said faintly. "I have to go now, and do significant things. Good-bye, Tom." I hung up the phone and leaned against the building.

SEEING A NICE GIRL? Who the FUCK had given him permission to "see" a nice girl? It had only been four months since we'd broken up! Did he have no sense of propriety? Was he an emotionless death robot sent from another planet to destroy my entire existence with a single phone call? What kind of a cold, evil bastard moved on from the greatest love of all time within four fucking months? I wanted to throw up. I wanted to punch a fist through a storefront window. I wanted to find the girl he was fucking and kick her repeatedly in the teeth, and then push *him* into a bubbling vat of something terrible and oozey.

Aside from a brief rebound dalliance in Texas with a twenty-year-old hippie who believed he'd been abducted by aliens as a child, I hadn't gotten back into the world of opposite-sex relations. I certainly hadn't been on any dates or "seen" anyone "nice." This meant that even though I was doing some interesting things in a cool city, Tom was winning. He was *winning.* And this was one thing I could not abide.

I needed to have sex with someone. Probably a series of someones. Or have a series of sexual encounters with a single someone who would then become a non-single someone because he would be my only someone and I would be his. The only problem was that I didn't know any straight young men in New York.

Well, that's not entirely true. There were two straight young guys in my program at Teachers College, but one of them only dated Jewish girls and the other one was caught up in a not-so-secret secret affair with a classmate, who reported to a friend of a friend that the gentleman in question had an enormous penis. I've never been a fan of big dicks, so this piece of information did not engender any lustful thoughts in my heart. I possess a vaginal model that takes a while to adapt to the shape and size of a particular phallus. It is made of a substance not unlike memory foam. When my equipment hasn't been used in a while, it returns to its factory setting. The lack of flexibility may be pleasing to my partners, but I often find it uncomfortable. I am told that upon having children, it will become as accommodating as a wind tunnel, but I'm no closer to that event now than I was at twenty-four. I preferred that my reintroduction to the world of cocks come in the form of an interaction with a medium-to-small member of the species.

My savior came in the form of Andrew, a guy I'd briefly

crushed on at my first college, Emerson. He was a senior when I was a freshman, and he'd been kind and quirky and smart and weird, and he was very good at writing. Back then, he'd had a long-term girlfriend, and I'd never entertained any serious thoughts of dating him. But when I ran into him at a pretty little bar in Brooklyn one night, I discovered that he was (A) newly single and (B) not opposed to talking to me at great length while I flirted shamelessly. I gave him my phone number, or maybe I asked for his, and somebody called somebody else, and eventually we set up a date.

I wasn't actually certain how to go about doing it on the first date. I assumed someone invited someone else home, and maybe a stop at the drugstore for condoms was involved. I wasn't uptight, but I'd never really enjoyed the non-oral type of sex—I was usually too tense, even after many months with Tom. I suppose it was a holdover from my seventeen years as a devout Catholic, when I regarded the prospect of a dick near my pussy with the same enthusiasm an ordinary human might reserve for a gun pressed to the back of her skull.

With Andrew, it was easy. We had a lovely dinner at a tiny French café on one of those Brooklyn streets where all the shops are aggressively adorable and the people look like the cast of a deliberately multiethnic GAP commercial. I avoided alcohol but encouraged his consumption, as I'd heard that getting the other person intoxicated was a good way to ensure that sexytime would ensue. We strolled along the promenade and held hands, and finally we sat on one of the wrought-iron benches and started making out. He was a good kisser, and I had flashbacks to when I'd thought he was so cute in college in Boston, long before I'd even heard of the town where I'd eventually meet Tom. I'd noticed Andrew in the fall semester then and it was the fall semester now, six years later. The air was crisp with the scent of dying leaves—my favorite smell in the entire world. Leaves are possibly the only things on earth that smell better as their corpses decay.

After kissing him for about twenty minutes, I pulled back and looked at Andrew conspiratorially.

"Would it be weird," I began, "if I asked you if we could go back to your—"

"Not weird at all!" he said quickly, and we both laughed. He stood up and offered me his arm like a gentleman. I took it, feeling like a genteel Victorian lady or at least a really classy fin-de-siècle whore. Together we paraded down the streets of his precious Brooklyn neighborhood, pausing casually to point out extravagantly useless items in cutesy shop windows ("Look at that pink unicycle!") as if we weren't totally on our way to a hot grown-up fuck session. I finally understood the modus operandi of those aging anorexics on that show with all the shoes and handbags and Detective Mike Logan working deep cover as a millionaire douche. I was going to have sex, and this was the city! I felt alive and vibrant and reasonably attractive. And I had shaved my legs, even *above my knees.*

Andrew shared an apartment with two good-looking guys who had been in a few of my classes in Boston. I'd been intimidated by them back then, because they were part of a very cool circle of writer-boys who wore slouchy vintage garments and wrote interesting poetry and short stories. They did hilarious things like invade Old Navy en masse and commence reading aloud the works of Richard Brautigan until they were asked to leave. They worked hard in restaurants and bars and spent their savings to self-publish their work, which they sold in bookshops around the city.

Andrew and I exchanged greetings with his roommates, who were polite enough to appear happy that I'd come home with him.

Perhaps they genuinely were glad for their friend—he'd gotten out of a stressful long-term relationship sometime in the past year, and I didn't get the impression it had been an easy breakup. At some point the roommates made their way to their respective bedrooms, and Andrew and I got on with the business at hand.

His room was small and had lots of books. I think I remember banging my head on a bicycle that was hanging from the ceiling. It was dark and not at all unpleasant, and we had gotten all the way to the part where he was actually inside me before I realized that something very terrible was happening.

It wasn't the sex that was bad. He seemed perfectly capable in that realm, and I probably made a reasonable contribution. But in that moment, I was privy to a great revelation, and I suppose revelations always arrive at rather inconvenient times. Moses probably had something on his daily agenda other than standing around listening to some fiery bush, and Mary likely had some weaving to finish when Gabriel interrupted her with the announcement that she was knocked up. And so it came to pass that I was in the middle of my very first grown-up pre-appointed New York City fuckfest when I was struck by The Truth: I had never felt lonelier in my entire life.

There I was, twenty-four going on twenty-five, a woman of reasonable intelligence and sophistication, with a funny, sensitive, artsy, non-sociopathic straight boy doing very adult things to my nether regions, and I felt horribly alone. Because as kind as he was, he didn't love me. And as desperate as I was, I didn't love him. I probably could have gotten there quickly, if he'd asked me on second and third and fourth dates and told me I was beautiful and held my hand in front of his friends, but none of that was going to happen. I'd been having sex for nearly four years, but this was almost certainly going to be my first-ever one-night stand.

There is as yet no book of etiquette on behavior during a one-time romp betwixt the sheets. Emily Post never addressed it, and I'm fairly certain Judith "Miss Manners" Martin would turn her nose up at the question. But I am positive that I broke one sacred (if unwritten) rule of conduct: I began to cry.

Picture, if you will, the tableau: a reasonably cute, consenting, single twentysomething brunette in missionary position beneath a reasonably cute, consenting, single, dark-haired twentysomething fellow on a reasonably non-squeaky IKEA bed in a reasonably clean apartment in a reasonably hip neighborhood in a reasonably legendary borough in a reasonably immortal city. Nothing in this scenario begs the question, "But which person will sob uncontrollably in the midst of the other's orgasm?"

Andrew paused in his labors, justifiably alarmed at my sudden change in demeanor.

"What's wrong?" he asked, horrified. "Oh no, did I hurt you?"

I thought about Tom, and how much I missed him and still loved him. I thought about school, and how much I didn't want to be a teacher. I thought about writing and how I hardly ever did it for fun anymore. I thought about my body, and how I still hadn't lost the burrito weight I'd gained in Texas. I thought about how I hadn't had a panic attack in a long time and how I (mostly) wasn't afraid to leave the house or get on an airplane, and how I was living on my own—something that had seemed impossible back when I was learning how to eat an entire meal again—and how I was still unhappy.

I sobbed, "This . . . just isn't . . . how I thought it would be."

I'm pretty sure he thought I was referring to his dick. Which, incidentally, he promptly withdrew from my undercarriage. We both looked at it at the same time and saw that it was wearing what appeared to be an Elizabethan ruff. And while my vagina is a cave of many wonders, it does not contain a Shakespearean costume closet. The condom, it seemed, shared my poor sense of timing.

"Oh my God," I said. "That is so fucking broken."

I'd had that happen before, back in college. I'd gone to Planned Parenthood and taken Plan B. It had been a frightening thing, and my Papist programming was so strong that I wasn't entirely sure I hadn't committed an unforgivable sin and paid for an extremely early and gentle abortion. But at least I'd had a boyfriend to support me through it. This was an entirely different challenge.

On the upside, I immediately stopped crying. I inherited my mother's ability to snap into crisis-response mode. On the downside, I think Andrew began to fight back tears.

"Let's not panic," I said in the voice I reserved for dealing with hysterical adolescents. "This is entirely fixable. May I use your computer?"

He looked at me blankly. I suppose my rapid transformation from emotional wreck to proactive project manager was rather unsettling.

"May I use your computer?" I asked again. "I need to see what time Planned Parenthood opens. I'll go and get the morning-after pill."

"Are you—are you sure that's necessary?" he asked hesitantly. "I don't want you to—I mean—I just feel so bad about all this. You were crying, and then the condom, and—"

"Well, it's better to be safe than sorry, right?" I patted his arm. "Don't you worry about a thing, Andrew. Everything is going to be all right." I rose, naked, and sat in front of his laptop at his desk. "And I do apologize for my earlier outburst," I said over my shoulder. "You're really very good at sex. I'm just in a weird place right now, emotionally speaking."

"I guess . . . I am, too," he said faintly. He watched as I went to

Planned Parenthood's website and looked up New York health centers.

"The Margaret Sanger Clinic opens at seven thirty on Saturdays," I said. "That's, what, four hours from now? It's in the East Village. I'll get a car service. Totally convenient."

Andrew looked at his hands. "What are we going to do until then?"

I lived on the Upper West Side, a good hour-long train ride away. I could call a car service, but I didn't relish the idea of riding around in a random town car with a stranger in the middle of the night.

"I'll stay here, if that's okay," I said. "I know it's weird."

"No, it's not weird at all," he said. Nice people tend to lie in these sorts of situations. "Let's go to bed."

As I lay beside him in the dark, with sleep utterly out of the question, I heard him begin to gently snore. Some guys will sleep through anything.

After a few hours of staring at the ceiling and wondering what would happen if the morning-after pill didn't work this time, I got up and shook him gently awake.

"I'm leaving," I said.

"Good luck," he whispered. I knew it was the last time I'd ever see him. I nodded and walked toward the door.

"Sara?"

"Yeah?" I turned around. He looked so cute there in the blue morning light, his eyes only half-open. I remembered how I'd giggled to myself back in Boston when he recognized me and said hi in the library.

"The front door locks automatically. Just make sure it's really shut."

I left.

As it turned out, I didn't even need to call a car service. A yellow cab happened to roll by as soon as I left Andrew's building, and I hurriedly flagged it down.

"Bleecker and Mott," I said.

As we glided through Brooklyn, I took the opportunity to assess the situation. I was exhausted, emotionally spent, and hungry. Everything seemed to whiz by quickly and crawl by slowly, all at once. And yet, somehow, I didn't detect panic anywhere inside me. Mostly I just felt confused and increasingly disoriented.

By the time we arrived at the Margaret Sanger Center, I was carsick, overtired, and glumly resigned to the fact that I was pregnant with three dark-haired triplets. On some level, I had always known that God would punish me for having sex outside of marriage. He'd allowed me to take the morning-after pill with success once before, but this time I was shit out of luck. Even if I took it, it wouldn't work. And then I would have to do the most terrible thing in the world and literally kill my babies, all three of them. Well, I'd pay some doctor to actually do it, but the fault would be mine and mine alone. I'd probably bleed out on the operating table like Penny almost did in *Dirty Dancing,* only Patrick Swayze wouldn't be around to ask Jerry Orbach to save me. And then I'd rot in the Hell I pretended not to believe in but still totally knew was real.

When I paid the cabbie and stepped out of the car, I was surprised to see a Santa Claus doppelgänger standing on the curb. He didn't have the red suit or the big sack of toys, but he did have the white hair, robust white beard, and round jelly-belly. He was wearing a pair of denim overalls and a plaid workshirt, and he looked just like one of the older farmers who sold his wares at the farmer's market outside the French Broad Food Co-op back in Asheville. There was something else familiar about him, too, though I couldn't put my finger on it. I felt relieved when I saw him. It was like he was waiting there just for me. And God, did I ever need to have a nice, normal interaction with a man.

"Good morning, sir," I said with a small smile.

Then I caught sight of his Bible.

However long this interaction was going to last, it was not going to end well.

The sad reality is that when you run into someone with a Bible on the streets of New York City, chances are your day is about to take a turn for the uncomfortable. The Mormon kids are usually nice, but I think they carry the Book of Mormon, which is a bit of a different game. Plus, you know they've chosen to do their mission year in New York City, so they're probably the weird, artsy and/or secretly gay ones from their synod back home in Utah or Missouri or wherever. They'd probably make nice dinner companions and would lend you money if you needed to get on the bus. But the folks with the Bibles aren't interested in selling you a membership to a modern desert cult with a kickass show choir. The folks with the Bibles—the *men* with the Bibles—want to tell you about Hell and why you deserve to end up there.

Have you ever been on the receiving end of authentic hatred? I don't mean resentment or rage. Anyone who's ever taught or raised a teenager has gotten those dirty looks. I'm talking about real-deal, genuine, wish-you-were-mauled-to-death-by-bears hatred. It's the kind of gaze that carries a physical force. It's palpable. Over the course of my life, I'd made plenty of people angry, exasperated, and unhappy, but I realized in that moment that I'd never truly known hatred. His eyes bored into me like a pair of drills. For a split second, I wondered if he was going to hit me.

Instead, he opened his mouth and let out the angriest sound I'd ever heard.

"MAAAAAAAAAAAAAAAAAAAAAWWWWWW

DDDDDDDRRRRRRAAAAA AAAAAAAAAAAWWW-WWW WWWWWWWWWWWWWWWWWWWWWW!"

I couldn't even make out what he was saying, so loud and deep and uncontrolled was his rage. He sounded like a demonically possessed grandfather clock. His hateful wail bounced off the buildings around the Sanger Center and echoed back in the early morning light.

Then he did it again, his eyes burning into me, and this time I caught his meaning.

"MMMMMUUUUUUUUURRRRRDDDDEEERRR EEEEER!" *Murderer.* He was talking about me. *Me.* Me, who hadn't even gone into the center yet. Me, who hadn't even taken a pregnancy test yet. Me, who hadn't even paid for the Plan B pill yet.

"MMMMMUUUUUUUUURRRRRDDDDEEERRR EEEEER!" Again! I was aghast.

If I'd been of sounder mind, I might have come up with something wittier. Instead, I went with knee-jerk honesty.

"Not YET!" I blurted out. "I don't even know if I'm pregnant!"

Apparently, this was not the response he was looking for.

He opened his mouth to yell again. I craned my neck wildly to see if another cab was coming, so that I could run away to my bed and bury my head in the pillows and make myself very small beneath the blankets, so that God and Satan and Santa Claus couldn't see me. I just really hated myself in that moment, maybe even more than he hated me, and it occurred to me that perhaps I deserved whatever was coming to me.

But before the old man could let out another hate-moan, somebody else piped up. Because where there are devils, angels are often present, too. And my divine guardians had arrived, albeit in a form I hadn't expected.

"Oh. My God," came a female voice out of nowhere. "I. Love. Those earrings!"

I turned my head to the left and saw two very pretty, stylish young women grinning at me. They had funky haircuts and perfect eye shadow, and they wore fun boots and skinny jeans. They looked a lot like the gorgeous people I'd seen on the street the night before in Andrew's cool neighborhood, with one major difference: they were wearing bright orange vests that read ESCORT.

I've never been a morning person, and by that point, my mind had accommodated all the new experiences it could handle. My powers of logic collapsed. Therefore, I came to the natural conclusion that these women were call girls. After all, that's what professional "escorts" are, right? Seven thirty A.M. on a Saturday, and I'd somehow stumbled into the center of the Venn diagram where sex workers and Bible thumpers overlapped. I had no idea what these high-class hipster hookers were doing wearing identifying vests, as that would seem to invite the attention of the vice squad. Were they that special feminist kind of prostitute, the ones who protested for legalization of the world's oldest trade? This was the East Village; it wasn't out of the question.

"MUUUUUURRRRRDEEEEEREEEEEER!" yelled Santa.

"They're so fun and dangly and they totally work with your outfit," Escort #1 said, smiling and walking up to me.

"But I feel like, also? They could work with something more formal," Escort #2 said, cocking her head to the side. "Like they could easily go from day to night, like if you had them on at the office you could change and just go to a party at night and you'd be fine."

"I caaaaan't handle how cute they are. Where did you get them?" Escort #1 demanded.

Now, I may have been utterly exhausted. I may have been

terribly scared. I may have been carrying three extremely small bastard children. But I was also a young woman who had spent most of her life in suburban New Jersey, where the chief recreational activity is shopping and the most sacred house of worship is the nearest mall. And these whores were speaking my native tongue.

"Target!" I said.

The girls gasped in unison.

"No way!"

"But they look vintage!"

"I *know,* right?" I said proudly. "Nine ninety-nine. I got them in El Paso!" Suddenly we were walking, as a little group, and I didn't know how that had happened but I didn't mind, because one of the harlots was telling me about the one-day sales at the new Target in Brooklyn, which apparently were epic and not to be missed.

"But you *have* to get there by ten A.M. because all the good stuff gets picked over after that," she said. "This is Carlos; he's going to check your bag and take you through the metal detector. We'll see you later; have a good appointment!" Startled, I realized she and her associate had somehow pried my frozen feet from the curb and walked me ten yards to the entrance of the Planned Parenthood Margaret Sanger Center. At the same moment Carlos the security guard greeted me, I remembered my friends who had volunteered as safety escorts for patients at the local Planned Parenthood health center back in Asheville. As Santa continued shouting in the background, the girls waved and shut the bulletproof-glass door behind me. They were like little feminist helper-elves, relying on their training and their knowledge of retail to get one frightened Jersey girl where she needed to go. And in that moment, I became a Planned Parenthood fan for life.

I entered my name in the log and waited my turn alongside a girl who looked to be about the same age as my ninth-graders back in Texas. Her boyfriend was with her. There were a lot of men there that day, waiting patiently or anxiously, listening to music or reading magazines. I learned that only patients were allowed beyond the second door, which was also bulletproof and rigged with an alarm.

Later, in the exam room, a nurse told me, "I don't think we've ever had someone come in just four hours after a broken condom. That's some impressive speed."

"I'm kind of neurotic," I said.

"Welcome to New York," she replied.

I went home with two pills and instructions to take them twelve hours apart. I took one combined with a Xanax, because by that point I was so tired I couldn't sleep. Lulled into a chemical slumber, I dozed peacefully for several hours, then took the second pill as directed. I prayed for support and forgiveness, but to the Virgin Mary, not God. I figured she'd be more sympathetic to the whole unplanned pregnancy thing, especially since she and I both knew I wasn't carrying any messiah. And I'd always had a sneaking suspicion it was Joseph who knocked her up, anyway, and the Archangel Gabriel thing was a less secular version of the stork story. The image of the Virgin of Guadalupe had been omnipresent back in Texas, so I prayed to that Mary as well as the more familiar Italian Catholic one.

When I didn't get sick from the pills, I felt relieved. But I also had this nagging feeling that the whole thing was too easy. Something was wrong. Something was missing.

A few weeks later, it became apparent that at least the latter prognostication was accurate. My period was MIA. Concerned, I called Planned Parenthood.

"You're a week late? Oh, don't worry," the woman said.

"Plan B can knock your cycle off for a month or two. You said you took Plan B a few hours after the incident? Well, statistically, chances are very, very slim that you're pregnant. If you get really worried, come in for a pregnancy test. It's free." I thanked her and hung up. As much as I'd enjoyed my interaction with the angelic escorts, I didn't greet the idea of a return trip with any enthusiasm.

I busied myself with school and student teaching. I ate a lot of chocolate, because I'd read or imagined that it could jump-start a period. Optimistically, I wore a panty-liner each day—just in case my period arrived. One month passed, then two. Nothing. Not even any cramps.

One night I was sitting in a graduate seminar listening to a girl named Rhoda Wasserstein explain how listening to Hot 97.1 (Motto: "Blazin' hip-hop and R&B!") for an hour each day really helped her relate to her class of thirty-five black teenage boys, when something inside me snapped like a wishbone and I began to bleed.

It was very sudden, and there was no warning, and then just a tsunami of pain. It was electric, coursing through me as if it were a power unto itself and I merely its conduit. I felt it in my uterus, in my stomach, in my pelvis, in my quadriceps muscles. I'd had my period since I was eleven years old, and it had never just shown up unannounced like this. There were always a few days of cramps and spotting before the main event. I remembered, dimly, that my period had arrived right on time after I'd used emergency contraception for the first time, back in North Carolina.

A classmate asked if I needed help—she said I looked like I "didn't feel so hot." I thanked her distantly, from some faraway place where my normal, polite self had gone on vacation. Abruptly, I excused myself from class. I forgot my winter coat, but no one noticed until later.

Out in the hall, I was shocked to feel my hands begin to tingle in the telltale way that augured a panic attack. My last one had come soon after I moved to Texas, when I grew overwhelmed by the seemingly endless sky. The embarrassment of having a sky-induced panic attack was mitigated somewhat by the fact that the attack was relatively light and manageable. I popped a Xanax and took some deep breaths, and it passed. Based on the warning tremors, though, this New York City panic attack was going to be bigger. And tougher.

"No, no, no," I whispered as I took halting, painful steps toward the bathroom. "No, no, no. It's been over a year. You're going on a year and a half without any. You can't have one now. Focus on getting to the bathroom. One foot in front of the other." I felt as if I were hip-deep in mud, so acute was the sensation of slogging through a thick, stubborn substance.

The bathroom door felt unnaturally heavy, and I leaned on it before it glided open. I was raised to avoid the handicapped stall at all costs—*What if a nice girl in a wheelchair needs to use it, and you and your perfectly healthy legs are hogging it?*—but tonight I needed it. I needed it because it was big, and because I was going to pass out unless I lay down. First, though, the toilet.

I don't remember how much blood there was. In my memory, there is none, not even a drop or a spot. But this seems unlikely. Still, I can't honestly say what I saw when I looked down between my legs. What I do remember is sitting on the toilet and rifling furiously through my purse, looking for the bottle of Xanax I always carried with me, like a talisman. I used it so rarely that the bottle always expired months before I emptied it, but I liked knowing it was always there.

Except that tonight it wasn't.

I dumped my purse upside down on the tile floor. Some loose change rolled into the next stall; a pen from my local bank branch skittered toward the sink. My wallet flopped open. But there was no familiar orange bottle with the white top.

There's really no convenient time for agoraphobia to flare up, but flare up it did, borne on the back of a rip-roaring panic attack, four floors up in an old stone building at the corner of West 120th Street and Broadway.

Fuck fuck fuck.

You know you're in a bad way when the thought of lying on a dirty public bathroom floor seems perfectly acceptable. You're in an even worse way when you curl up beside the public toilet and start to cry.

What do you do? Do you yell for help? Do you stay on the tile floor with the tampon wrappers and the stray pubes and the dirt from two hundred New York City shoes and mewl like a kitten? Can you survive there? How long until someone discovers you and tries to make you leave, without understanding that you really and truly can't go?

And what if you get the courage to get out of there? Do you get up, take the creaking elevator down to the ground floor, and ask the security guard to call for an ambulance, even though St. Luke's is only a few blocks away? Do you go home and wait it out? What if you don't even know what *It* is?

I had to leave. It was never going to get better unless I left. But what if *It* didn't get better? What if leaving made *It* worse? I wanted to stay there for a while, like forever, and maybe die on the floor, or pass out. Maybe I could pass out from the pain and someone would find me and I would wake up hours later in a lovely private hospital room or in my bedroom at home or in some beautiful safe rehab facility somewhere, a home for well-intentioned but slatternly young public school teachers.

Giving up seemed like such a nice idea.

Then came another stab ripping through my body. It was so

jolting and so raw that I cried out. And that is when from the depths of my soul, like an irradiated plant-human hybrid emerging from a toxic swamp, came a voice I had locked away in a cage built out of literature courses and wry detachment and books recommended on NPR. It said, "*Madonna mia,* you did not move to Manhattan to sit and cry on a dirty friggin' ladies' room floor. Get the fuck up. Splash some water on that hair and scrunch it, it looks like bullshit. It's like you got *agita,* just . . . in the front." And somehow, for just a moment, I caught the faint scent of cannoli. (Look, we can't all have madeleines.)

I let the pain propel me from lying on the floor to sitting up and then, gingerly, to standing.

I focused on each step. I talked myself through the motion, the way I'd done walking meditation back at my parents' house in Jersey. Heel rolling to toe, heel rolling to toe, step, step, breathe. Every few steps, I had to stop and lean on something for support—first, the bathroom door, then the elevator wall, then a marble pillar in the hall, then a garbage can near the main entrance, then a utility pole outside in the icy rain. It was cold and I wore a long-sleeved T-shirt and jeans. I got soaked. But I kept going, from one buoy to another, until I reached the corner of West 120th and Amsterdam, where I hailed a cab.

"Columbus and . . . and . . ." I groaned a little as another wave of pain churned through my innards.

We just sat there, and the car didn't move.

"Are you . . . okay?" the driver asked, craning his neck around to look at me worriedly.

"No sir," I said, with effort. "Sick."

"You make . . . a vomit?" He mimed puking.

"No, no, not that kind of sick."

"I pull over, you make vomit, we keep go."

"I *promise* I don't have to vomit."

"Vomit so hard to get out of seats. Gets stuck in seat belts. I clean with toothbrush, last time."

"I have cramps!" I said loudly. "I have really bad cramps! And I need to go home now!"

"Stomach?" he said. "No vomit in my cab."

"Woman's problems!" I said with a sob. "I am having woman's problems. Female troubles." I pointed, for emphasis.

"Ohhhh, baby," he said, nodding sympathetically.

Now New York is full of folks from all around the world, many of whom do not speak or understand English. But a language barrier was not our problem. I was stuck in a car with a man who was perfectly capable of understanding me. He simply wasn't *listening.* And because I had been in similar situations with past boyfriends, I knew it was time to take the very direct approach.

"NO BABY!" I screamed. "MY PERIOD! ONCE A MONTH! BLOOD! FROM MY VAGINA!"

"Oh my God!" he said, horrified.

Then he hit the gas pedal and we screeched into the night.

We sped all the way home. We did not pay attention to traffic lights. We did not pay attention to pedestrians with the right of way. He mumbled to himself furiously in a language I didn't understand. I preferred this to our torturous interactions in English. When he dropped me off, I attempted to hand him a twenty. He took it gingerly, as if I were offering him the tail of a wriggling rat. I'm pretty sure that after he left me off, he had to call a shaman from his homeland to do some sort of mystical cleansing ritual on his vehicle. A pigeon may have been sacrificed; I don't know. He may have just set the cab on fire and run away screaming.

I lived in a third-floor walk-up, and I knew I couldn't make it upstairs on foot. I crawled, which gave me a close-up view of all the dog hair the super's vacuum didn't reach. I couldn't see straight enough to put the key in the lock, so I knocked on the door as loud as I could, which wasn't very loud.

Eventually, my pretty roommate and surrogate older sister Aimee, whom I adored, heard me and came to the door.

"What's wrong, Sar?" she asked, looking shocked.

"Sick," I said in one shallow breath. I brushed past her without another word and stumbled to the bathroom medicine cabinet.

I swallowed a small pile of Advil, and I took a few Xanax, and I lay down in my bed in the quiet dark. For the first time in years, I sang an old hymn from church. It had been my favorite when I was a child.

Be not afraid
I go before you always
Come, follow me
And I will give you rest.

I clutched my stuffed yellow giraffe, a toy I'd had since I was two weeks old. It played music; I wound it up and listened to the familiar tune for perhaps the ten thousandth time. And I rocked myself back and forth, back and forth. I slept for twelve hours. When I awoke, it only hurt a little bit. And then I just had a period, or something like it. Just blood, in small trickles and drips, for a few days. Then it was all gone.

Logic dictated that I see a professional ASAP, so I waited two weeks and then went to see a psychic named Aubergine, on Ninth Street and Second Avenue. She assured me that it had just been a really bad period. Phew! Then she asked me if I wanted a $500 chakra-clearing session. I passed.

I still don't know if I miscarried. Some of my friends say it was obviously a miscarriage. Others say it was just a crap period because the heavy dose of synthetic hormones had thrown my body off. It sounds absurd, but I'm honestly not sure which idea I want to be true.

I know women who've miscarried. Some of them keep it a secret and mourn silently on the anniversary of the day each year. Some of them are glad it happened, relieved that they didn't have to take on a burden they might have resented. Once in a great while, some of them joke about it among friends, because after all, comedy is tragedy plus time, right? They laugh because they can't cry anymore.

I read an article by one of my usual hippie-dippie self-help gurus who said that children choose to incarnate on this mortal plane, and that sometimes a miscarriage occurs when a child realizes that its timing isn't quite right, that its mother isn't ready for it yet. It's probably utter bullshit. But part of me wants to believe. Because if I actually was pregnant, and if the hippie's theory is true, then I had one smart little bundle of cells in the oven. It takes fully grown adults years to realize their partner is not a good long-term choice, and my teensy tiny accidental fellow-traveler got the message before it even got a *brain*.

I hope the kid comes back one day, when I'm ready. When I meet her, the first thing I'm gonna do (after demanding a bottle of wine to complement the effects of my epidural) is give her a high-five. And then I'm going to hold her wrinkly little red face very close to my own, and I'm going to whisper so just she and I can hear, "Thank you for giving me another chance."

CHAPTER TEN

Funny Business

On the first day of class at Columbia University's Teachers College, I broke into tears when it was my turn to introduce myself during a small seminar.

"I'm sorry," I blubbered into a tissue someone hastily produced. "I'm just not sure I'm supposed to be here. I don't think I want to be a teacher."

My professors at Teachers College were almost uniformly encouraging and helpful. They believed in me, even though *I* didn't believe in me. As I bonded with my classmates and grew more comfortable around the staff, I found that my favorite part of the day was recounting the most ridiculous thing that had occurred during my hours as a student teacher. Nothing pleased me more than to relay a story that sent my classmates and professors into fits of laughter. Hearing them giggle and guffaw made all the pleasure centers in my brain light up. When I cracked them up, I felt warm and alive and energized. And I had plenty of tales to offer up for their amusement.

Thanks to the efforts of the head of the program, I received my first-semester student teaching placement at an upscale public school in Manhattan. Unfortunately, my "cooperating" teacher was anything but cooperative. Instead, she was bitter, resentful, and all the other qualities one so often finds among teachers who would really rather be doing something else. I understood her dilemma, but not her meanness. Today, I'd tell her to fuck off, but I was younger and sweeter then. With my usual desperate need for approval from authority figures, I wanted her to like me. She responded to my polite overtures by rolling her eyes and shooting me disgusted stares from the back of the room when I taught my mini-lessons. To her credit, she was a good teacher. To my discredit, I showed up late a few times. But I'm still fairly certain her veins were filled with briny pickle juice rather than human blood.

One day before class, she told me she was going to assign the seventh-graders an essay with the title "The Most Important Day of My Life."

"Well, that sounds fun!" I chirped.

"Wait 'til you see the shit we get back," she said, her voice tinged with disgust. "Most of them were in third grade at a downtown school on 9/11 and they saw the planes hit. They all had to evacuate. Do you know how many fucking 9/11 essays I've had to read this year? 'The smoke cloud, Daddy cried, we had to move,' and blah blah blah blah *blah*. They make everything about 9/11. It's like, enough already. You're in middle school now. I don't want to read about this shit. Can we please move on, already?"

"Yeah, what a bunch of fucking pussies," is what I should've said.

Instead, I said, "Well, they are still little kids. It's kind of a huge trauma."

That was not the correct response. She made a disgusted sound in the back of her throat and pounded a coffee. Later that day, she announced that no one in the class was allowed to write about 9/11 for the rest of the school year.

I knew I didn't want to end up like her.

I just didn't know how I *did* want to end up.

I was sure I wanted to be a writer. I'd always known that. Most writers are born, not made. Bawling, they emerge from the sticky, wet womb slick with some combination of material effluvia and literary ambition. The main trouble for born writers, as for born painters and sculptors and actors and musicians, is that art doesn't generally pay the bills. I didn't want to work in an advertising agency. I didn't want to produce diet tips for some soul-killing women's magazine. I didn't want to churn out instructional manuals for tech companies. I wanted to write. And I wanted to do something else, something attached to writing but somehow different, though I had yet to identify exactly what that was.

A graduate school classmate ended up providing me with the answer. Some of my fellow students found my class-clown tendencies offensive and irritating, but a few seemed to find me entertaining, even refreshing. A woman a few years older than me stopped me after class one evening.

"Have you ever tried stand-up comedy?" she asked. On my tearful first day of our seminar, she'd told us she had just left her job at Comedy Central's talent department in order to make a difference through public-school education.

"No," I said. This wasn't strictly true. I had done stand-up comedy once at an Emerson College benefit for a food pantry. I think my chief joke involved a dolphin impression. I don't remember who asked me to do it, nor do I remember why he or she thought I would be any good at it. I just remember blowing the light (ignoring the light that indicates a comedian's time is up) because I didn't know what it meant or why it kept flashing at me. I would later learn that blowing the light is one of the most irritating etiquette violations a comedian can commit. But I wasn't a comic—I was just a girl who had been asked to tell jokes onstage for some reason. Finally, one of the actual comedians got in front of the stage and started waving his arms at me. It wasn't exactly the most fabulous debut in the history of the jester's craft, and I had regarded it as a strange little one-off, almost entirely forgettable.

But now this former comedy-industry professional seemed to think I was funny.

"You shouldn't be teaching," she said. "You should be doing stand-up."

"Can you make any money doing that?" I asked.

"Not usually," she said. "But I bet you'd be happier."

We became friends, and she introduced me to her former co-workers at Comedy Central. These were the women who decided what went on air at a channel I'd been watching since I was a kid.

"Sara's thinking of trying stand-up," she told them.

"Cool," they said, and then we drank wine and ate burritos.

I still didn't try stand-up. I'd been doing pretty well in New York with the mental health stuff, and I didn't want to upset my wobbly brain-canoe. Stand-up comedy seemed like a ton of pressure. It was just you and a microphone up on that stage, emotionally naked in the blinding spotlight in front of a crowd of strangers. What if I had a panic attack in front of everybody?

When the next semester rolled around, I moved on to a much happier student-teaching placement at the super-competitive

Bronx High School of Science. I still didn't know if I wanted to try stand-up, but I enrolled in a sketch-writing course at the People's Improv Theater downtown. The instructor, Kevin Allison, was a member of the legendary sketch comedy group The State, which had spawned the films *Wet Hot American Summer* and *The Baxter* as well as the television shows *The State, Stella, Reno! 911* and *Viva Variety.* I loved the class, and made friends with Avi, a handsome and hilarious recent college grad who worked at one of those hip boutique ad agencies that exist in loft spaces around Manhattan; Callie, a tiny blond bombshell, who also toiled in advertising; Geoff, a nude art model (he put on clothes for class) and reality TV cameraman; and Andrea, one of those casually beautiful girls who walk around New York City as if it were normal to have perfect bone structure. (She was also a black lesbian real estate agent. Obviously.) They were my first friends in New York besides my roommate and my Teachers College classmates. They were the first New Yorkers I met who also had a strange compulsion to make other humans laugh. It can be really comforting to meet someone who shares your mental illness. I met four someones (plus Kevin).

We sat around my graduate-school seminar one night talking about what we did to blow off steam after long days of work and class. Drinking was a popular option, as was knitting. I mentioned my class at the PIT. Out of nowhere, a girl asked me if I might be interested in doing stand-up at her dormitory as part of a women's comedy night.

"I volunteered to help book the show," she said. "We already spent our budget on the real comedians and I need somebody cheap to open the show. Do you want to do it?"

Without thinking, I nodded yes.

"Great!" she said. It wasn't until she'd walked away that I realized what I'd done.

Before I could come up with a creative way to back out, she e-mailed me with all the details. It turned out that the "women's comedy night" was part of her dormitory's celebration of the United Nations' International Women's Week, during which various heads of state and Madeleine Albright were scheduled to speak. Her dorm was International House, a big fancy residential building for international students attending any one of New York's kajillion graduate schools. It was comprised of seven hundred students from more than one hundred countries. Its board of trustees was headed by a Rockefeller. Past chairmen of the board included Henry Kissinger, Dwight D. Eisenhower, and Gerald Ford.

In other words, this was not a casual evening of laughs in the study lounge beside the soda machine.

I e-mailed her back and asked what she thought the crowd would be like.

"Mostly Pakistani and Indian med students," she wrote in response. "Well, some of them are scientists."

I groaned and told my PIT class about it the next day. Avi, Callie, Geoff, and Andrea immediately said they were coming and bringing a camera.

"I'm pretty sure it's going to suck," I said.

"How many minutes do you get?" Avi asked. Avi knew more about comedy than anyone else I'd ever met. He idolized Jack Benny, and his bedroom wall was decorated with a black-and-white photo of someone named Bill Hicks. He wanted to be a writer-director-editor-producer-actor (and also a stand-up).

"Fifteen minutes," I said. Avi started laughing.

"Is that not a lot?" I asked.

"For your first time? Fifteen minutes is *forever.* Do you *have* fifteen minutes?"

"What, like, right now? I'm not busy."

"No, do you *have* fifteen minutes of jokes?"

"No. I don't have any minutes of jokes."

"And when is this event?"

"In a month."

"Well, you'd better get writing," Avi said. He told me to carry a notebook around and be prepared to write down anything funny that I saw or thought about. He also told me to watch my favorite comedians online, or to buy their DVDs and watch them.

I went out and got Denis Leary's one-man show, *No Cure for Cancer,* even though Avi claimed Leary stole half the show from Hicks. I didn't know if that was true, but I knew I dug Leary. I also picked up Margaret Cho's concert films, *I'm the One That I Want* and *Notorious C.H.O.* I got an old favorite, John Leguizamo's *Freak,* even though Avi said Leguizamo was a monologuist, not a stand-up comic. I picked up some Lenny Bruce, Richard Pryor, and Eddie Murphy, because Avi said this was required viewing. Finally, I bought some of George Carlin's HBO specials. I'd always liked Carlin.

We'd gotten into the habit of going to a club on the Lower East Side, called Rififi. There was a room behind the bar that could fit about fifty people, seventy if most people stood. It was the hippest comedy club on the face of the Earth. Avi pointed out the different comedians who shuffled through to perform at $5 shows like "Invite Them Up" and "Oh, Hello." "That's Patton Oswalt," he'd say. "That's Brian Posehn. That's Michael Showalter. That's Christian Finnegan. That's Aziz Ansari. That's David Cross. That's Nick Kroll. That's John Mulaney. That's Greg Giraldo. That's Reggie Watts. That's Zach Galifianakis."

"Who?" I asked, confused.

"Galifianakis. He's amazing. Oh, and that over there is Louis C.K."

"He has initials for a last name?"

While their delivery and content varied, most of these comics had one thing in common: they all had dicks. I didn't have personal knowledge of any of their dicks, although a few of my ever-expanding group of girlfriends did. Some material I liked; some I didn't. Some styles appealed to me; others didn't. But I didn't spend a lot of time watching women perform live. There just weren't that many of them onstage at the shows I regularly attended.

I figured the thing to do was to write down funny stories I wanted to tell, and then cram them all into a fifteen-minute speech. Avi said I had to practice, so I did. I practiced in front of my full-length mirror. Using a water bottle as a microphone, I practiced in front of my roommate and her dog and cat (she laughed in all the right parts). Finally, I practiced in front of Avi in his bedroom.

"Make eye contact with me," he said. "You keep staring at the ground. It makes it seem like you're nervous."

"I am nervous," I said.

"Just pretend you're not," he said.

I pretended I wasn't. He laughed in some of the right parts and gave me pointers on the other parts.

By the time the big day rolled around, I was consumed with nervous energy. In the classroom, I flitted to and fro like a coked-up hummingbird. My digestive system attempted to evacuate every hour on the hour. It didn't have much to work with, because my appetite generally disappears when I'm excited. I headed back down from the Bronx to Teachers College for an early-evening class, and then a group of girls and I marched over to International House. There we met up with my comedy buddies, and my two little New York City worlds mixed together for the first time. Looking around, I realized that after eight months in New York, I'd actually made quite a few friends. It was a good feeling, warm and comforting. Then I looked around the room.

The downstairs café/performance space at International House was designed to hold about seventy-five people. Apparently, the United Nations' International Women's Week Comedy Night was quite a draw, because people kept filing in even after all the seats were taken. By the time the bartender shut the door, there were about a hundred people in the room. True to my classmate's word, most of them appeared to be of the subcontinental Asian persuasion.

I was opening, which I had originally thought was the most prestigious position. Avi had explained to me that the person who closes is actually the biggest deal. The middle person is called the feature, and the opener is, well, the opener.

"The opener warms up the crowd," he'd said. "It's the shittiest spot to have, and it's the one they always give newer comics."

This was apparently true even at the United Nations' International Women's Week Comedy Night at International House. The woman performing after me was a professional comic about five years older than me. She had a TV show on a cable channel. The headliner, also a pro, was about five years older than the feature act. She'd done lots of television, including a few of the big late-night shows. If I hadn't been so nervous, I might have been thrilled to perform with two actual professional female comics. I was too nervous to introduce myself to them before the show, so I sat in the corner sipping a ginger ale and quietly studying my notes.

One of my classmate's friends hosted the event, and when she took the stage, I felt my gut lurch. But then something odd happened. As she spoke from the stage about what an honor it was to have three great female comedians in the room, and what a night of fun everyone could expect, and how hilarious all the performers were going to be, I found myself scooting toward the edge of my seat. But to my immense surprise, I didn't detect the makings of a panic attack. And I wasn't bracing myself to run for the door. In fact, I was instinctively aiming myself in the direction of the stage. Through some magical physiological alchemy, my nervousness rapidly transformed into enthusiasm. When she called my name, I burst out of my seat and practically ran onstage, grabbing the microphone gleefully.

"And how the hell are *you,* you sexy foreign bastards?" I asked the crowd. The men laughed and hooted, and the women giggled. And then, by some comedy miracle, I killed. I mean, I motherfucking *killed* it. It helped that I had written my entire set for them. I did jokes about grad school. I did jokes about the 1 train. I did jokes about the different languages represented in the crowd. ("For those of you who don't have the best command of English, we'll be redoing the entire show in Farsi at ten and in Urdu at eleven. You're welcome, Axis of Evil." That one blew the roof off the place.)

My timing was horribly off. I was jumpy and giggly in places where I ought to have been smooth and polished. I was raw and wordy and I went over my allotted time. I looked at my feet a lot. But when I did, I grinned at my shoelaces. I was awful, and I had a great time. Avi laughed at everything from behind the camera he'd brought, even the bits I knew he wasn't too keen on, and he and my other friends enthusiastically led or joined in on the waves of laughter.

By the time I got off the stage to pulse-pounding applause, I had reached a record-high emotional altitude. I was sweaty and energized and gloriously, loudly alive. They had *laughed.* They had laughed when I *wanted* them to laugh. Even now that I was offstage and the host was back on the mic, some of the people in the crowd were glancing at me appreciatively and smiling when I made eye contact. People in New York didn't just smile at you like that unless they knew you. Did they know me now? Or did they just feel like they knew me because they'd spent fifteen minutes listening to and laughing at my stories? These strangers and I had connected somehow, and for a quarter of an hour I'd held their attention. Now *that* was power.

The other comics did well, but their jokes about marriage and motherhood and aging didn't go over like my jokes about MLA style had. Every comic has had the experience of doing poorly or only moderately well at a show where another comic, one with a ton of family and friends in the audience, has killed. It's annoying, because no matter how shitty the other comic is, his or her loved ones are going to laugh. And since laughter is contagious, some of the other audience members will laugh just to be a part of the crowd.

On my first real night as a stand-up, I didn't know that the graduate students in the crowd may as well have been my friends and family. I didn't know that what we often find funnier than anything, even the most well-crafted jokes, is familiarity. Those students may not have known me personally, but they knew my type—young, nerdy, hopeful. I was their type, and they were mine. I was familiar.

After the class, my comedy friends and my teaching friends came up and wrapped me in a series of great big hugs.

"You killed it," Avi said. "You wanna do it again?"

"Definitely," I said.

"You have to look up more next time," he said.

I shared a cab home with the headlining comic and my friend Geoff. The headliner had gotten progressively drunker throughout the evening.

"You know how old I am?" she slurred.

"No," I said. "How old are you?"

"Thirty-fucking-seven," she moaned.

"You don't look it," Geoff said.

"Thirty-seven is hot," I said. "Jennifer Aniston is thirty-seven."

"Yeah, and she ain't married either," the headliner said, unleashing a hacking cough. "Christ, I need a cigarette. And my period. God, do I need that fuckin' thing to show up." She look at Geoff and said, "Sorry, buddy."

"No problem," Geoff said. "I'm sure your period is coming soon."

I relaxed into the seat as we zoomed down Broadway, listening to a real working comedian in the midst of a premature midlife crisis. I didn't know her, and I didn't imagine we'd ever be friends. But right then, in that moment, we were coworkers headed home from the office after a great day of work. And I finally knew what job I really wanted.

CHAPTER ELEVEN

The Only Living Girl in New York

Fresh from moderating a couple of panels at a new media conference, I grabbed a cab to a gig downtown.

"I'm going to Comix at Fourteenth and Ninth," I said. "Thanks."

The cab driver was silent, which wasn't unusual. I didn't find it insulting. I imagine that you get tired of small talk after ten hours behind the wheel in the bitchiest city in the world. New Yorkers are many things, but first and foremost we are complainers. It's always too hot or too cold, too sunny or too overcast, too loud or too quiet.

We were at a red light when he said it. He didn't even turn around. He just said it.

"Do you know what is panic attack, man?"

I froze in the middle of texting whatever boy I was trying to make fall in love with me through sheer force of will. Rationally, I knew the driver couldn't possibly know what panic attacks meant to me, how they had overruled my best instincts for so many years. He couldn't know the embarrassment they had brought me, or the shame, or the stress they had put on the people I loved most. He couldn't know that I'd ever even *had* a panic attack. And yet, I wondered for a split second if he somehow knew me—knew everything about me, knew that even now, when I traveled to colleges and little theaters around the country, when I cracked one-liners on TV and radio about politics, sex, and popular culture, there were moments before my day began when I curled up in a ball under the covers and breathed slowly and steadily, reciting to myself, "You can do this. It's okay. You are safe. You can do this. It's okay. You are safe," and that was just to get my ass to sit up in bed.

The question hung in the air.

Do you know what is panic attack, man?

Yeah, I knew what is panic attack, man. I just didn't know why he was asking me, of all people.

"Sure," I said faintly.

He launched into a tirade.

"Yesterday I am driving. I feel like I am going to die. My heart is like to explode out my chest. You know this, man?"

"Yes," I said. "I know this."

"I go to hospital. St. Vincent's, in the Village. You know this, man?" I knew St. Vincent's. From its founding in the nineteenth century, it had been known as a charity hospital. It had been the admitting hospital for the majority of the injured on September 11, 2001. A victim of budget cuts, it would close within six months.

"I know this," I said.

"I think I have heart attack, man. They tell me I have panic attack. They try to give me drug. I say no."

"Why did you say no?" I asked. I figured so long as he was sharing this much personal information, I had the right to ask.

"Because I do not want drug, man!" he practically shouted. "I tell them I do not want drug. I tell them I do not want anything for panic, man. And they look at me and they check everything. For four hour I am there. Four hour!"

"Wow," I said, thinking of my time at the emergency room back in Asheville. "It's got to suck to be in a New York ER for that long."

We came to another stoplight, and he turned around to look straight at me. Something in his eyes, or maybe around his mouth, was momentarily broken.

"I think they lie to me, man," he said. "Do you think they lie?"

"No," I said. "I don't think they lie."

And then we talked. About the fear, the growling voices, and the shame. About recovery, management, setbacks. About pills. After about ten minutes, I think I'd actually convinced him that panic attacks were real. After about twenty minutes, I think I'd actually convinced him that the doctors had diagnosed him correctly.

We neared my destination, a posh comedy club with excellent food cooked by a real, trained chef. The place was a true anomaly in the comedy world, where most clubs serve expired chicken wings fried in the sweat of the mustachioed, molester-chic owner. I'd spent the past year and a half hosting a weekly live show, "Family Hour with Auntie Sara," in a small but tidy space in the basement beside the lavatories. Comedians came to my show and told true stories about their families. It was one-part performance, one-part therapy. It was usually hilarious. Best of all, it was free. Actually, that may have been one of the club's many problems. Never financially solvent, the club was in major trouble. It would close within a year.

"You think it is real, man?" he asked me as he pulled to the curb. I could see some people I knew, and some people I didn't, filing into the club. Some were headed to the main room upstairs, where I performed once in a while. Others were bound for my show in the basement. I saw some regulars stealing a smoke with the bouncer, James.

"I absolutely think it is real," I said.

"And you had this?"

"Oh, yes. I had this. Sometimes I still have this." I paused and considered whether to tell him the most colorful part of the story.

"You know," I said, getting out cash to pay the fare, "there was a time when I had so many panic attacks that I was afraid to leave my room. I was even afraid to leave my bed. Like to go to the bathroom. I was too afraid to go to the toilet."

He whipped his head around and stared at me, wide-eyed. He nodded for me to continue.

"I even stopped using the toilet," I said. "For real. I would pee in bowls. In my bedroom. That was before I took the right drugs."

His already wide eyes got even bigger, until they looked like two teacup saucers glowing in his face.

"Holy shit," he finally said. "That is fucking crazy, man."

"Yeah," I said. "I had a lot of problems." I gave him his money, and he gave me my change.

"Take care, man," I said.

He drove on to the next passenger, and I went into the club, both of us wondering how we'd ended up this way.

The Thing at the End of the Thing

At present, gratitude is my only religion. With that in mind, let's go to church!

Thanks to my parents, Lillian Janine Teresa Benincasa Donnelly and Jonathan Steven Donnelly. You gave me life, you saved my life, and you're very cool people to boot. Thanks to my brother, Steve, who took me on walks and made me eat raw kale while I finished this book.

Thank you, Scott Mendel, my über-mensch of a literary agent, and his lovely wife, Sara. You are delightful humans and I'm enormously pleased to know you.

I'm fortunate to work with the funkiest, most enthusiastic and dedicated comedy management team in the world: Keri Smith-Esguia, Sarah Martin, Emily White, and everybody else at Whitesmith Entertainment. My agent at Keppler Speakers, Sean Lawton, is a magical wizard. (FACT: I am available to talk to your college, company, knitting club, or private militia. We will laugh and maybe cry and then laugh again, and hopefully high-five each other at the end.)

Some of the material in the book was performed at the People's Improv Theater in Manhattan; Ars Nova in Manhattan; Largo at the Coronet Theater in Los Angeles; Theatre 99 in Charleston, South Carolina; the Norwegian Storytelling Festival in Oslo; the Los Angeles Comedy Festival at the Acme Theater; Dirty South Improv in Carrboro, North Carolina; the Ladies Are Funny Festival in Austin; the Women in Comedy Festival in Boston; San Francisco Sketchfest; the Playground Theater in Chicago; the Brick Theater in Brooklyn; the D.C. Arts Center; and the Comedy Central Stage in Los Angeles. A hearty thanks to all the folks who brought me into their wonderful venues—especially Ali Farahnakian, Jeff Lepine, and Teresa Bass at the PIT, my comedy home.

Thank you to the badass superhero editing team of Cassie "Batman" Jones and Jessica "Robin" McGrady. Mary Schuck designed the raddest, reddest cover, and Jan Cobb took one fabulous photo. He also photographed JWOWW's cover, which means the man has an instinctive feel for Jersey-related literature. Hair and makeup sorceress Rhona Krauss worked beautiful wonders. The hardcore sexy bitches at Pinup Girl Clothing are responsible for that pill-poppin' red housewife dress. Kickass publicist Ken Phillips (also my future husband) hooked it up. Thank you legal eagle Melanie Jones and copyeditrix Olga Gardner Galvin.

Grazie to all the following humans and entities: the Francis family; Aunt Jeri and the Kozielec family; Johnny Benincasa; the Donnelly family; the Faerstein family; the Hodnett family; Gee; Karen; director Paul Stein at the Comedy Central Stage; my "Sex and Other Human Activities" podcast cohost and producer, Marcus Parks; Rebecca Trent at the Creek and the Cave; all the wonderful "SaOHA" listeners; the insane hordes of Wonkette commenters; Jen Schwalbach and Kevin Smith; Kambri Crews; Benari Poulten; Sam Apple; Mandy Stadtmiller; Dean Obeidallah; Aimee Kreitzer; Warren Wilson College; Margaret Cho; John DeVore; Beowulf Jones; James Urbaniak; Hillary

Buckholtz; Diana Saez; Sean L. McCarthy; Rose Miley; Nate Sloan; Todd Hanson; Zach Ward; Carolyn Castiglia; Rob Delaney; Melissa Cynova; Livia Scott; Josh Marshall at TPM; Pat Wiedenkeller at CNN; Patrice, Mona, Alyona, and all the other hotties at RT TV; Larry and Julie Bauer; Liz Gallagher; Baratunde Thurston; Gretchen Bauer Stanford and Tim Stanford; the staff at the Pisgah Institute and at Mission Hospital; anyone who has ever paid me to be funny; anyone I've ever paid to sort my brain troubles out.

A final thank you to Katherine Kelly Henk Baxley, Alexandra Jebet Fox, Prozac, and all cats everywhere.